VIKA KIRCHENBAUER

WORKS, SCRIPTS, ESSAYS 2012–2022

EDITED BY EVA BIRKENSTOCK, FANNY HAUSER & VIKTOR NEUMANN

2012

2022

VIKA KIRCHENBAUER

WORKS, SCRIPTS, ESSAYS

PREFACE

EVA BIRKENSTOCK, FANNY HAUSER & VIKTOR NEUMANN

Conceived as a monographic reader, *VIKA KIRCHENBAUER: WORKS, SCRIPTS, ESSAYS 2012–2022* compiles for the first time an extensive, decade-spanning collection of Kirchenbauer's seminal and profoundly perceptive essays, the scripts of her widely celebrated moving image works in conjunction with selected video stills, as well as exhibition views. This volume offers substantial insights into the Berlin-based artist, filmmaker, writer and music producer's research inquiries and aesthetic vocabulary. It also includes Kirchenbauer's two latest texts, exploring the relation between violence and visibility within the Western paradigm as well as the complex entanglements of European religious music and colonialism—research that has also fueled her solo music project *COOL FOR YOU* since 2015. This compendium is extended through novel essays by Oakland- and Los Angeles-based archivist, curator, and artist Leeroy Kun Young Kang and by Warsaw-based feminist philosopher and activist Ewa Majewska. While Kang looks at the social, affective and political implications of distance and proximity that Kirchenbauer so eloquently unfolds as powerful and meaningful techniques inherent in relations of oppression and emancipation, Majewska analyses the artist's elaborate and tortuous negotiations of violence and non-violence as lived and performed experiences.

/ *VIKA KIRCHENBAUER: WORKS, SCRIPTS, ESSAYS 2012–2022* is structured through thematic proximities—complementary and in relation with another—between the artist's essays, scripts and works, providing a thorough overview on how she approaches, through different media, wide-ranging topics and socio-cultural phenomena such as opacity, transparency, and translatability; the commodification of experience, memory, and difference; the intersection of negative affect and political agency; the symbolically and politically loaded fields of art production and presentation from perspectives of gender and class; as well as the contemporary politics of the gaze and of spectatorship and their historical implicatedness in coloniality or technocracy.

/ The volume, even though released independently, follows the production of the artist's two solo exhibitions from 2021, presented subsequently in Düsseldorf and Vienna; two exhibitions that are closely related with this volume, as the shows were configured around the works discussed within: the survey exhibition 'FEELINGS THAT MOVE NOWHERE' at Kunstverein für die Rheinlande und Westfalen in Düsseldorf (pp. 26–33), and the concentrated 'VIOLET BUT MORE RADICAL' at Kunstverein Kevin Space in Vienna (pp. 34–41). The selection of video stills together with the installation views of both exhibition projects offer insights into the aesthetic vocabulary of Kirchenbauer's moving image works, their spatial manifestations and her site-specific interventions. They are constituted, amongst other aspects, of her ongoing critical investigation into the cultural traditions of transferring the non-graspable into the normative frame of vision, and propose to rethink the relation between representation, personal and collective memory as much as non-remembrance, and trauma. / By bringing together Kirchenbauer's essays and scripts, and by putting them into dialogue with additional voices and the idiosyncratic visual repertoire of her works, we hope to provide further entry points to her practice, and wish you, the readers, joy in spending time with this volume devoted to an artist whose thinking, acting and artistic articulating radiates an empathetic intellect of profound transformative potential. /

Finally, we would like to genuinely thank those who helped make this publication possible. We extend the artist's deep gratitude to the Berlin Senate Department for Culture and Europe for its generous support. Thank you Leeroy Kun Young Kang and Ewa Majewska for insightful contributions, thank you Studio SMS (Katharina Shafiei-Nasab and Alix Stria) for the design, Judith Sieber and Nancy Chapple for content and copy editing, and Mousse Publishing for including this volume in their programme. Last but not least we would like to thank you, Vika. Having been fortunate to be collaborating with you over the past years, we are particularly grateful to have been invited to support the production of your first monograph and, thus, continue our close dialogue.

AT A CLOSENESS

LEEROY KUN YOUNG KANG

Darling, let me share with you
my unresolved emotions.[1]

I remember feeling very happy, excited, and honored the day I received Vika's invitation to contribute to this publication, but it didn't take long for other emotions to surface. Anxiety, fear, and the shame I attach to writing seemed to soon dominate over anything else. In her essay "Writing Shame",[2] Elspeth Probyn writes, "to care intensely about what you are writing places the body within the ambit of the shameful: sheer disappointment in the self amplifies to a painful level." These words rang true after weeks of sitting with these difficult feelings, as it became clear that my deep investment in Vika's work and her artistic practice provoked the anticipated disappointment (and also embarrassment) of what I may produce. But what also loomed large was not only the task to somehow write commensurately with Vika's work, but to do so from my proximity to her as a close friend. Naturally, we want to please our friends and make them proud, but it is also true that our own emotional entanglements are often implicated within these desires. The measurements of worth and expectation that we place on

1 Vika Kirchenbauer, *YOU ARE BORING!* (2015).

2 Elspeth Probyn, "Writing Shame" in *The Affect Theory Reader*, Melissa Gregg and Gregory J. Seigworth (eds.) (Durham: Duke University Press, 2010), p. 73.

ourselves are always relational to others and to larger social structures, and so when asked to produce or perform within this dynamic, it can leave much room to dwell in one's own sense of imposture. The mere thought of delivering a less than satisfactory contribution to what is undoubtedly a great achievement in my artist friend's career plagued me, while I also considered the risks associated with deepening "professional exchanges" between friends. /

Throughout my experience within educational settings, I have often heard people talk, in one way or another, about the sense of ease that comes with writing on subjects that are somewhat distant from themselves, and conversely, the difficulty that comes with addressing intimate subjects within one's own work. Despite a recent turn towards more self-reflexivity within contemporary discourse, certainly, entire scholarly disciplines including the development of the empirical sciences and, concurrently, art history have traditionally been predicated on maintaining an "objective" distance between the writer-researcher and their subject(s). This approach to writing (or "making work" more broadly) on subjects positioned at a distance to one's own experience or to one's own intimate community(ies), seems to communicate a couple of central messages in my observation. One is often framed as a practical measure, which suggests that the closer you are in proximity to your subject, the higher the risk of sacrificing productivity (i.e., you'll never finish that manuscript or dissertation!), and the other being the belief that a distanced approach inherently produces "better" work. / The lack of affective burden placed upon one as a distanced observer can provide an uninhibited ground on which to write and produce more freely with little to no emotional attachment. With distance, the often fraught conditions of having to negotiate one's own position as both researcher and "insider" can be curtailed altogether. Furthermore, the clear lens of objectivity and neutrality is often seen as achievable through distance, a perspective long upheld as measures of true and valid scholarship, as well as of some forms of artistic production.

/ So then, how *does* one write from a place of closeness? What are the greater social, economic, and political risks, affects, and ramifications implicated within working from this position of proximity? From what place do these difficult feelings emerge and where do they settle?

/ What I came to find in my own confrontation of difficult feelings enmeshed in this very writing process was a way back to some of the most central questions and concerns that have surrounded Vika's work for over a decade. From her work in moving image, installation, music, and writing, Vika's wide-ranging practice provides an uncompromising meditation on the precarious negotiations between distance and vulnerability as positionalities, resources, and affectual conditions steeped within violent structures of power. In her work, she interrogates *who* and *what* can hold themselves "at a distance" to remain unaccountable to pervasive abuses of power, while also laying bare our own implications in the maintenance of violent structures through the gaze we place onto ourselves and onto others. By thinking and feeling through Vika's practice, I am wondering how we as both creators and spectators might engage "at a closeness" to the subjects we are so deeply invested in with both criticality and care, while learning to wade in the difficult feelings that move nowhere[3] yet still tickle down our spines.

The chronology is clear,
the narrative coherent.[4]

I'm watching *YOU ARE BORING!* again, but this time in Vika's studio. While sitting alone in a swivel office chair wearing a pair of 3D glasses and with window blinds drawn closed, I feel a moment of irony in how radically contrasting this scene is from the intended environment of a darkened gallery space occupied by strangers. Perhaps it's the added effect of viewing it in 3D or being in this unfamiliar yet intimate setting, but I'm immediately struck by how notably different it is to experience the work now versus the very first time back in the fall of 2015, the same night I met Vika during a screening of her work at UnionDocs, a documentary art center in Brooklyn, New York. As I'm watching the work, I find myself pleasantly surprised that there are moments in it that I don't fully remember, or perhaps more accurately, that I remember differently. At some point, I become particularly fixated on how I can taste urine as I watch the "golden shower scene" featuring Max Göran, Lauren John Joseph, and the legs of an unidentified performer.
/ It is now spring, in 2022, and I'm in Berlin for the first time. Everyone was right: May *is* the best month to be here. I've spent the week enjoying the many lush and vast spaces designed for public life in the city, meeting new friends through old friends, visiting art galleries, and walking virtually everywhere (the latter being something I've greatly missed since moving from New York to Los Angeles). Despite how wonderful my experience has been, I still feel utterly out of sorts and jarred by my sudden immersion into a large unfamiliar city, moving through streets filled with people after over two years of an ongoing global pandemic. This particular timing of my visit makes me all the more grateful to spend so much time with Vika, and to see a bit of the city through her eyes. It gives me another glimpse into my friend's life and the context of her work. It allows me an opportunity to reflect on what has transpired since we first met. /
On the night of her screening in 2015, Vika showed five works: *LIKE RATS LEAVING A SINKING SHIP* (2012), *KINGDOM COME: RITUALS* (2014), *CONVENIENT, SACRED, BLESSED*

3 In reference to Vika Kirchenbauer's solo exhibition, 'FEELINGS THAT MOVE NOWHERE', that took place at Kunstverein für die Rheinlande und Westfalen, Düsseldorf, 29 May–5 September 2021.

4 Vika Kirchenbauer, *LIKE RATS LEAVING A SINKING SHIP* (2012).

(2015), *PLEASE RELAX NOW* (2014), and *YOU ARE BORING!* (2015). One of the primary themes addressed in these works dealt with the troubling power dynamics inherently located within practices of "looking" and "being looked at". From this central premise, the works utilised a range of formal and aesthetic approaches, including essay film, experimental video, performance, and direct address, to explore opacity in relation to representation of the othered. With a particular attention to the affective contours of institutionalised power and its impact on marginalised subjects, the works also addressed the camera as a visual apparatus of violence (for instance, as used in modern drone warfare), and how queerness and gender non-conformity can be interchangeably claimed as expressions of self-agency as well as forms of currency within the context of contemporary art. Opening with the earliest work in the series, *LIKE RATS LEAVING A SINKING SHIP*, a polyvocal and nonlinear essay film about the artist's clinical diagnosis of gender dysphoria, the program continued on to show later works like *PLEASE RELAX NOW* and *YOU ARE BORING!* that featured Vika and/or her co-conspirators in front of the camera in the form of direct address to confront the perverse nature of spectatorship and participatory culture. /

Experiencing these works that night and listening to Vika speak about them was like a lamp—an illuminating heat that resounded under my skin. And amidst the backdrop of a year saturated with the hypervisibility of trans life, and its utterly flattening effects exacerbated by mainstream media and the art world alike, I felt an immediate sense of kinship that I had been longing for through the biting clarity and rigor within Vika's work and in her life practice as an artist. Since that time, Vika's continued artistic practice and our many conversations as now friends and collaborators have been incredibly generative in my own continued thinking around how issues of difference, visibility, affect, and institutional violence manifest within the work and everyday lives of marginalised people. /

As both an archivist and film curator, I often think about how to create meaningful modes of access, while minimising the potential harms of exposure to the artists and communities I work with. When I speak of "exposure", I mean the process by which a certain compressed legibility is rendered by institutions to facilitate the material and intellectual theft and co-option of artists' labour, particularly of those within minoritised positions, for their own economic and political gains. The tension that exists between artists' desires and needs to resist these institutional forms of legibility, while also creating sustainable means of visibility and recognition within them, is a central concern that I frequently explore in my work and in tandem with others. This has often required me to work slowly, with duration, and in intimate settings, to establish trust and forms of care with both artists and institutional actors, as these complex issues attach to very real material and affective consequences. My investments in these concerns have led me to consider more deeply how aesthetic and relational forms of opacity, absence, and invisibility can generate methods of personal and collective agency. While working with these concepts in my curatorial practice, I find it crucial to also apply them towards dismantling the violent forms of erasure that attach to them through histories of colonialism and forced displacement.

/ In the spring of 2021, I had the pleasure of curating a series of programs for Los Angeles Filmforum[5] that featured Vika's work alongside the work of New York-based Korean-American filmmaker Caroline Key. Titled *What We Imagine in Its Absence*, the programs brought together these two artists in their shared interests in exploring constructions of alterity and otherness through the framework of opacity to posit how forms of medical, institutional, and state violence exist and permeate beyond visual capture. Having known both Vika and Caroline separately since 2015, the series also served as an experiment to consider what could be generated by bringing two artists and their works together across geographical contexts and different positionalities, given that they share central concerns within their artistic practices.

/ Featuring the virtual Los Angeles premiere of several works by both artists, the first program, dedicated to Vika's work, included her early essay film *LIKE RATS LEAVING A SINKING SHIP*; two videos employing infrared technology produced as part of her music project, *COOL FOR YOU*, titled *SHE WHOSE BLOOD IS CLOTTING IN MY UNDERWEAR* (2016) and *SHAME/HUMILIATION* (2018); a piece featuring scripted performance as institutional critique commissioned by the Schwules Museum titled *WELCOME ADDRESS* (2017); and her newest work at the time, *UNTITLED SEQUENCE OF GAPS* (2020), a personal essay film on trauma-related memory loss through reflections on light outside the visible spectrum. The second program featured Caroline Key's feature film *GRACE PERIOD* (2015, co-directed by KyungMook Kim), an experimental documentary centering a group of women sex workers in the Yeongdeungpo district in Seoul and their resistance to South Korea's Anti-Sex Trade Law, and *KHÔRA* (2019), an experimental short that utilises "surgical waste" footage to question the visibility and knowability of the body within the medical gaze. Together, through their forms and themes, the works address ongoing concerns attached to the Western world's demand for transparency and its troubling relationship to issues of difference and image production. /

These concerns are taken up by Édouard Glissant in his notion of opacity and his claim to "the right to opacity for everyone"[6] as a relational framework that refuses the Western world's demand for transparency and its forces of extraction upon colonised and other marginalised peoples. In the concluding artists discussion[7] of *What We Imagine in Its Absence*, both Vika and Caroline addressed the colonial and post-colonial

5 Los Angeles Filmforum is the longest-running organisation in Southern California dedicated exclusively to the ongoing, non-commercial exhibition of independent, experimental and progressive media art.

6 Édouard Glissant, *Poetics of Relation*, trans. by Betsy Wing (Ann Arbor: University of Michigan Press, 1997), p. 194.

contexts of Glissant's work, discussing how discourse around opacity must consider one's own proximity to power and privilege. In particular, Vika noted how when taken up within the context of Euro-American positions of whiteness, ideas of opacity can be used to excuse problematic forms of appropriation, such as the justification of withholding or concealing to evade accountability to abuses of power. As the ability to withhold or conceal freely is an automatic "right" reserved for those who create and maintain systems of power, the artists further discussed how Glissant's particular framing of opacity can be utilised by those in marginalised positions as a form of resistance to the violent demands for their transparency and knowability as subjects. / As both artists intentionally align their work within the realm of non-fiction rather than documentary, they discussed at length the latter's long-standing and troubling approach to spectatorship and authorship in relation to issues of proximity, intimacy, and distance. In many ways, these issues in documentary can be traced back to the form's early roots in anthropological practices of ethnography through what Fatimah Tobing Rony has described as "fascinating cannibalism",[8] the voracious appetite of Euro-American spectators to consume images of the racialised Other through the mix of desire, horror and fascination brought upon by the ethnographic gaze. /

In regards to her own work, Vika described these fraught dynamics attached to working in modes of non-fiction as the process in which one "can crawl into someone else's skin without the risk of getting stuck in it," to express the spectator's desire and ability to momentarily inhabit forms of difference without "the disruption of hegemonic comfort".[9] Within this arrangement, those in privileged positions are able to engage with subjects outside of their own social realities through the superficial registers of proximity and intimacy that these images can create, while still maintaining the distance necessary to disengage when they please. /

How these very dynamics played out through the wide reception and success of her film *LIKE RATS LEAVING A SINKING SHIP* gives greater context to Vika's decision to shift her focus towards meeting the unmet gaze of the privileged spectator as seen in works made from 2014–2018 like *YOU ARE BORING!*, *WELCOME ADDRESS*, and in the use of infrared technology in the works produced through her music project *COOL FOR YOU*. While these works confront issues of spectator relations and critique directly, Vika also revisits personal narrative and the essay form nearly a decade later through her work *UNTITLED SEQUENCE OF GAPS*. While returning to subjects of a personal nature in the form of fragmented memories from Vika's past, the work is produced within a different set of

7 *What We Imagine in Its Absence, Part 3: Conversation with Vika Kirchenbauer and Caroline Key*, Los Angeles Filmforum, 27 May 2021: ›https://www.youtube.com/watch?v=mSjKYJUBIOo‹ [last accessed on 11 July 2022].

8 Fatimah Tobing Rony, *The Third Eye: Race, Cinema, and Ethnographic Spectacle* (Durham: Duke University Press, 1996), p. 10.

9 Lauren Berlant, "Intimacy: A Special Issue", *Critical Inquiry*, vol. 24 no. 2 (Winter, 1998), p. 287.

terms that asks the viewer to meditate on how violence can be understood not only through what we can visualise, but through what is invisible, unremembered, and unknowable from our particular social positions and subjectivities.

/ In her newest work, *THE CAPACITY FOR ADEQUATE ANGER* (2021), Vika takes up similar themes as she reflects on a return to her home village through the form of montage and narration to address issues of class and queerness in relation to affective formations of shame. Produced as part of her first institutional solo exhibition at Kunstverein für die Rheinlande und Westfalen, Düsseldorf, Vika self-reflexively meditates on the irreconcilable distance she feels from her past and the current realities of her career as an artist, as she asks, "What if it was possible to speak and be heard without the prerequisite of social ascent?"[10] I was very grateful to be able to attend the US premiere at the New York Film Festival alongside Vika after a long stint of travel restrictions due to the pandemic. This occasion also marked the first time being in the city together since our initial meeting in 2015. /

Knowing how unpleasurable it often is for her to watch her own work, I wonder how Vika feels as she sits behind me in the theater as a room full of both friends and strangers look at images of her childhood. As Eve Sedgwick tells us that, "shame is itself a form of communication,"[11] I wonder what Vika can detect from her view. Through the exaggerated and pulsating twinkling eyes of a cartoon figure, I am reminded of my own gaze across this screen, but also the many screens and seating arrangements in which I have viewed Vika's work. From this view, I wonder what I might feel, taste, and remember differently again in our future encounters.

10 Vika Kirchenbauer, *THE CAPACITY FOR ADEQUATE ANGER* (2021).

11 Eve Kosofsky Sedgwick, *Touching Feeling: Affect, Pedagogy, Performativity* (Durham: Duke University Press, 2003), p. 36.

VIOLENT, NON-VIOLENT, VIOLENT.
VIKA KIRCHENBAUER AND THE PERFORMATIVE COMMON

EWA MAJEWSKA

"I think that if I can still address a 'we', or include myself within its terms, I am speaking to those of us who are living in certain ways beside ourselves, whether in sexual passion or emotional grief, or political rage."

Judith Butler, *Precarious Life: The Powers of Mourning and Violence* (New York: Verso, 2006), p 24.

In my childhood, there was only one way to access the mysterious knowledge of "does he love me?"—it could only be gained in the process of meticulously plucking the petals of a flower. This small act of violence against the innocent plant was strongly gendered—it was always performed by girls (perhaps their younger brothers participated in it too, as they would sometimes play with us rather than with the older boys) about boys, not the other way around. I am not sure what boys did to guess whether a girl fancied them. I vaguely remember one boy jumping into a pond to get a beautiful water lily for me when I was eight years old, but this is probably not always the case. At the time it was happening, we were all mostly preoccupied with his mother's screams and the fear that he might drown, as it was not a safe place to swim. Only some years later did I actually see, or perhaps experience, the cordial affect behind his heroic act. / The acts of violence permeate the acts of love, as in an emotional roller coaster, a version of enumerating, of "drowning by numbers", to borrow the expression Peter Greenaway used as a film title. The plucking of flower petals is an act of violence, subtle, girlish, pretty, and yet the flower does not survive such an emotional workout: it is dead when we are done counting. The "loves me, loves me not..." mantra is one that might be safely located in our childhood, but it sometimes resurfaces as a version of affective matrix in adult life as well. It delineates the "distinction", in the sense given to the term by Pierre Bourdieu when he discussed class differences, the operation of "abjection", as depicted by Julia Kristeva, who emphasises the process of distinguishing between "me / the subject" and "the other / the object" as a central part of the psychological process of individuation.[1] The "loves me, loves me not" ritual is a cruel path to knowledge, in which girls would even tear a petal up into smaller pieces if, in the process of counting, the "loves me not" was awaiting at the end of the game. / In my reading of Vika Kirchenbauer's inspiring and powerful artistic practice I do not try to immerse myself in every piece she has produced. Instead, I would like to offer a modest journey addressing a small collection of her recent works, with a focus on violence and non-violence, as constructs, ideals, and experiences. I believe her works allow a great variety of experiences in which the focus can move among childhood memories, flashbacks and the relations between the individual and the social. Kirchenbauer's videos create a collective experience without necessarily creating a collective, and offer a more complex set of implications than many other works of art we see today. They seem to resist an all-too-easy identification practice and as well resist the erasure of difference and discomfort.

THE TICKLISH SUBJECT, AND WHAT IS SUBVERSIVE?

My first reaction to the work of Vika Kirchenbauer was that one has to come closer, to shorten the distance, as her narrator's voice is quiet, and the images she offers sometimes seem a bit perplexing in their combinations and montage. Watching three people tickling each other for 35 minutes in the video *THE ISLAND OF PERPETUAL TICKLING* (2018) is an exercise for one's patience, as one has to look at it up close, because, before the exercise begins, the participants explain what might seem their experience and preferences concerning tickling. What comes next might become reason for embarrassment for the audience, as the sounds of the ticklish persons might be taken for those of a sexual orgy. Or torture. The whole game lasts for some 35 minutes, and it might make us wonder: is it hysteria? Perversion? Both? / The similarities and differences between perversion and hysteria have long been discussed in the field of psychoanalysis. In Jacques

1 See Pierre Bourdieu, *Distinction. A Social Critique of the Judgement of Taste* (Cambridge: Harvard University Press, 1987); Julia Kristeva, *The Powers of Horror. An Essay on Abjection* (New York: Columbia University Press, 1982).

Lacan's work, as well as in that of Slavoj Žižek, the ticklish subject is one of a hysterical nature—they find no satisfaction (or do they?), and thus their *jouissance* consists in refusal. In his book *The Ticklish Subject*, Žižek confronts perversion and hysteria, claiming that only the latter has subversive potential, while the pervert only confirms the status quo.[2] /

In *THE ISLAND OF PERPETUAL TICKLING*, we participate in a somewhat frivolous activity of three persons, who tickle each other in turn, following some instructions given in advance. The exercise should thus, I believe, be witnessed as a mixture of perversion and hysteria, especially in the case of the tickled person wearing neon green, who explicitly announces what gives him pleasure at the beginning of his turn. Based on this work by Kirchenbauer,[3] the sharp divide between hysteria, as the futile quest for pleasure with subversive potential, and perversion, as the affirmation of the status quo to come offered by Žižek, can be contested. As the distinction between perversion and hysteria is blurred by the doubts we might have observing the tickling on screen, the dimensions of the subversive act can also expand and complicate themselves. In Judith Butler's work, where she depicts drag queens, the emphasis is not only on the failure of performing gender. It is also, albeit Butler does not express it explicitly in *Gender Trouble*, the pleasure of being other, of crossing the gender borders, of accessing the *eternal feminine* by cis-male crossdressers as drag queens.[4] In short: the subversion of drag queens consists, I believe, in their crossing of the gender binary divisions and ability to fully acquire perfect womanly looks, but also in the joy of embodying the feminine for their own pleasure, which is perverse par excellence, as it violates straight men's monopoly on pleasure. This point was made clear to me by Agata Zbylut, a Polish feminist artist working with body transformations and the feminine looks, now experimenting with drag.

/ In *Sade, Fourier, Loyola*, an exercise in search for the discourse of pleasure, as I like to think of it, Roland Barthes reminds us of various forms of perversion—the sexual, religious and rationalist utopian, all immersed in bodily practices.[5] Pleasure seems to be a subversion in its own right. Of course, pleasure and the lack of it should not be confounded with violence and non-violence. But they can be compared. In such comparison, the impossibility of accessing pleasure could be understood as a version of violence in the perverse paradigm or as lack of violence, if we see pleasure solely as the joy of the hysteric, which Žižek seems to suggest.

2 See Slavoj Žižek, *The Ticklish Subject* (London: Verso, 2000), p. 247.
3 I use the artist's family name, never just the first name, in order to avoid the popular diminishing of women, who, like, e.g., Rosa Luxemburg or Angela Davis, often become Rosa or Angela in writing, differently from Vladimir Lenin or Martin Luther King Jr., who never become Vlad or Martin under such circumstances.
4 See Judith Butler, *Gender Trouble. Feminism and the Subversion of Identity* (New York: Routledge, 1990).
5 See Roland Barthes, *Sade, Loyola, Fourier* (Berkeley: University of California Press, 1989).

RITUALS OF CHILDHOOD, WITCHES AND THE FIRE

Vika Kirchenbauer's first persona essayistic narrator, recapitulating what might sound like elements of the artist's biography, sometimes mentions how she left the small town she grew up in and how, the one time she returned after more than a decade, she avoided her father and dreamed that he shot her with a rifle. In the video *UNTITLED SEQUENCE OF GAPS* (2020), the narrator also tells how huge haystacks were built and a witch figure made to slide into the stacks every Summer Solstice until several years ago, when this sad and cruel tradition was finally ended. Seeing those huge fires was an experience of brutality, very different from a ritual Solstice feminist fire I once witnessed and participated in building. Perhaps the village fire was bigger, perhaps it was the scary costumes that made me feel frightened, I am not sure, but since I saw that image some months ago, it permeates all the other images created by Kirchenbauer. The women disguised not just as witches, but as the worst stereotypes of witches, abound in the (supposed) reconstruction of a village summer festival in the video, scaring the children, the viewers; they are a performative re-appropriation of the figure of the witch by village women, including the artist's late aunt, a lesbian. The life-size straw witch sent into flames, symbolically, but in a visually persuasive way, somehow marks the limits of women's emancipation, as there is the reappropriation on the one hand and the burning on the other. "The witch" stands for many things in European culture, including: femininity, old women, women's wisdom, feminine disobedience, gender crossing, magic, excluded knowledges, alternative medicine, etc. Yet it is also always connoted with the violent act of burning. Watching *UNTITLED SEQUENCE OF GAPS* made me think about other forms of violence, also those associated with childhood, my own or in general. I was wondering to what extent these experiences influence our perceptions of gender and identity, and I realised how important it is, and how greatly Kirchenbauer performatively guides us through childhood—her own / her video character's, but also our own. As we witness the memories depicted, we probably revisit our own past as well.

/ In *THE CAPACITY FOR ADEQUATE ANGER (2021)* the images of childhood and adult memories, and baroque references, are shuffled and mixed with pieces of a feminist Communist manga series by Riyoko Ikeda, *The Rose of Versailles* (1979), presenting French Revolutionary times in reference to a book by Stefan Zweig on Marie Antoinette.[6] Among other excerpts, Kirchenbauer's video features snippets from a scene in which the non-binary character of Lady Oscar, a girl who was raised as a boy in order to provide a male heir to the family, is sexually assaulted. The shuffling of the historical manga series, the stories about aristocrats, peasants, as well as

6 Stefan Zweig, *Marie Antoinette: The Portrait of an Average Woman* (New York: Viking Press, 1933).

the artist's supposed memories narrated in the video, seem like a roller coaster. It is aimed to complicate identification with real or fictitious historical characters as well as with the artist, working in turn as an invitation to revisit one's own theirstory. In such revisiting, the common experience is at the same time collective and individualised, as the viewer is not invited to inhabit the artist's past, but to be moved/inspired/transformed by the narrated fragments.

STAGING POVERTY

The tale of violence does not stop there. It was there already in the smooth clip-like videos related to Kirchenbauer's music project *COOL FOR YOU* (2016–ongoing), in the tickling video, in *UNTITLED SEQUENCE OF GAPS*, as already depicted, and yes, it abounds in *THE CAPACITY FOR ADEQUATE ANGER*, which integrates the topics of labour and inequalities embedded in various forms of work. To that aim perhaps, the images used by the artist partially lose their sensuality, and become sensual in a different way, appropriate to illustrate sport or the aristocratic dreams of the 18th century to fashionably embody the fictionalised and idealised lives of shepherds or shepherdesses. Their dream was indeed coming true, as while pursuing it, they could drop some of the baroque outfits, build comfortable bowers or, God forbid, even sit on the grass. While watching Kirchenbauer's video, I wondered about famous past stories of upward mobility. Such a lavish version of the idyllic peasant life was probably not known to the philosopher of German idealism, Johann Gottlieb Fichte, who in the late 18th century, somewhere near Dresden, embodied the ordinary, most popular version of a shepherd, simply a poor yet very clever boy. His intellectual potential was discovered by accident, as he was asked to repeat what the sermon in the nearby church had been about, and explained it with such finesse and wisdom that the local aristocrats decided to sponsor his education. And this is how we got someone who invented passports and conceptualised in large part the nation-state. I wonder whether he ever experienced what most women know as "imposter syndrome", as his first book was published without the author's name by the same publisher who printed Immanuel Kant's books. At first, it was also perceived as Kant's; only later was it attributed to its actual author. Already in this historical example, never discussed in Kirchenbauer's work but somehow recalling it in my own memory, several layers of privilege and exclusion were reshuffled—since what we understand as "poverty" can mean so many things—from material deprivation to lack of access, even being denied one's signature under one's own work. / Poverty is a form of violence, a deprivation of comfort, safety, food, shelter and dignity, as well as access to cultural and political power. In the 19th century, economic capital also defined other symbolic or cultural capital, at least for the majority of the European population. Today we usually follow Pierre Bourdieu in discussing several versions of capital, and how they do not necessarily all depend on possessing financial resources. In this sense, poverty does not necessarily mean scarcity of resources necessary to survive, but definitely less education, cultural competence or access to power positions.[7] Poverty does not have to be painful, but in most cases it causes shame, even if it is just relative —perhaps especially in such cases. Poverty is the experience; class is the structure. Precarity, sometimes debated by Kirchenbauer in her essays, also contains that version of violence, or the frightening risk of it. However, the artist is very hesitant about today's discussions concerning precarity, particularly in the art field, as in her view they often lead to illegitimate equivalences between actual poverty and the experiences of insecurity among financially, culturally and politically privileged people in rich countries. Similar doubts were expressed by the feminist philosopher Isabell Lorey at the Former West conference in Warsaw in 2015, when she discussed precarity as a condition in which the majority of people were pushed throughout centuries as the "others" of the European Subject, shaping his autonomy through othering, exploitation and marginalisation.[8]

/ The experience of working in local factories, sometimes mentioned by the narrator of Kirchenbauer's videos, is presented as one of relative poverty, small cultural capital, perhaps lack of mobility. The account of a conversation with her grandmother is particularly telling—the essayistic narrator seems arrogant, and her explaining of the kind of work she does as an artist definitely goes beyond anything the old woman can imagine; there is impatience and perhaps even anger, marking the newly established class distinction between the two speakers particularly sharply, and probably deliberately. The artist's concern about the structural limitations of using art as a political tool is perhaps expressed here as well.

"I WAS OFTEN THE ONE THE OTHERS THOUGHT WOULD 'GIVE THEM AIDS'"

Children are cruel creatures. Their mechanisms of allying and dividing, of inclusion and exclusion, are sudden and unmediated, and they often focus on criteria we find strange as adults. The figures of Freddie Mercury and Magic Johnson bring the AIDS topic to Kirchenbauer's video *THE CAPACITY FOR ADEQUATE ANGER*, making it sound at first like a distant phenomenon. Its proximity becomes clear, as the stories of children "fearing AIDS" and the dentist asking whether she was HIV-positive appear in the narrative. Another proximity of a supposedly distant and abstract phenomenon of class division arrives with the topic of dental flossing, narrated as an

7 See Pierre Bourdieu, *Distinction: A Social Critique of the Judgement of Taste* (Cambridge: Harvard University Press, 1984); Zygmunt Bauman, *Globalization. The Human Consequences* (New York: Columbia University Press, 1998).

8 Isabell Lorey's presentation at the "Former West" conference at the Museum of Modern Art in Warsaw, Poland, 9 October 2015.

imagined upper-class habit. The general impression the video leaves with the viewer is that supposedly invisible, abstract and complex phenomena, such as class distinction or homophobia, are perfectly tangible in the lived experience of those most affected by them. I am not sure whether we can speak of an exercise of "visual phenomenology", but I think those words could aptly describe the effects of Kirchenbauer's art. The artist sometimes references Sara Ahmed in her writing, and I believe a version of "queer phenomenology" also happens in her video work. It enables a version of the "veil of ignorance", like, for instance, while revisiting childhood, the village life and customs, the dentist, we are confronted with the artist's / narrator's memories, which in turn conjure up our own memory work, and more general perspectives. Thus, by the power of supposedly simple storytelling, the viewer is thrown into topics normally conveniently obscured by media, public debate and theoretical knowledge, but now somehow stripped of all those layers of knowledge and habit the viewer previously had.

/ In psychoanalysis, working with fairytales was often seen as making it easier to approach trauma. Bruno Bettelheim is perhaps the best-known author in that line. Clarissa Pinkola Estés also collects tales, but in her work, especially the writing, the stories merge with experiences of her actual patients to provide a systematised collage, working on the reader and her experience on several levels simultaneously.[9] In the movie *Waltz with Bashir* (2008), Ari Folman employs animated film technique and storytelling by multiple narrators to recall his memories from the war in Lebanon in 1982, in which he fought as an Israeli soldier.[10] The videos produced by Vika Kirchenbauer often employ a reverse strategy—they recount the childhood events as a story, mix it with other references, taken sometimes from childhood, sometimes from popular culture or history, usually in some connection to the key factors shaping the artist / narrator's identity. For the viewers, these fragments become a version of a contemporary fairytale about contemporary reality—they remain "fictitious" as in "nothing like that ever happened to me" and yet they feel "real" as in "I also had dreams / to overcome something or / to struggle". I believe positioning Kirchenbauer's work in such a psychoanalytic line of thinkers, therapists and artists makes sense, as she works with identity formation on the level of her own and other individual experiences, as well as on the level of culture. Touching on the experiences of sexual and gender minorities makes her storytelling peculiar—it can be shared, but not necessarily comfortably. It might offer some generalisations, but perhaps not to all viewers, and differently depending on their proximity or distance from the mainstream. In *THE CAPACITY FOR ADEQUATE ANGER*, the story built on snapshots of memories and cultural references is told in a quiet, somewhat shy voice, which makes it necessary to intensify the focus and shorten the distance: we are seduced into a mode of

9 Clarissa Pinkola Estés, *Women Who Run with the Wolves* (New York: Ballantine Books, 1996).

10 *Waltz with Bashir*, dir. by Ari Folman (Ger-Fr-Is, 2008).

heightened attention. With this stronger focus, the stories of gender disobedience, the dreams and rebellions, meticulously crafted with different images and references, are received with stronger intensity, although probably differently depending on the viewer's own specific past experiences. As in the intercultural process of translation, there are more layers than just the two different languages that need to become a re-united vessel. As Gayatri Spivak argues in *Politics of Translation*, one should not assume that in Kirchenbauer's videos or performances, "she is just like me".[11] Most probably she is not, though we might have something in common; that makes the experience of her work even more complicated, as it resists mere consumption. / The ambivalences of childhood, class, tickling are mediated; they do not have, or only sometimes can have any direct connection with the audience's experiences. Some of our usual defences are left behind. We participate—Kirchenbauer's videos are definitely of an interactive nature—but the hells that might open in this participation are not those depicted by Claire Bishop. We are not abused, our suffering is not appropriated by others; if we experience intense emotions, memory work or address past traumas, we do it individually, on our own account.[12] While some versions of participation in art have indeed been involved in stripping the participants / public of dignity or of profit, here the experiences of vulnerability and pain are our own, as is the community we might suddenly feel with other viewers possibly experiencing similar affective shifts.

SOLIDARITY OF THE VULNERABLE?

There is a kind of common ground built here by the narrator of Kirchenbauer's videos / the artist herself, supposedly telling us her own memories, sometimes sharing sexual fantasies or the *Unheimlichkeit* of ticklishness, in a quiet voice, sometimes with laughs and screams. We merge in a common world, with our common, our experiences, as different as they might be, because the possible common denominator does not consist in shared facts, it consists in shared affective states: those of shame, ecstasy, fear or pleasure, in the turbulent building of our exceptional individuality as a collective process. In returning to childhood, to violence, to trauma, the storytelling provides a platform for an audience's desire for universalisation, where the particular set of experiences is set up as a platform for others to merge in such a universal and fundamental process as individuation. The artist's intention, however, and this I find particularly interesting, is to provide a universalisation as in "to make accessible", but not as in "to offer for easy appropriation". / In the past ten years Kirchenbauer has been preoccupied precisely with making her

11 Gayatri Spivak, "Politics of Translation", in *Translation Studies Reader*, Lawrence Venuti (ed.), (New York: Routledge, 2012).

12 See Claire Bishop, *Artificial Hells: Participatory Art and the Politics of Spectatorship* (London: Verso, 2012).

videos less easy for "cis-hetero audiences" to swallow her personal experiences and stories; in the more recent productions it can be seen that the viewer is perhaps invited to participate, but not necessarily to appropriate. There is affect and there are perhaps some points of possible identification, but there are also elements that make the viewer's experience unstable, just as the issues addressed by the artist usually are. Paradoxically, the symmetry between vulnerable or brutal events and affects narrated in the videos and performances and the visual and audio means chosen to stage them adds to the contradictions in the reception of Kirchenbauer's works. They seemingly perform gender, identity and class as trouble, not as a "ready-made" to be swallowed and colonised by the public's normalising and appropriating gaze. In her essay *FEELING DIFFERENCE*, the artist explains her disagreement with the plethora of commodified experiences ready to be purchased, suggesting that their enhanced readiness for immediate consumption is dangerous.[13] /

Several elements assure the success of Kirchenbauer's resistance to catharsis on the one hand and appropriations of minoritarian experiences by the often mainstream audience on the other. Reminiscent of Bertolt Brecht's "distancing effect" (Ger. *Verfremdungseffekt*), her montage and remixing strategies, playing with a plethora of references and storytelling which—while supposedly telling a consistent story, in fact tell pieces and fragments integrated only by the viewers with a great deal of effort, makes it hard to proceed with identification, and thus—also appropriation. /

The clarity and novelty of addressed complex phenomena, obtained with the visual queer phenomenology; the storytelling leading us to a childhood, which in the careful, silent account becomes "the childhood" of many of us in the public, but at the same time remains the artist's particular story; the choice of ordinary, common experiences, such as parents, tickling, summer fests or sport practice, builds proximity. But the specificity remains in place, as a warning that perhaps "she is not just like me".

THE SCARY RURAL LANDSCAPES AND THE VIOLENCE OF DISTINCTION

The interesting question in the context of Kirchenbauer's work is what the possible results and implications of such works as hers are. Does it offer a catharsis? A version of reconciliation with the painful, violent social world? Is its possibly therapeutic work directed at providing some sort of internalised acceptance of the status quo? Or is it rather further expanding the impossibility of acceptance, thus following Adorno's classically avant-gardist path? / I believe some interesting contradictions might be a result of her practice,

13 See Vika Kirchenbauer, *FEELING DIFFERENCE* (2019) in this volume.

combining a therapeutic moment with the impossibility of healing. What comes to the forefront in experiencing Kirchenbauer's work is a contradiction, combining the mixed feelings of connecting—with the narrated story, with the artist/voice on the one hand—and the perpetuation of the disconnections with the forms of violence at the core of the traumas the works address. In the videos discussed, I did not see the premise of a "happily ever after"; it perhaps allows some sense of empathy and community in the past experiences, but it is a precarious community. It lasts only for the moment of revisiting some past experiences or traumas, but is immediately dismantled as soon as the video is over: the world is still the same. Perhaps it did not change while I watched the video, but maybe I have changed, and this change consisted in sharing the common space with other vulnerable beings, without appropriating their experiences. This could, in turn, bring some change, but one that does not announce itself with big declarations and grand gestures, as was popular in critical and avant-garde art of earlier times. Now we are all "the people", also in the sense of being confronted with perhaps painful moments of growing up. Now we are perhaps "the vulnerable people", as opposed to the heroic, macho and exclusive people announced in past decades by some more privileged individuals in the name of all. Such "vulnerable people" obviously preserves differences, but perhaps allows for solidarity, understood not as an all-too-easy identification with the Other, but as solidarity—being many, together, but not the same.

FEELINGS THAT MOVE NOWHERE

KUNSTVEREIN FÜR DIE RHEINLANDE UND WESTFALEN • DÜSSELDORF
29 MAY–5 SEPTEMBER 2021

CURATOR	EVA BIRKENSTOCK
CURATORIAL ASSISTANCE	GESA HÜWE
FINANCE/ADMINISTRATION	HANNA WELZEL
TECHNICAL MANAGER	MARIUS COMANNS
MEMBERS DESK	SIGRID KONOPKA
INTERNSHIP	SUMRU TEKIN ANN-KATHRIN STUMPF
EXHIBITION MOUNTING	NINA NICK VALERIE BUCHOW DAVIT CHAGANAVA
EXHIBITION DOCUMENTATION	MAREIKE TOCHA

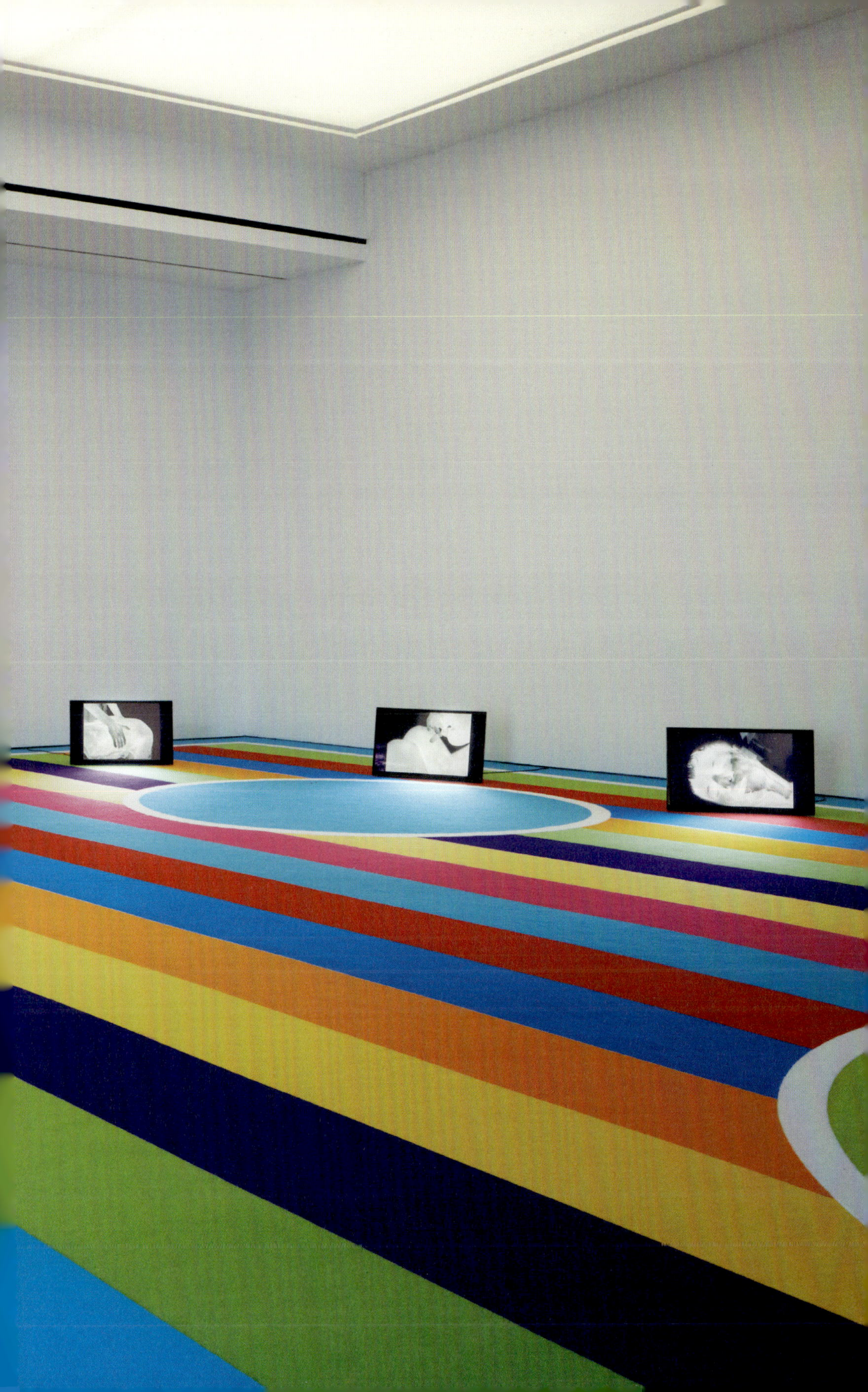

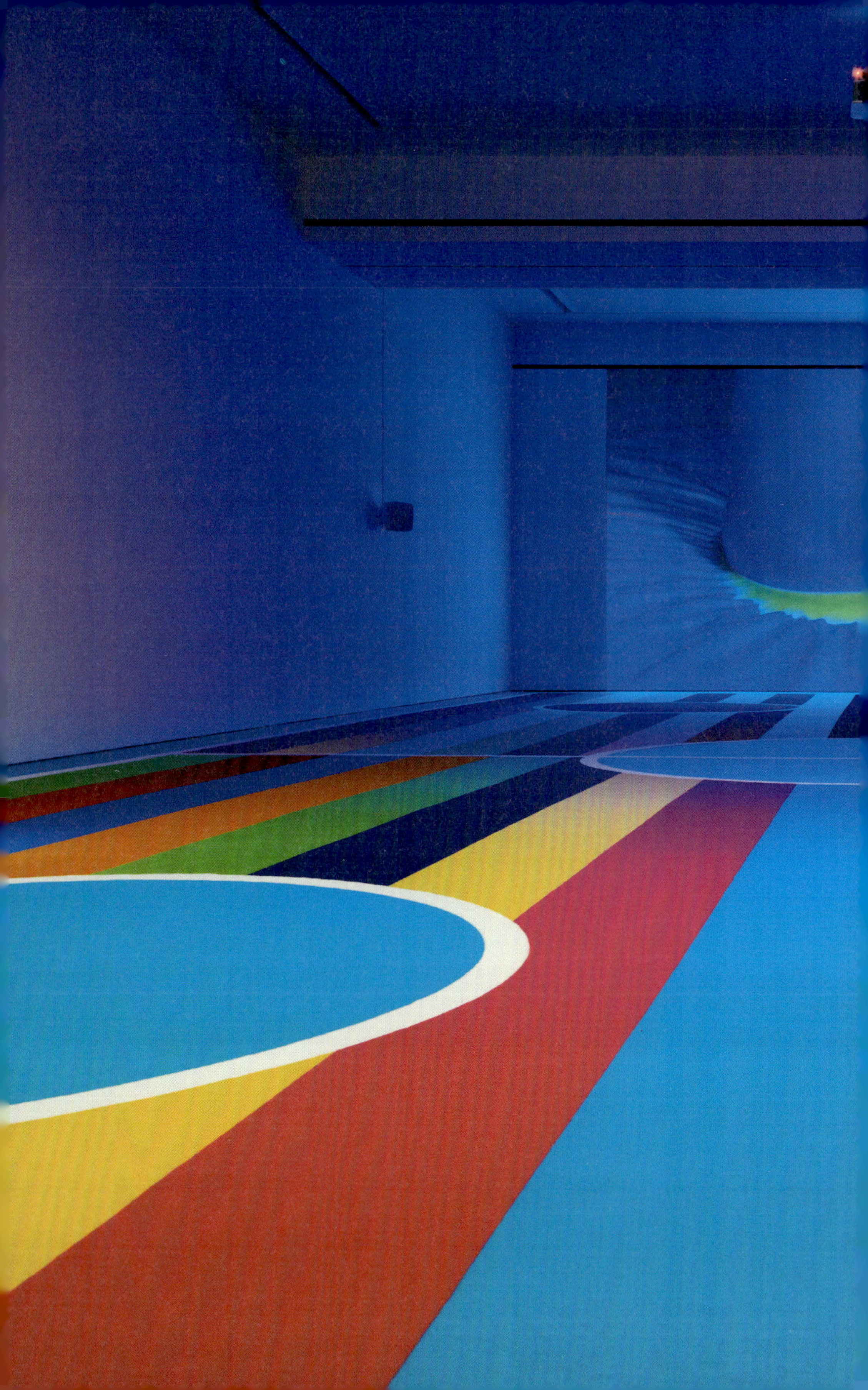

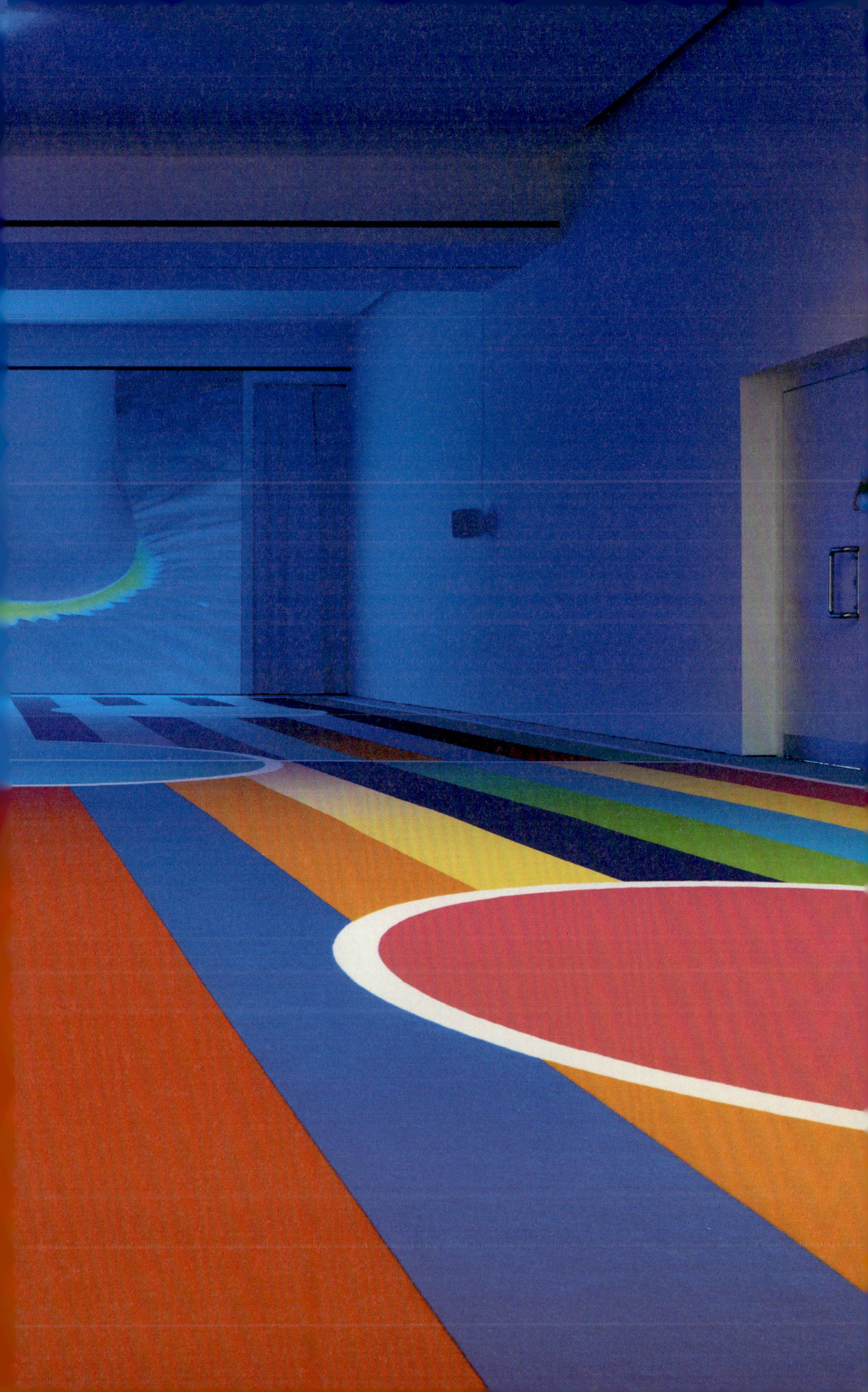

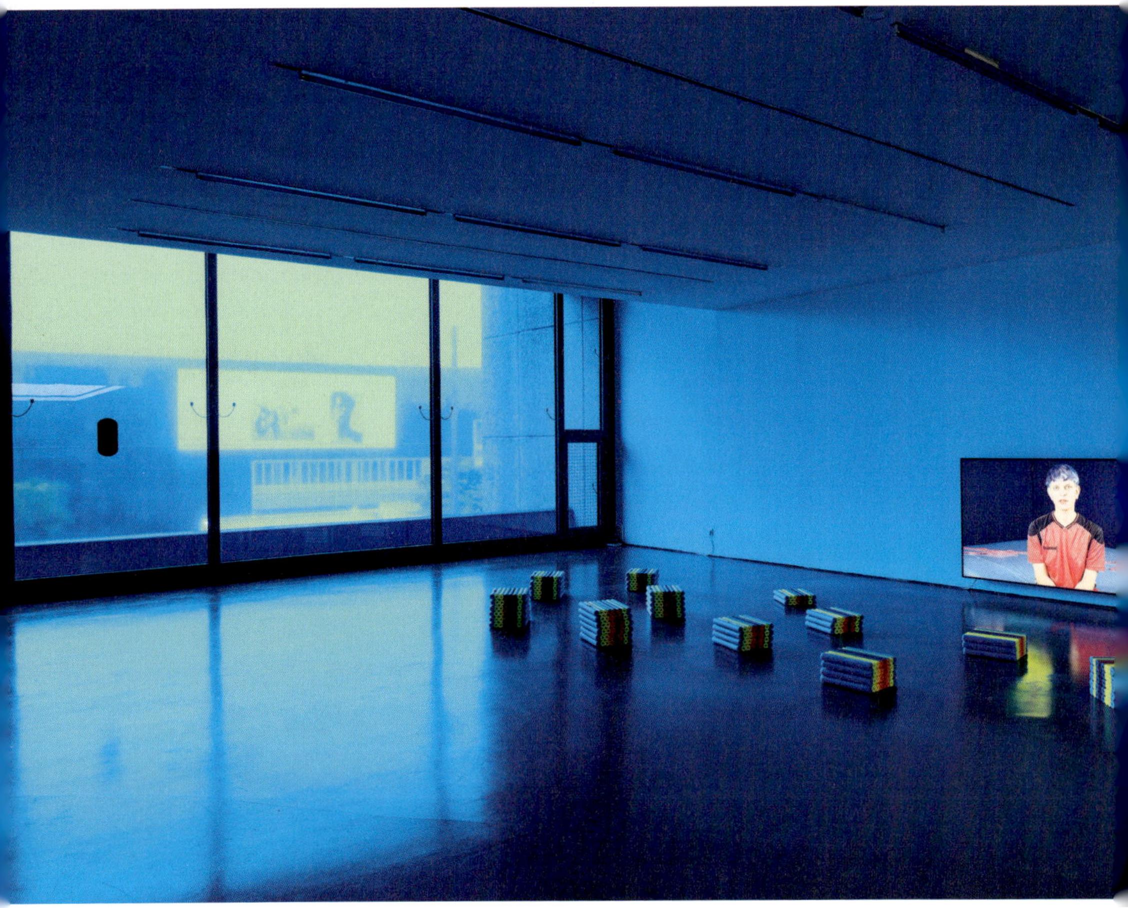

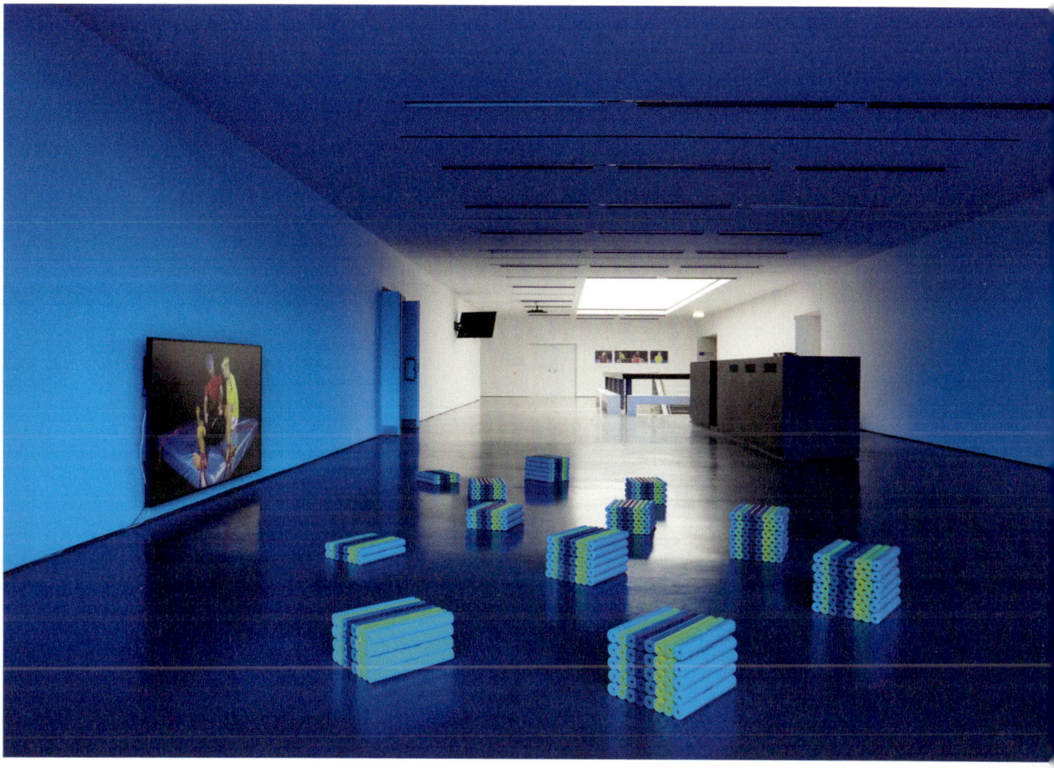

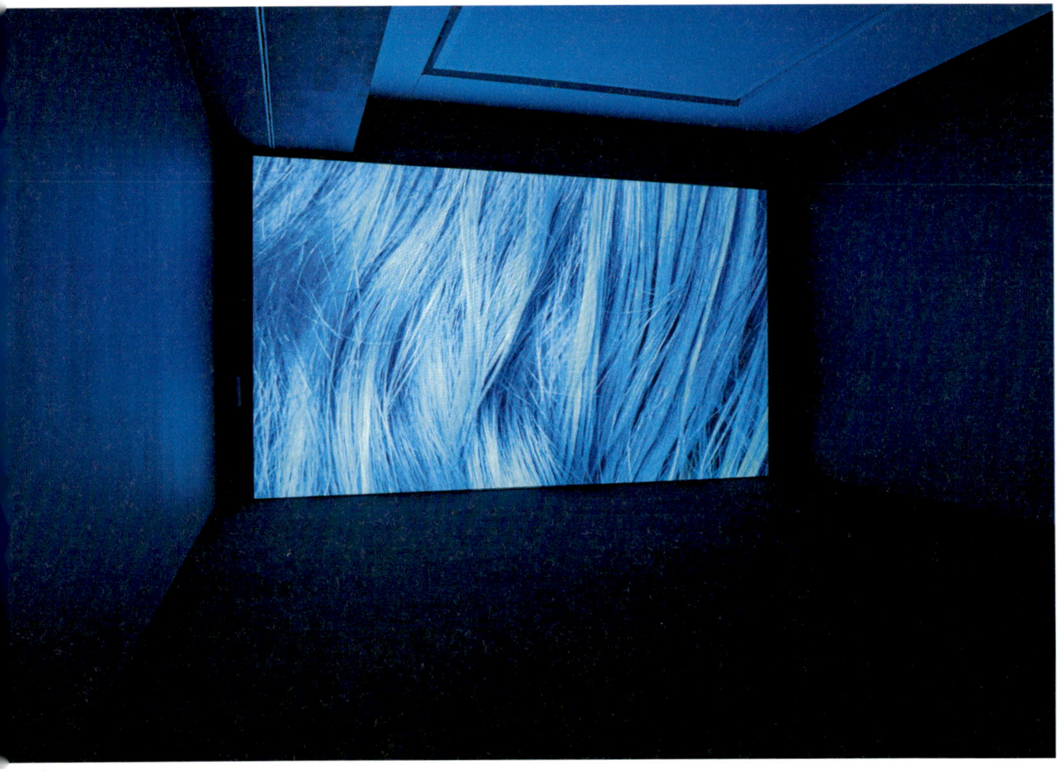

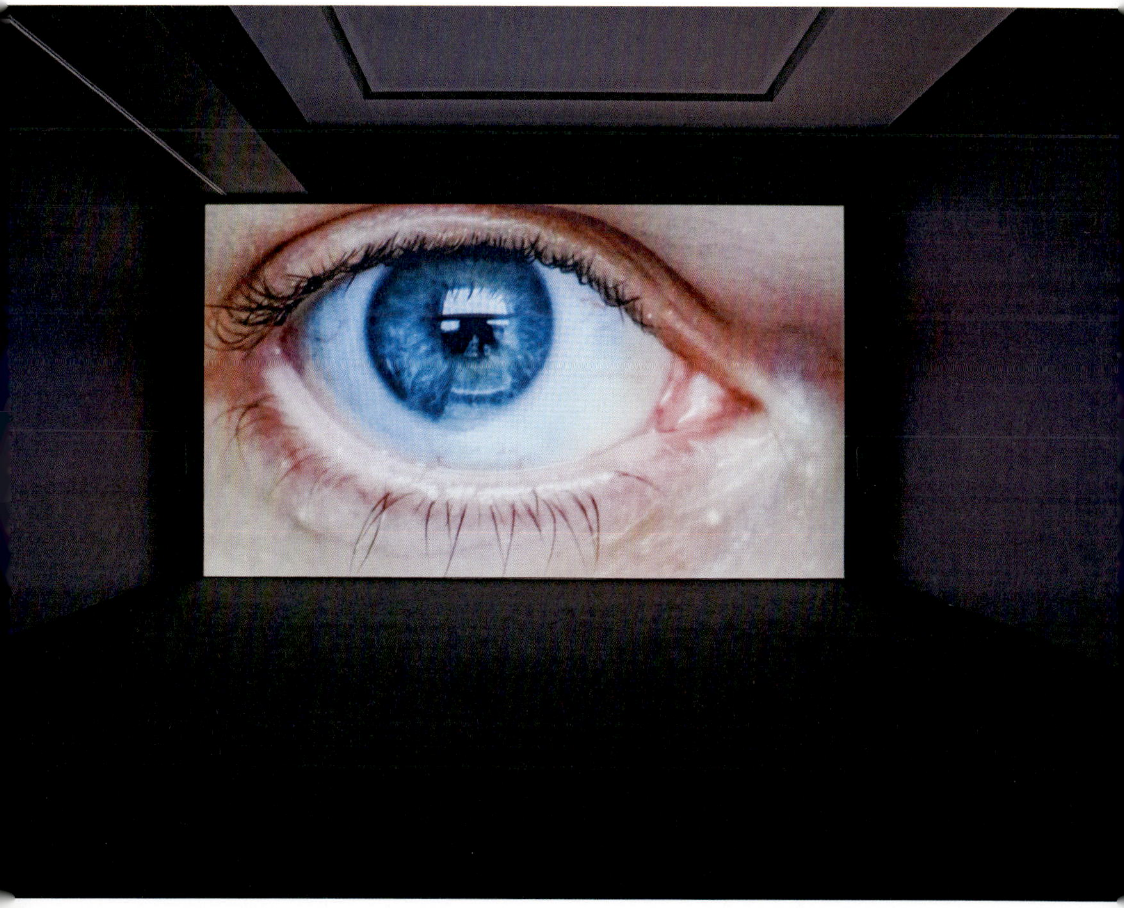

VIOLET BUT MORE RADICAL

KUNSTVEREIN KEVIN SPACE • VIENNA
19 NOVEMBER 2021–29 JANUARY 2022

CURATORS	FANNY HAUSER VIKTOR NEUMANN
TEAM OF KUNSTVEREIN KEVIN SPACE	FANNY HAUSER CAROLINA NÖBAUER DENISE HELENE SUMI FRANZISKA SOPHIE WILDFÖRSTER
EXHIBITION DOCUMENTATION	MAXIMILIAN ANELLI-MONTI

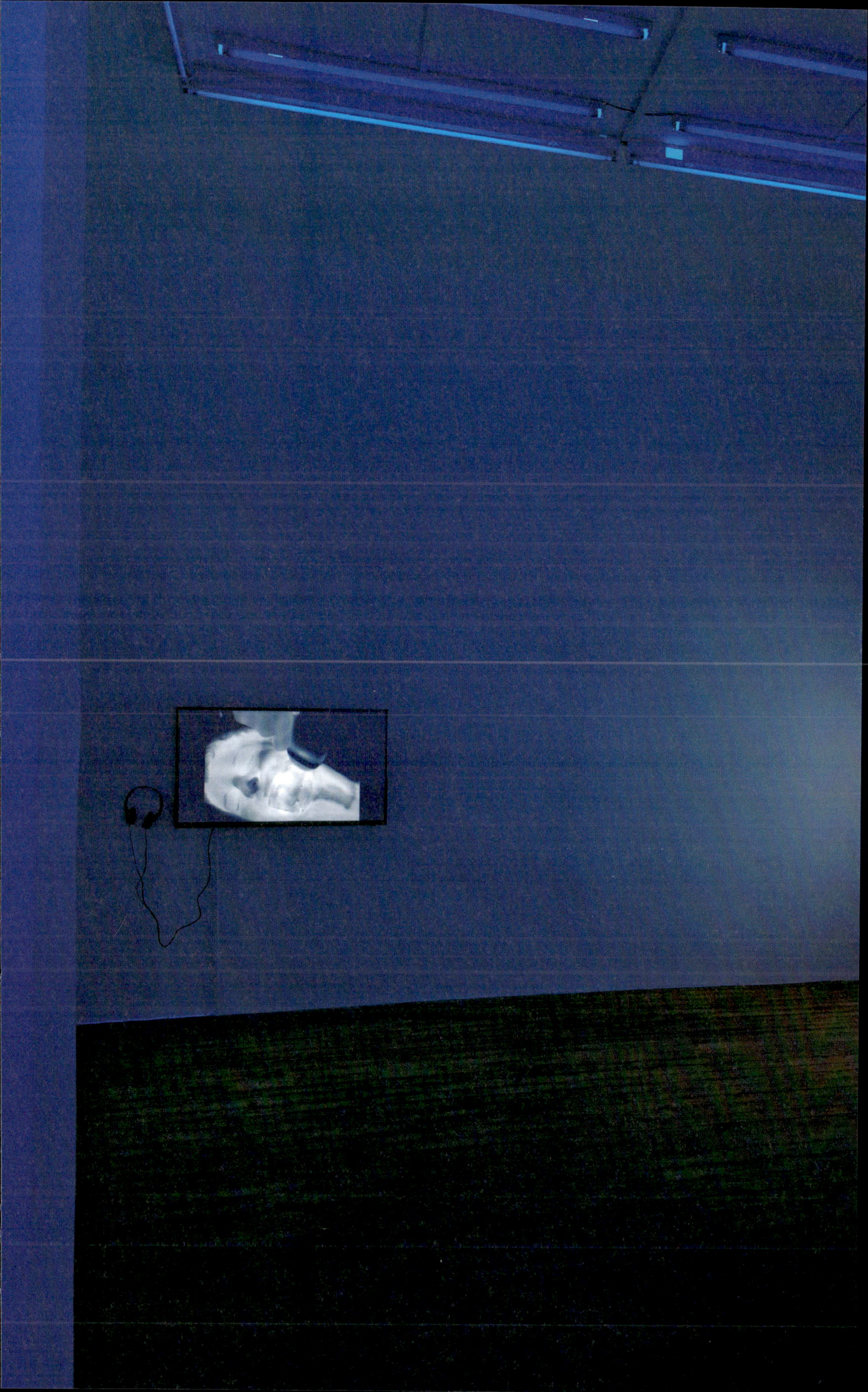

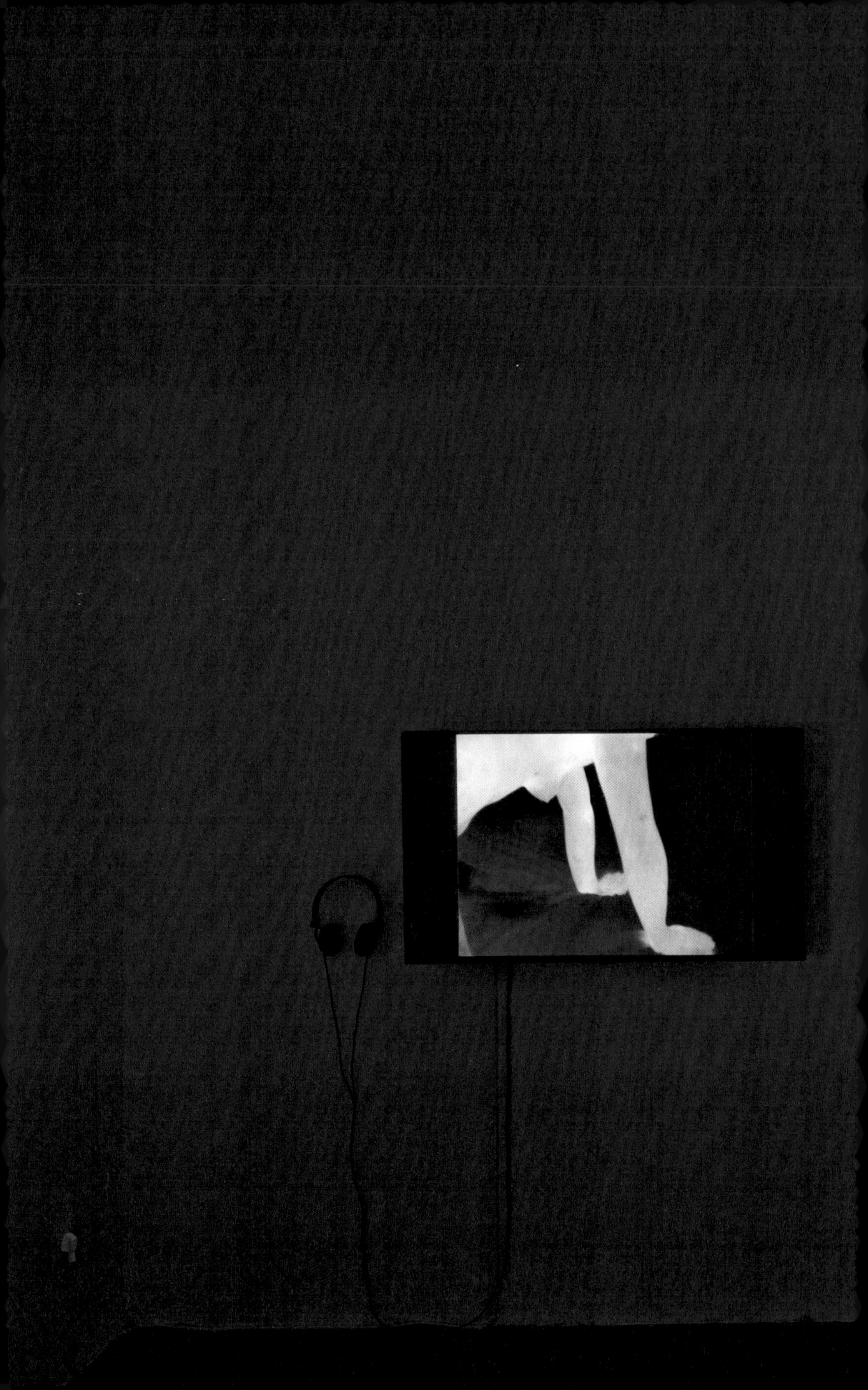

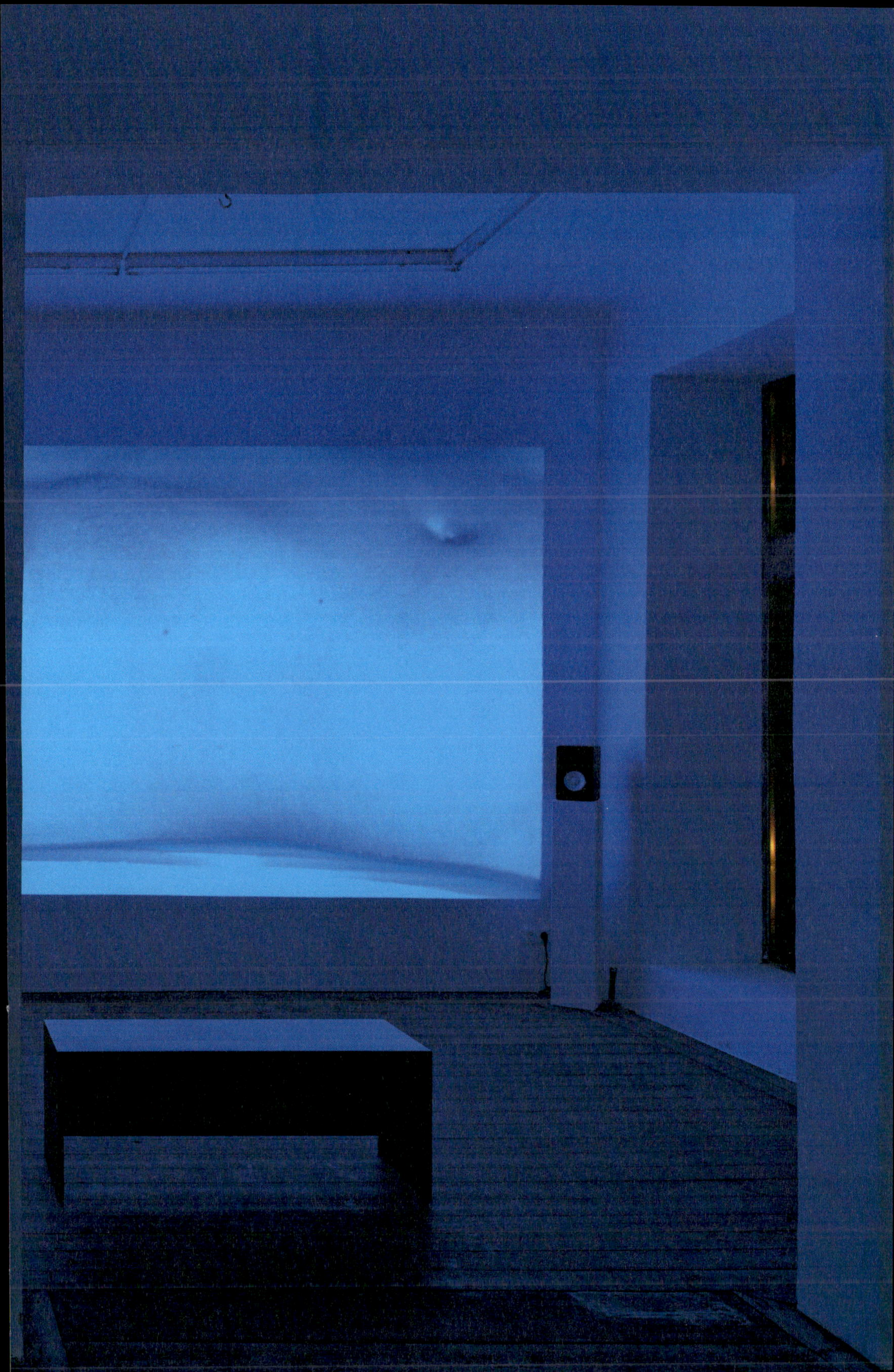

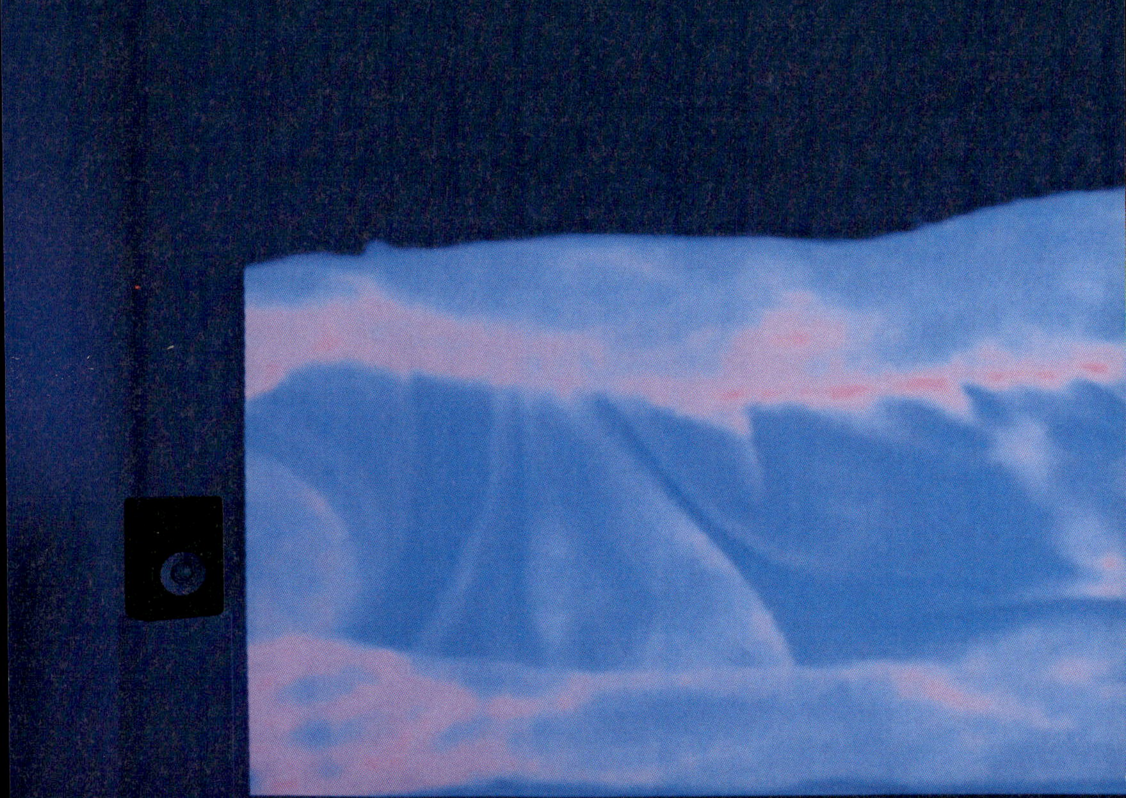

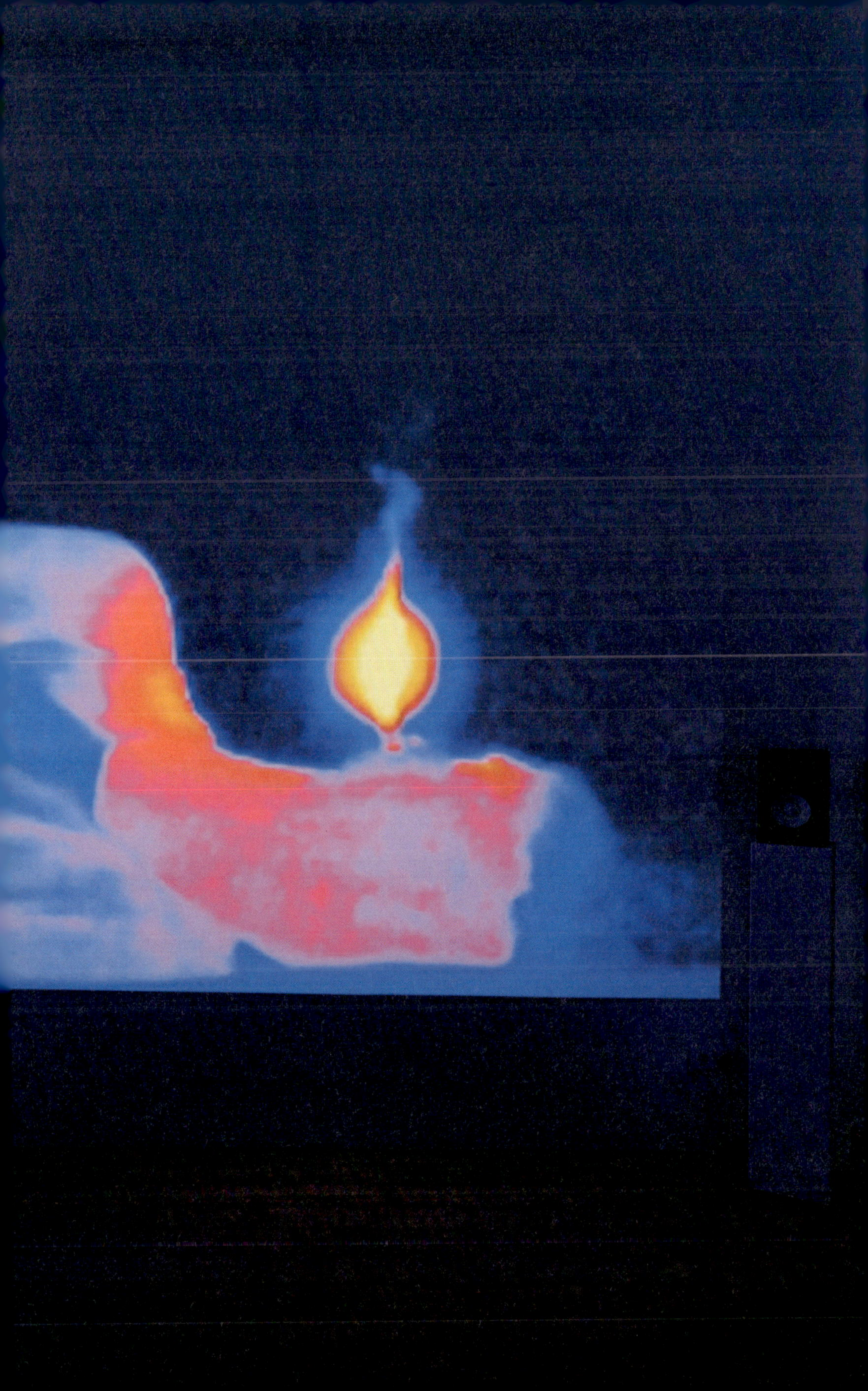

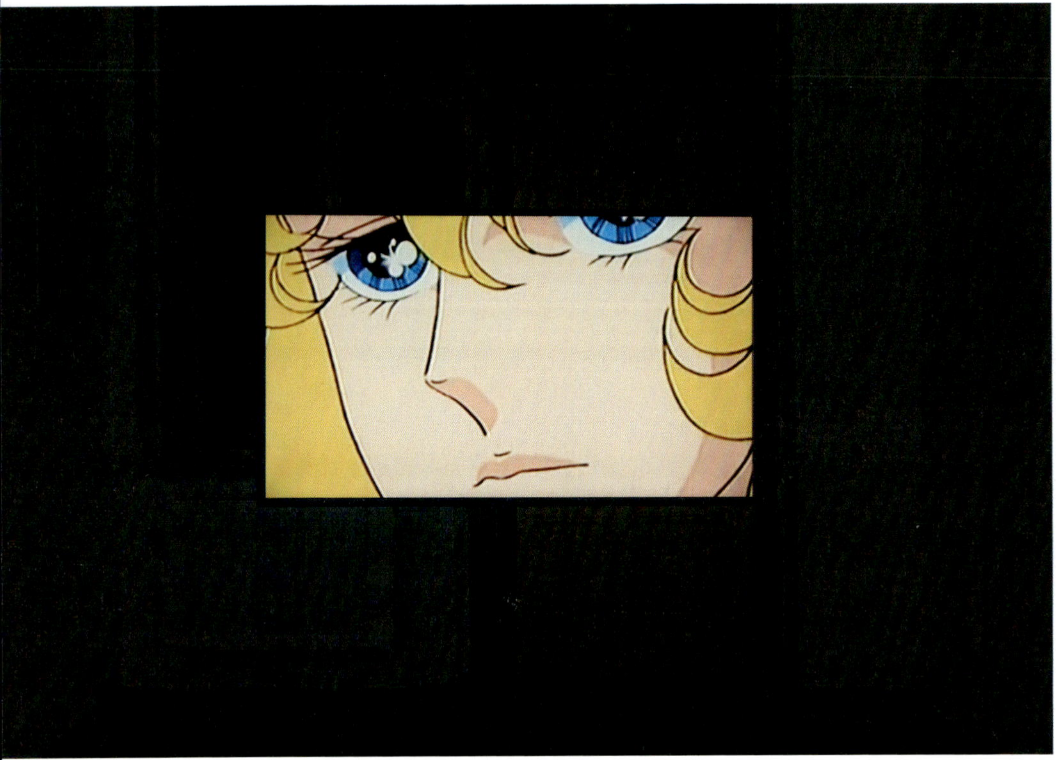

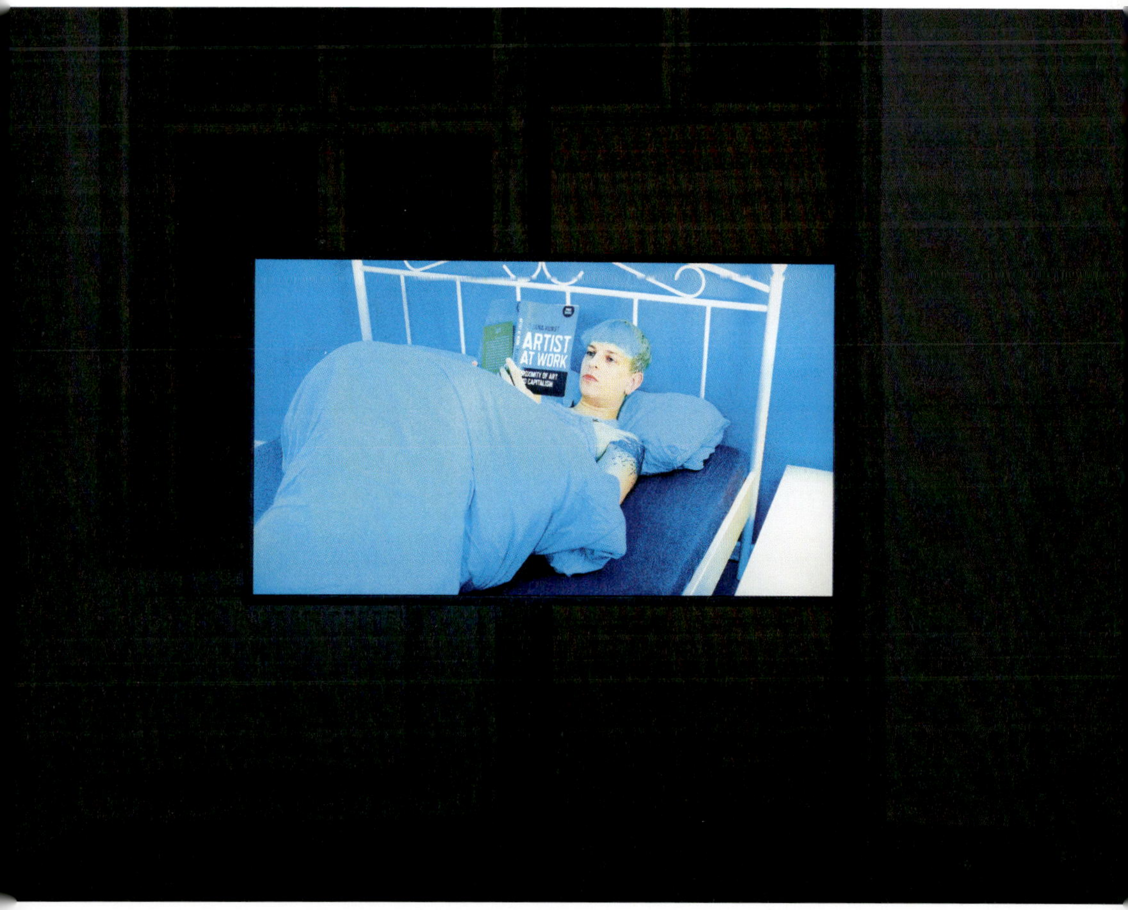
ARTIST
AT WORK

ON VIOLENCE AND VISIBILITY

VIKA KIRCHENBAUER · 2022

PRIVATISED PAIN: THE STRUGGLE OVER WHAT ENTERS THE PUBLIC POLITICAL SPHERE

In the art field, as in other professional fields, sexual violence is not only a gender issue, but also a labour issue. Freelancing arrangements are common in artists' studios and megastudios as well as in private galleries, even when those formally self-employed work exclusively, permanently and indefinitely for one individual or business. This frequently goes for registrars, studio managers, administrative workers, facility managers, chefs, artist assistants, as well as for researchers, cleaning personnel, art installers, etc. Such freelance setups leave those without an appropriate employment contract with little job protection, and in a poor position from which to take the risk of standing up for themselves. These conditions also result in a lack of formal structures through which complaints concerning sexual harassment and assault could possibly be processed. In addition, power is very concentrated in contemporary art, so that, independently of specific work arrangements or contracts, it must always be feared that those with accumulated connections may assert their influence in the field to ruin somebody's professional, artistic, personal or moral reputation in the event they do speak up. / Within the art field, power structures are upheld by means of informal networks and unwritten agreements. For instance, remarkably few artists have any written contracts with the galleries representing them, sometimes handing over their entire body of work in a leap of faith. Those occupying the more powerful position in such partnerships favour the vagueness of verbal promises over binding written arrangements, a setup that works to their advantage in instances of conflict. These states of informal connectedness create personal and professional dependencies that often result in implicating many people in known transgressions, at the least through their inaction and silence. Under such circumstances there exist various painful public and private secrets, and—as has been observed over the past years, especially in the European context—each time the perpetrators are about to be exposed, the issue suddenly and swiftly disappears again. /

In Germany—to focus on one example in the European context—specifically within the artistic and cultural field, only few cases of sexual violence have been publicly exposed in the wake of the global #MeToo movement.[1] The question as to why that is provokes many answers, which are not the same for each and every context. A shared foundational condition is, however, the following: German law places the honour and reputation of those accused above the free speech and expression of those affected. Unless the perpetrator is convicted in court, publicly accusing a person of sexual violence or misconduct is punishable as slander or defamation of character.

/ If the law protects first and foremost the honour and reputation of someone accused of sexual violence, it also means it protects their privacy. Privacy is a public issue, and the question as to whom or what it is bestowed on remains a site of continued political struggle. On a legal level as well as in social debate, some sex acts are made private, while others are made public. In this regard, acts of intimacy—whether violent or consensual—are always publicly mediated. Up until 1997, German law did not criminalise marital rape, relegating such violence to the protected sphere of heterosexual privacy.[2] In contrast, until their decriminalisation in 1994, in (West) Germany consensual acts of intimacy between men—even if they took place in a private home—were not private affairs but occurrences of legal, and thus public concern.[3] Heterosexual sex, conversely, remains linked exclusively to the institution of personal life, structurally differentiated from the public, political or professional sphere.[4] This in turn means that instances of sexual violence in heterosexual constellations are historically situated within this solidified conception of a private and personal zone, a place from which survivors must wrestle them into the public political sphere if they seek justice. The way in which the law protects the privacy of alleged

1 The movement was initially started by Tarana Burke in 2006, and developed into a broad-based international movement over a decade later, in 2017.

2 Under both East and West Germany criminal codes, rape was defined as forcing a woman to extramarital sex, meaning that marital rape was not criminalised. In July 1997, marital rape became criminalised in unified Germany by removing the word "extramarital" from the definition of rape in the Criminal Code. This change happened after the German Bundestag voted to criminalise marital rape on 15 May 1997, and to include men as possible victims. Following a heated debate, 138 of 643 MPs voted against criminalisation, including former Interior Minister Horst Seehofer, and current CDU party leader Friedrich Merz. See the minutes of the session ›https://dserver.bundestag.de/btp/10/10175.pdf‹ [last accessed on 16 May 2022].

3 In the GDR, homosexual acts were only punishable under § 151 from 1968 on if they involved minors.

4 Lauren Berlant and Michael Warner, "Sex in Public", *Critical Inquiry*, vol. 24 no. 2 (Winter, 1998), p. 553.

perpetrators (independently of their gender or sexual orientation) is therefore closely connected to heterosexual culture's institutions and ideologies of intimacy. /

Different legal circumstances in regard to allegations of abuse and sexual violence produce different specific systems of silencing in their respective contexts. In the United States, for instance, the right to free speech is generally valued more highly in legal terms than it is in Germany and most other European countries. While the American conception of free speech constitutionally protects all kinds of misinformation, hate speech, right-wing propaganda, conspiracy narratives and verbal assaults, at the same time it also to some extent facilitates the possibility for survivors of sexual violence to confront their abusers on public platforms, and thus alert and protect others. /

As a global audience has learned through a wide array of documentary streaming series[5] as well as newspaper and online articles focusing on prominent and powerful men, wealthy US celebrities accused of sexual misconduct usually use settlement agreements to stop those who are potentially ready to speak out against them. These contracts generally include confidentiality clauses—often referred to as nondisclosure agreements—that, alongside substantial payments, often suffice to ensure that not more than a handful of people ever learn about the accusations. Breaking a nondisclosure agreement incurs a stiff financial penalty, which makes such instances rare, given that abuse and sexual violence are facilitated in the first place by conditions of unequal distribution of power and wealth. This system of payoffs and nondisclosure agreements allows abusers in possession of the necessary means to continue preying on other people who have no warning.

/ If in Germany—to stick with the context I am most familiar with—relatively few perpetrators have been exposed,[6] the conclusion should not be that these things do not happen here, but that there are reasons why they only rarely spill into the public realm of information. Here, the system that serial perpetrators with access to legal teams deploy differs from the strategy of their North American counterparts. Rather than gagging those affected by their violence with money and nondisclosure agreements, financial threats serve as the tool of silencing most used. On the basis that no public allegations of abuse are allowed if the perpetrator has not been convicted, in Germany it is common practice for law firms to send out cease and desist letters. These letters are received not only by those naming perpetrators publicly, but also by those sharing information about a specific perpetrator's occupation or branch of business that could lead to them being recognised. The cease and desist letters usually include threats of lawsuits not only on the grounds of alleged slander

5 Among several, the most prominent might be *Untouchable* on the Harvey Weinstein case, *Leaving Neverland* on the allegations of childhood sexual abuse against Michael Jackson and the docu-series *Surviving R. Kelly*.

6 Some notable exceptions from the wider field of the arts in which the names of the accused have been publicly exposed are the cases of comedian Luke Mockridge, director Dieter Wedel and rapper Samra.

and defamation of character, but also for compensation payments for the economic "losses"[7] the accusations may have ensued. Potentially having to recompense for the (speculative and hypothetical) economic "losses" of a person with ample business activity puts most people at risk of financial ruin. For those receiving such letters, the alternative to costly—and potentially ruinous—court procedures against high profile law firms is to sign the cease and desist order, declaring never to repeat any of the accusations. By signing, they also agree to pay the law firms for their efforts in drafting the threat, which adds insult to injury. Yet, understandably, paying a three-figure sum rather than possibly being ordered to pay tens of thousands will be most people's only feasible choice. The result is that conversations around specific cases vanish quickly from social media platforms, if they even appear in the first place.

/ In light of these silencing strategies, the most promising option for exposing powerful abusers is the press. Abuses are rarely isolated incidents; instead, they follow a predictable pattern and logic within systems that enable and sustain these violent practices. If dedicated journalists can establish such a pattern, they can publish a story even in the absence of a court conviction, and without disclosing any of their sources. This is possible under a strict protocol if the independently collected evidence is overwhelmingly strong and beyond any reasonable doubt. However, journalists are not public prosecutors and they operate within an attention economy. The media outlets they work for will only allocate time and resources to a case if the perpetrator is well-known enough for the revelations to generate broad public attention. If a person's abuser is not sufficiently well-known, the only remaining option is the justice system, through which only about 1% of the total number of rape cases end in the perpetrator's conviction.[8] Such court cases with extremely limited prospects for conviction take place at the expense of potential re-traumatisation of the survivors, so instigating them is not a decision taken lightly.

/ If an abuser inhabits a position of significant influence and power, this often manifests in their ability to prevent the violence they exert from entering the public realm of knowledge. It is often within such privatised spheres that violence can do its workings in the most unobstructed way. In addition to the prevailing structural, systemic and economic realities that privatise sexual violence, significant resources are mobilised in specific cases to keep allegations from becoming public. The feminist struggles of recent years are a direct response to this, and in many ways stand in the feminist tradition of critiquing the untethering of the ostensibly private zone from the public political sphere. As such, #MeToo follows a form of activism that seeks to make commonly and publicly visible what is otherwise relegated to

7 I put "losses" in quotation marks because I do not agree that a projected, but unrealised profit can automatically be considered a loss.

8 In Germany, about 15% of the total number of rape cases are brought to court, of which about 7.5% result in conviction, according to data from 2014 to 2016, evaluated by criminologist Christian Pfeiffer in: Christian Pfeiffer, *Gegen die Gewalt* (Munich: Random House, 2019).

individualised experience. Such a strategy can be powerful, in that it can lead in some cases to convictions, and perhaps even more importantly, give a sense of connectedness and agency to people who might have previously regarded their experiences as isolated from a political dimension. Together, this can shift public discourse and sensibility around what is tolerated and what is not. Yet, in addition to the struggles for the accounts of (sexual) violence experienced or observed to enter the public realm of knowledge, it is also important to examine the social conditions under which any resistance to the privatisation of pain and trauma takes place. One fundamental question in this regard is whether a painful and embodied experience can be made commonly and publicly visible at all, and if so, at what cost.

OFF THE RECORD: ON THE POLITICAL CONCEPTUALISATIONS OF OPACITY AND TRANSPARENCY

In light of the circumstance that only a fraction of cases of sexual violence end in the perpetrator's conviction, it must be stated that within current legal frameworks these crimes are hardly prosecutable. Western legal systems are constructed upon a notion of intelligibility, in the sense that they presume that violence can be evidenced and proven in general terms, and that it can become legible and verifiable beyond the specific, embodied and situated experience. If someone has experienced sexual violence, in addition to the crime often having been relegated to the private realm without witness or evidence, the affected person may also not become cognitively aware of the crime immediately, if ever. Past experiences, amnesia, a state of freezing as well as self-questioning often contribute to making it a long process until a survivor of assault, coercion, abuse or rape can trust their feelings enough to place and name what they experienced. Memory resists the linearity of a timeline, and trauma can put gaps in places the mind is not prepared to revisit. Consequently, despite its having occurred, the experience of violence cannot necessarily be proven even to oneself. It is nonetheless expected of survivors to verifiably prove themselves and their case. Thus, the courageous act of speaking up always comes accompanied by the heightened pressure of making oneself transparent under public interrogation. This stands in opposition to the way the perpetrator is positioned, who defends their chartered right to privacy and honour, and who is equipped with the legal foundations to do so. It is significant to note who departs from a space of self-evident opacity, of not having to disclose anything, and who can only seek justice under the condition of making themselves transparent. / The political conceptualisations of transparency and opacity are deeply embedded in Western thought. The ways in which they structure relations are often indicative of how privilege and power are distributed in a specific context. In his writing, when Martinican philosopher Édouard Glissant "clamor[s] for the right to opacity for everyone",[9] it is in response to a Western subjectivity set on making the Other transparent through processes of knowing and understanding. The Other is assessed according to a Western scale of measurement; using that scale, legitimacy can only be achieved through transparency. This process takes place within a hierarchical relation in which the subjects of understanding need not explain themselves, while the objects of understanding are reduced and rendered knowable. The claim for the right to opacity is therefore not a call to strip the powerful of their privileges, but to generalise these privileges and extend them to everyone by effectuating equal relations predicated on opacity that "[d]isplace all reduction."[10]

/ The violence of imposed transparency can be observed at the example of colonial ways of relating, yet Glissant's philosophy describes something so fundamental to Western subjectivity that it can be found structuring all realms of relation in a hierarchical manner. Opacity—the right not to be understood and reduced—is granted only to some in all Western societies, while those situated lower within constructed social hierarchies are only legitimised if making themselves transparent. Somebody who seeks asylum will need to relay their most traumatising experiences to convince the body of people their safety and survival depends upon, while somebody naturally considered a citizen simply enjoys inalienable rights without first having anything to prove. Somebody who is transgender needs to make themself legible and intelligible in order for the judicial and medical system to grant them legal personhood, while somebody who is cisgender is not required to endure psychiatric assessments for their identity to be adequately represented in their passport. Somebody who applies for the unemployment benefits they are technically entitled to generally needs to grant the state access to their bank account, while somebody who is wealthy and feasibly owes large sums in taxes can often protect their financial information as part of their privacy. Someone who has experienced sexual violence needs to provide solid evidence in vivid and painful detail under interrogation in a court setting, while a perpetrator can simply be silent on the matter and insist that their name not be tarnished. /

Especially when it comes to sexual violence and the ways in which justice or accountability can be sought, the constellations around private/public and opacity/transparency are marked by friction and ambivalence. On the one hand, sexual violence is relegated to a private and personal realm, from where it needs to be wrestled into the public political sphere for any kind of justice to be found. On the other hand, this shift into the public sphere takes place under conditions reproducing the violence of transparency onto those who on top risk a doubling of traumatic events. It is a precarious position, in which those affected by sexual violence are rarely granted any right to opacity,

9 Édouard Glissant, *Poetics of Relation*, trans. by Betsy Wing (Ann Arbor: The University of Michigan Press, 1997), p. 194.

10 Glissant, p. 190.

at least almost never in conjunction with the exposure of perpetrators in the public sphere. As mentioned earlier, rare exceptions in this regard are the instances in which journalists can establish a pattern of abuse and publish a story citing people who spoke off the record—a notable circumstance in which survivors are not required to expose themselves publicly as a precondition for a perpetrator to become known. In view of this, it is incumbent to conceive of further ways through which cases of abuse and injustice can become known in the public realm without forcing transparency upon those affected. This would also mean expanding upon the notions about how violence relates to visibility in more general terms, in order to radically challenge the conditions that produce the unequal relations and positions around transparency and opacity in the first place.

VIOLENCE BEYOND VISION: DIFFICULTIES REPRESENTING THE STRUCTURAL

For a broader consideration of how violence relates to visibility, it makes sense to move on from the textual realm of law and journalism, and contemplate the ways in which violence is approached within practices that make use of images, still or moving. The conceptualisation of images is historically linked to the ways in which, for centuries, the Western eye has been attached to the idea of making visible, legible and intelligible. Within this notion, what is invisible to the eye is regarded as veiled or hidden, ready to be uncovered or excavated. This impulse has also informed contemporary artistic as well as activist strategies from within this Western legacy. When seeking to address the social workings of violence, much faith is usually placed in the power of the image to make violence and injustice visible. By framing the image as evidence, these strategies position seeing as the main way of knowing, and become complicit in maintaining and solidifying empirical notions of the visual—while generally offering little acknowledgement of the approach's limitations. Though such strategies can in many instances be efficient in mobilising people through or around a commonly visible object, their effectiveness ends at the point where vision begins to fail. /

This Western conception of the visible presumes that violence is something that can be seen, at the very least through images and verifiable traces of its effects. But oftentimes, violence is only felt by those affected by it. Across differences, violence can rarely be seen and witnessed from all positions and perspectives. Depending on where we stand, we might be unable to perceive specific instances of violence that are first-hand for others. Thus, we often remain oblivious to the ordinariness of violence others are subjected to. If violence cannot be seen from where we stand, that does not indicate it doesn't exist. Hence, our desires for wanting to be made to see should make way for modes of justice not reliant on making the pain of those affected generally visible. /

Not all forms of violence manifest in a visual way, and not all instances of violence can be commonly witnessed. Furthermore, violence fundamentally relies on structures and systems enabling it. Such complex formations can hardly be conveyed by means of conventional representational methods. Within the logic of the visual, the symptomatic then often ends up standing in for the systemic, while blurring it significantly. Indirect and immaterial aspects of structural violence shape our world's often very concrete and material injustices. For those invested in artistic practices around (moving) images, such forms of structural violence operating outside the representable realm bring about fundamental challenges. Knowing that these kinds of structural violence cannot be captured in an image does not solve the question as to how to address them. To confront the intricate systems in which violence and injustice emerge, operate and ripple into the future, I believe it is necessary to imagine different ways of conceptualising moving image practices, perhaps by decentralising the visible, or by establishing images capable of being sceptical of themselves.

/

Power can manifest in the ability to keep violence away from public vision, and it can also manifest in the ability to make violence itself invisible. Within established social hierarchies, the more economic, social or political power a person holds, the more they are able to affect the lives of others, particularly also in indirect ways. Or, to put it differently, the violence they exert can work through structures, and thus outside the directly visible or observable realm. Their policies and actions may, for instance, cause someone to be denied work, housing, or social benefits. Yet despite impacting the lives of people intimately, their active role and responsibility may not necessarily manifest in immediately traceable and directly observable ways.

/

This very much relates to systems of social stratification, within which many people are only able to confront structural violence through immediate resistance. While the violence working through structures may not show, the visible response to it is frequently framed as aggressive. When then, for instance, entire social groups are stigmatised as rowdy and violent, they are accused solely of their social status, and the associated structural limitations on being violent beyond the immediate and visible. To focus on the visible realm of violence thus often means to focus disproportionately on those without the structural opportunities to exert violence beyond the visible.

/

The present is shaped by personal and collective instances of (past) violence that resist visibility, which tasks us to rethink the relation between representation, gaze, memory, and trauma. Within artistic practices that employ the moving image, it is necessary to leave behind the assumption that violence and trauma can be adequately represented within the visual field. Instead, it may be more appropriate to imagine the totality of violence and trauma as the negative space that shapes and defines the little that becomes commonly observable. This negative space itself might not be captured; yet again, this circumstance in no way negates its presence.

In making moving image work we often try to fix and stabilise an object into steady form, but—to quote Lauren Berlant—"objects are always looser than they appear (...) only a semblance, a seeming, a projection effect of interest in a thing we are trying to stabilize."[11] The practical and discursive terms of stabilising and visualising may be too limiting a conception to approach the complex formations around violence and trauma. In moving image practices, perhaps it could be more generative to depart from an understanding of the weakness of one's tools, and question one's own impulse to transfer the non-graspable into the normative frame of vision. /

Infrared imaging technology is quite allegorical for the desperate impulse to make visible. There exists a common misunderstanding around infrared imaging technology, namely that it makes us see infrared radiation. It does not, because nothing can really make us see anything beyond the light spectrum physically visible to us. Infrared imaging technology is not a representational medium, but a compound measuring tool and data visualisation system. A thermal sensor array measures the amount of infrared radiation emitted, transmitted and reflected by an object. In a somewhat simplified manner, each pixel of an image can be imagined as a single temperature measurement, with software translating these measurements into a visual display. The human eye is and remains unable to see infrared radiation, so all information measured needs to be represented within the visible spectrum. To this end, infrared imaging technology lets the user choose among various visualisation models in which, for instance, red stands for hot while blue stands for cold, or black stands for hot and white stands for cold, or the reverse. While promising to make us see more, infrared technology reduces, compresses and translates what we cannot see into our limited spectrum of vision. This is where it becomes emblematic of many visual strategies that try to drag what resists representation into the frame. /

In the pursuit of seeing more, we refuse to see the limits of our vision. Yet in order to imagine ways to justice and accountability applicable beyond the narrow field of empirical intelligibility, it is a prerequisite to acknowledge the limited spectrum in which violence can in fact become visible. Moreover, it is crucial to let go of the faulty notion that violence outside visibility can be shifted into the visible realm for it to become generally knowable from all positions and perspectives. When those affected by violence are only legitimised by making themselves and their pain transparent, this is always connected to an ideology of the visible that refuses to come to terms with its limitations. If it were instead commonly recognised that not all violence can be made visible, it would also become illogical to demand transparency from those affected by it.

11 Lauren Berlant, 'The commons: Infrastructures for troubling times*', *Environment and Planning D: Society and Space*, vol. 34, no. 3, June 2016, p. 394.

VISIBILITY & DISTANCE: PERSPECTIVES OF CLASS MOBILITY IN CONTEMPORARY ART

In a last step, I want to invert the initial question that has made me think through these thoughts. Instead of asking how violence relates to visibility, I want to consider how visibility relates to violence, moving from notions of minority visibility to questions around class mobility in relation to contemporary art. Demands for visibility have been central to many kinds of identity-based activism for several decades. At the same time, members of the social groups demanding social and political visibility find themselves already frequently burdened with the experience of hypervisibility in the everyday, since difference from dominant, unmarked identities is often socially codified based on visual notions. This hypervisibility in the public sphere often leads to increased exposure to violence. It is then hoped that representational visibility will curb the ordinariness of the violence that minority groups are subjected to. The underlying assumption is that representational visibility of the under-represented is followed by enhanced political power. However, this direct and absolute connection between representational visibility and political power is doubtful, since institutions of power usually grant visibility only in an individualised and rarefied sense, rather than in a collective and political one. The social acceptance of a visible representative of a social group does not necessarily influence the life conditions of the demographic ostensibly represented. /

Increasingly over the past decades, hegemonic institutions of contemporary art have prided themselves on "giving visibility" to artists from various minoritised positions, whose difference the institutions' curators or boards measure based on their own scale. The idea of "giving visibility" presumes that people only become fully visible on an elevated platform, and within a specific context. The cause for someone having previously remained unseen from a certain position and perspective is usually attributed not to the limitations of the looking subject but to the alleged invisibility of the object. Additionally, such a politics of visibility presupposes that subjectivity and identity are per se visually representable—even though queerness, for instance, might fail to appear in the representational field, residing rather outside the rainbow that constitutes the visible spectrum. /

Those who like to "give visibility" usually also like to "include", the concept of "inclusion" being by necessity self-centralising. The art field perceives itself as the desirable centre to which representatives from the margins are admitted, while at the same time negating that the supposed margins are most people's centres. All kinds of cultural formation irrefutably possess an aesthetic form, whether or not they are regarded as artistic. Yet the art field is disinclined to regard sites of cultural formation and aesthetic practice that are less socially valued as alternative centres on an equal level. Instead, through inclusion it aims to reproduce its own legitimacy and centrality as well as the hierarchical structuring it allegedly seeks to subvert. The artists or art collectives included then often stand in for the demographics they are tasked with representing. / The democratic notion that an individual is capable of representing the perspective of a larger social group within a public field can be generative, also in contemporary art. Representation is capable of creating important affective binds of identification along the lines of many social markers. It can influence and instigate important discourses. Seeing an aspect of oneself reflected by means of representational visibility can also provide a variety of the optimism required for sustained political struggle. Yet representation itself does not guarantee any structural changes capable of accommodating political demands.

/ This becomes particularly apparent when within a hegemonic cultural field, such as the art field, individuals come to serve as representatives of a class reality from outside the field's own environment. Minority categories intersect with structures of social class, and identity is never as stable and fixed as processes of othering suggest. Yet, while within social minority categories—such as within gender, sexual, racial, religious or otherwise othered minorities—the representative generally remains part of the represented group despite social ascension, things are different with regard to the structure of social class. A person's relation and positioning with class systems can significantly shift as their economic, social and cultural circumstances change. Predicated on this is the notion of social mobility, which in turn causes some fundamental, perhaps irresolvable problems in regards to, for instance, artists from working class backgrounds in contemporary art. / There is a structural limitation as to what kinds of artistic perspective can be represented within the field of contemporary art in regard to class experiences from outside its own sphere. The societal structure in which different kinds of cultural practices are hierarchically ordered presupposes and produces notions of class mobility predicated on distance. For an artist socialised within a class socially considered lower to become legitimised and "visible" within the artistic field, it is a prerequisite that they first establish significant distance to their class origins by obtaining distinctive educational and cultural capital. Passing within the field of art requires knowledge of its codes, as well as specific social skills. Who does one kiss on the cheek? Do the cheeks touch or not? Who do you hug? Who do you shake hands with? Who do you smile and nod to without interfering? Once legitimised, included, and elevated onto the platforms on which the field of art "gives visibility", the artist gains an outlook from a class position quite distanced and distinguished from the one originally inhabited. /

The distance to one's own class background need not be permanent or absolute, but possible. One may return but must be able to leave again; one must be able to move in society rather than be stuck in it. The skill of code switching between different social contexts speaks of a kind of mobility that stands in stark contrast to how inter-class immobility often marks working class realities. In that sense, mobility itself can be understood as a marker of distance, a distance that is not necessarily static but can be established at will. Distance is considered a prerequisite for seeing, analysing and reflecting, as well as for critical or artistic engagement. In contrast, life in the working and poverty classes is often characterised by the absence of cushioning against violence: it is the lack of distance that makes bodies intimately vulnerable to politics and its effects. By necessity, within the realms of contemporary art, one can only be presented with the artistic perspective of somebody who was not crushed by the violence of a class-based society. It is the position of someone for whom, despite obstacles, things have gone relatively well. If things hadn't gone well, the person would not have a recognised artistic practice, and consequently would remain unseen in that field. Visibility within contemporary art is predicated on personal success, not on collective politics. / Autobiographical novels of people leaving the classes considered as lower have fascinated and entertained formally educated and economically privileged audiences for centuries. In recent years, in addition, it is remarkable that a notable number of novels on class and social ascent have been published, many of which were later adopted into theatre plays or essay films, all forms of culture that are directed at and consumed by privileged classes.[12] These forms of cultural production usually have two audiences: those born into class privilege, and those who have experienced social ascension and can identify with the author's or artist's struggle as well as sense of alienation. An audience that remains unaddressed consists of the classes excluded from higher education and legitimised forms of culture. / In such cases, the visibility of individuals who have found success can signify a violent insult to the many they supposedly stand for, and whose lives they make legible to those implicated in shaping their social conditions. As Chantal Jaquet writes in *Les transclasses ou la non-reproduction*: "The rare examples of social mobility are frequently used to mask and reinforce immobility. Individuals from the working classes who move up the social ladder are used as mascots or symbols to consolidate the social order (...). They are used as political showcases and alibis to dismiss collective claims and to stifle the feeling of injustice."[13]

/ The individual example of social mobility made visible within the artistic field serves a double function. Firstly, it draws up a model of fairness in which the individual chance to success supplants a collective right to political, social and economic equality. Secondly, showing that someone can rise from the bottom to the top creates a

12 The tenth edition of the international theatre festival Brandhaarden, for instance, was dedicated exclusively to stage adaptations of the books of Édouard Louis (Amsterdam, 19 February–3 March 2022).

13 Chantal Jaquet, *Les transclasses ou la non-reproduction* (Paris: Presses Universitaires de France, 2014) p. 10. My translation, original: "Les rares exemples de mobilité sociale sont fréquemment brandis pour masquer l'immobilisme et lui servir de caution. Les individus des classes populaires qui connaissent une ascension sociale sont utilisés comme des mascottes ou des symboles confortant l'ordre social (…). Ils servent de vitrines politiques et d'alibis pour récuser les revendications collectives et juguler le sentiment d'injustice."

generalising illusion of meritocracy, suggesting that most people's success is not inherited but deserved. Those who have experienced social ascent are thus simultaneously presented as aspirational exceptions to the rule, and as a form of disavowal that such a rule exists. The scarcity principle under which visibility is produced thus serves the reproduction of capitalism, as well as the hierarchical social and global structures on which it depends. /

When notions of upward mobility intersect with the spheres of legitimised culture, it can be observed how each visibility produces its invisibilities, and how visibility afforded within a representational field can be reproductive of violent inequalities. In contemporary art this invisibilisation is frequently very concrete. Behind one artist's name there vanishes the work of many. Often, the more perfectly and effortlessly an exhibition is presented, the more invisible becomes the labour and effort of the many who installed and constructed it. A similar focus on the visible output can be observed in most examples of art criticism. Rarely do critical reflections on the work's display and distribution extend to the economic circumstances of its production. The representational logics of contemporary art hide many behind a singular person, voice or image. Beside the power to make violence invisible, or to exert violence invisibly, there is thus also the violence of invisibilising. In participating in a form of refined culture that delegitimises other cultural practices it considers lower, one's own visibility within such a sphere can be the violence felt by those kept at a distance from it. Justified by notions of exceptionalism, uniqueness and differentiation, individualised visibility often comes accordingly at the expense of the invisibilisation of collective political demands. In such instances, representation has little bearing on the structures that reproduce marginalisation and violence in the first place.

LIKE RATS LEAVING A SINKING SHIP

VIKA KIRCHENBAUER · SINGLE-CHANNEL VIDEO · 24:33 · 2012

PR-1 RS	PSYCHIATRIC REPORT 1 VOICE: ROBERTO SANTAGUIDA
VO VK	VOICE-OVER: VIKA KIRCHENBAUER
PR-2 LY	PSYCHIATRIC REPORT 2 VOICE: LAURIE YOUNG

00:00:06 PR-1 RS

The assessment subject arrives punctually to the scheduled meeting. She talks and moves in a feminine manner, female breasts are clearly visible under a relatively wide shirt. Along with green trousers and sneakers she wears a t-shirt featuring a zebra print; when seen as a whole, rather gender-neutral clothing. On her mouth she exhibits a lip-piercing. During the assessment she is fully oriented, with clear consciousness, and there are no indications of formal thought disorders or delusions. During the course of the conversation she provides information openly and in detail. The general atmosphere is pleasant.

00:01:43 VO VK

It's hard to remember and prove with childhood facts
when you don't really remember much anyways.
Everyone wants you to suffer, have suffered and still
suffer more.
How much does it hurt?
Show me your soaking wet pillow please,
so I believe!
Freaks and abnormals need to suffer.
Nothing else would make any sense (to them).

But there's a liberty in having no past, no home to return to, no memory to get absorbed in.
And the flattering joy of breaking the laws of what we call nature.
By choice, not by destiny.

00:02:32	TITLE	LIKE RATS LEAVING A SINKING SHIP BY VIKA KIRCHENBAUER
00:04:03	VO VK	Drag your feet onto the streets of autumn's low and blinding light. Just for a minute, forget to be constantly self-conscious.
00:04:33	PR-2 LY	General questions: • Appetite is good • No food intolerances • Difficulties falling asleep • Bowel movements and urination are normal • No allergies • Mr. Kirchenbauer smokes approximately 10 cigarettes per day • Mr. Kirchenbauer does not drink coffee and consumes alcohol only socially Psychiatric result: • Well-groomed patient, alert and with full orientation • No consistent mnestic deficits, no confusion of the sense of time • Concentration and attention intact • No indications of perceptive disorders or sensory illusions • No formal thought disorder • No significant depersonalisation or derealisation disorders • Even-tempered, drive is focused
00:06:03	PR-1 RS	The chronology is clear, the narrative coherent.
00:06:32	PR-2 LY	Mr. Kirchenbauer was born on October 19th 1983, as the second of two children in Germany's south-western provinces. During childbirth there was insufficient amniotic fluid and the umbilical cord had become wrapped around his neck. Early childhood development was unexceptional.
00:07:02	PR-2 LY	The personality profile test was conducted. The applicant revealed the following profile: Mr. Kirchenbauer is relaxed, passive, self-confident and sociable.
00:07:26	PR-1 RS	Furthermore Vika K. displays no consistent signs of neurosis and overall has a normal stress profile. Since childhood a slight tic disorder has been present.
00:07:58	PR-2 LY	His father tried to prepare him for his future as a "football star". His remuneration was performance-based: For every goal he received 50 Pfennigs, for every assist 1 Deutschmark.

00:00:15

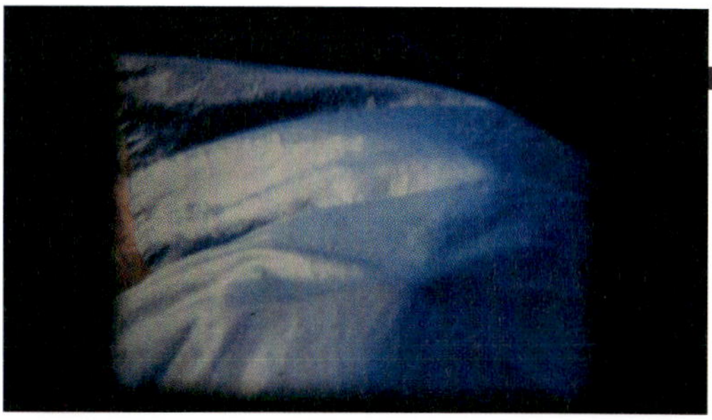

00:01:01

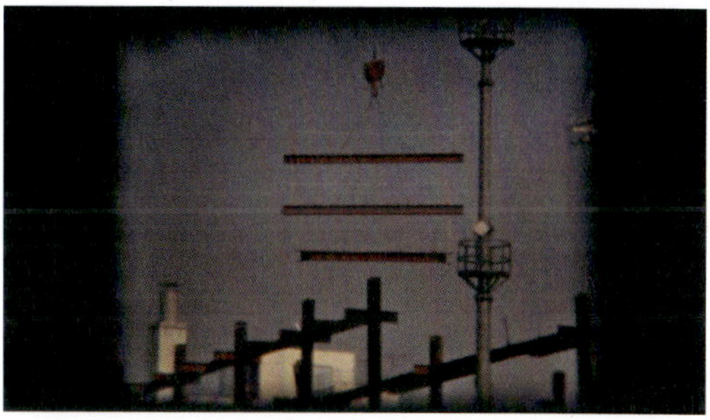

00:01:58

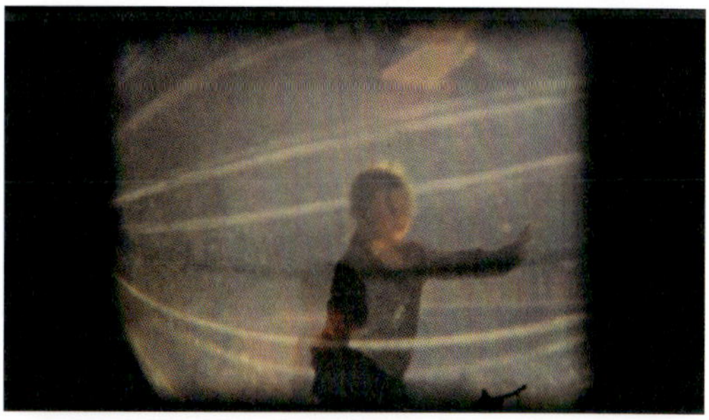

00:03:00

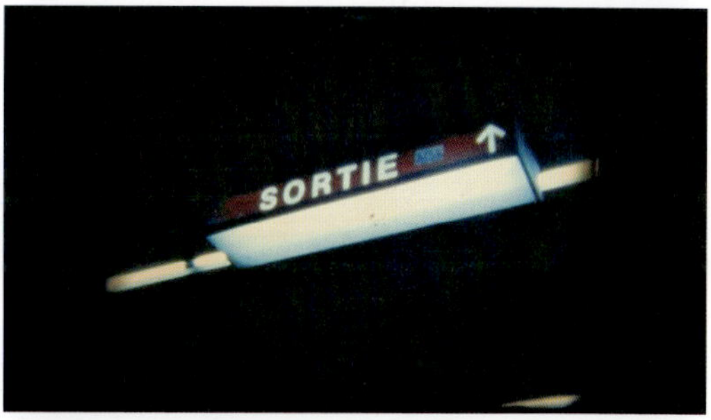

00:03:50

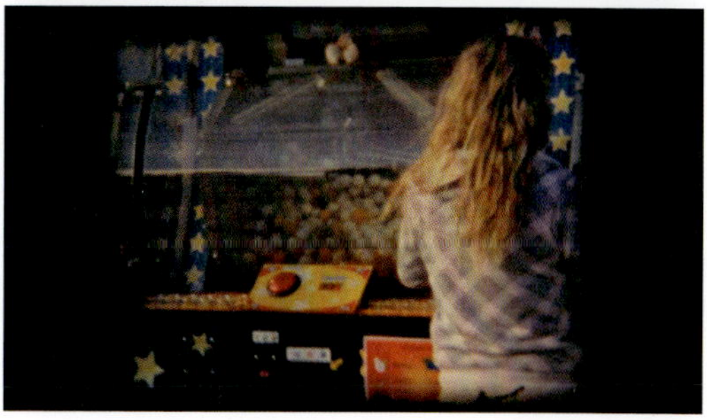

00:04:12

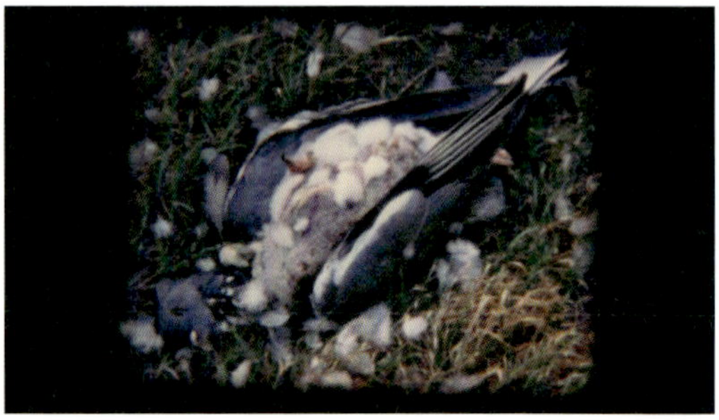

00:04:35

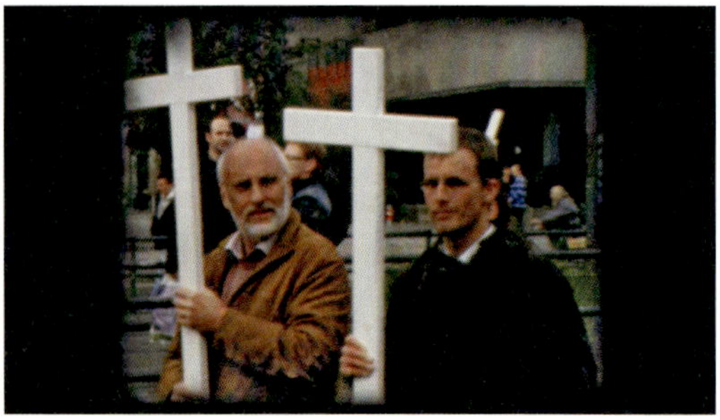

00:05:36

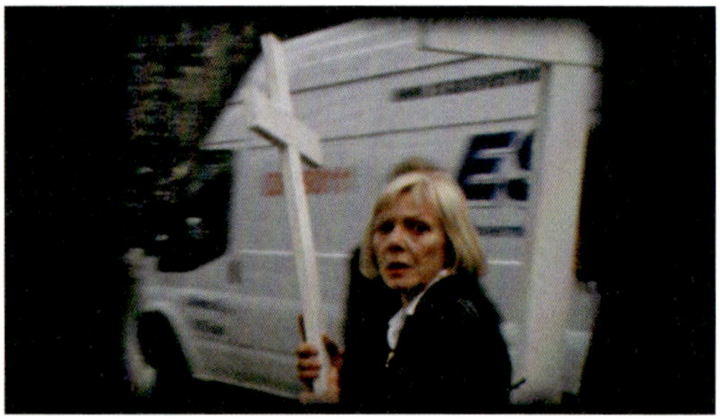

00:05:45

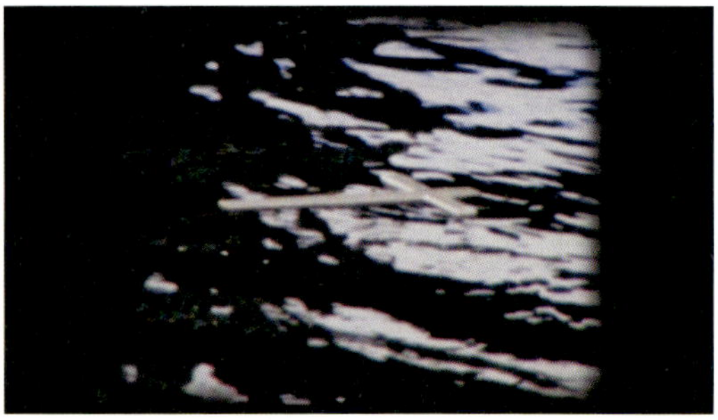

00:06:12

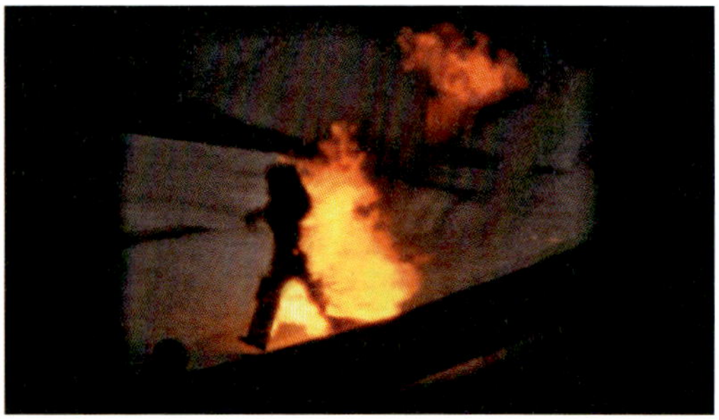

00:08:24 PR-1 RS

In an important match when she was 10 or 11, she was booed by outraged fathers (e.g., "Who made this girl the captain!?"), which made her cry.

00:08:50 VO VK

I have no clear recollection of most things. I'd find photos of myself in drag that I never knew existed. They serve as proof but don't make up any memory. On a note I once found on the street it said: "All of life's possible excitements; instead: middle-class."

00:10:22 VO VK

When I was little I used to dream about the cute little goalie of my football team. Each night I'd hide under my blanket, think of him and fart—wishing that he could be there to share this moment of intimacy.

00:10:58 PR-1 RS

So as to no longer be perceived as weak and girlish, she started consuming large amounts of alcohol at the age of 13. Up until the age of 18, she drank up to half a bottle of liquor per day.

00:11:26 PR-2 LY

He was very self-contained. When under the influence of alcohol he used to join groups of roaring men at beer festivals. Otherwise he was alone.

00:12:19 PR-1 RS

Following her A-levels she moved to Portugal for two years in order to perform voluntary work. She had constantly varying sexual encounters with both boys and girls. She could not accept compliments directed to the "handsome boy". She even despised those who found her sexually appealing as a boy.

00:13:09 VO VK

You don't go there because you want to
but because there's no other choice.
You go to the judges and doctors and specialists
who know the official answers
to what's a man
and what's a woman.
It's not about fun, you learn.
And it isn't fun when they
make you get naked,
touch you, squeeze and measure your genitals
"for reference".
What reference?

They'll analyse your DNA to find out
what you really are.
You'll learn not to say that
you are what you are
but that you are what you are not.

You'll learn to focus on the right
insignificant moments of your model life.
You'll learn to say the right things,
have the right biography.

00:06:21

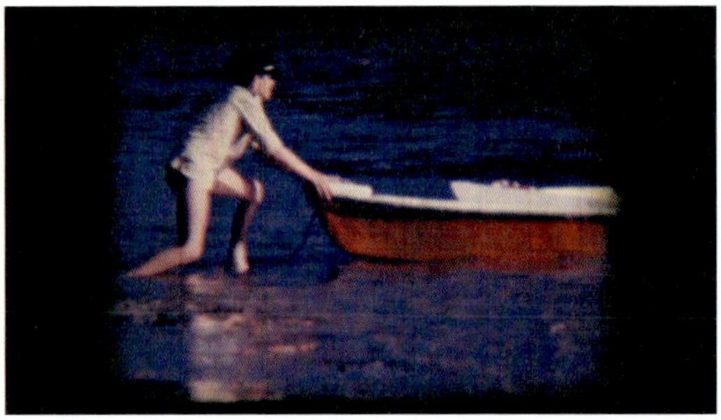

00:06:43

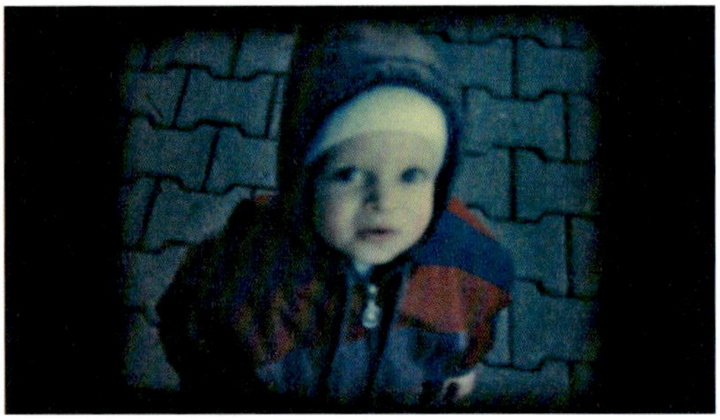

00:07:28

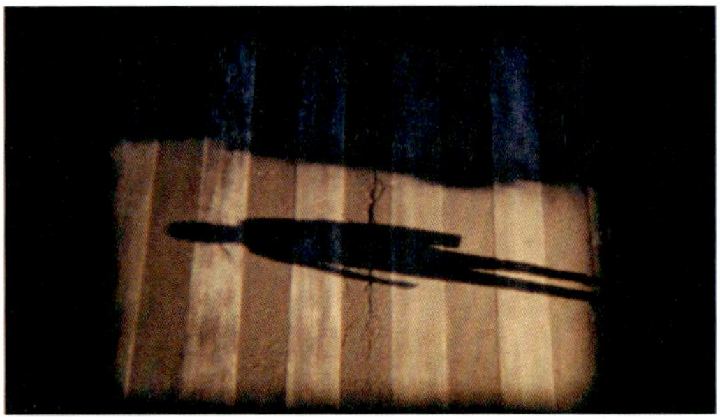

00:08:07

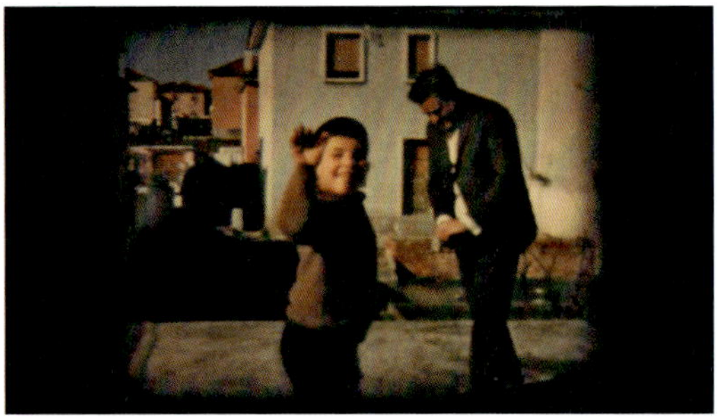

00:09:08

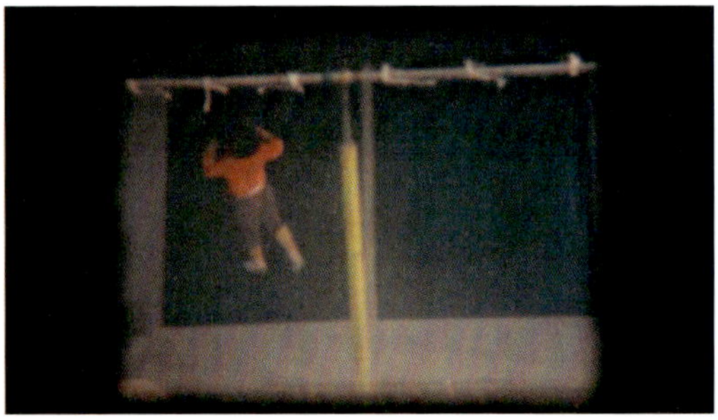

00:10:06

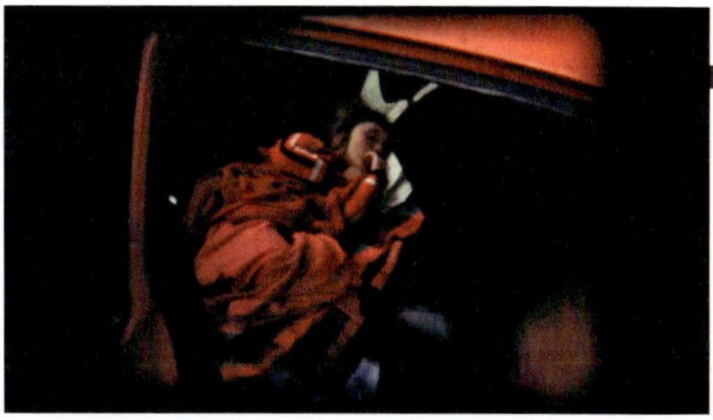

00:10:48

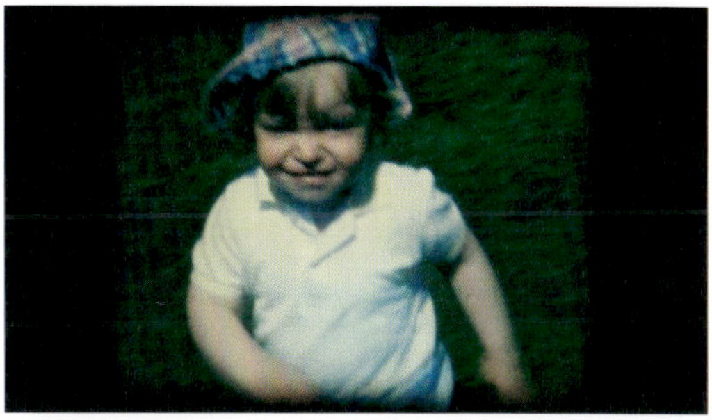

00:11:22

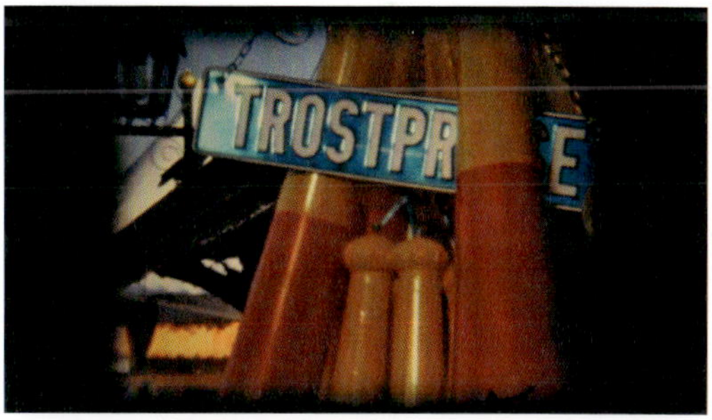

00:12:43

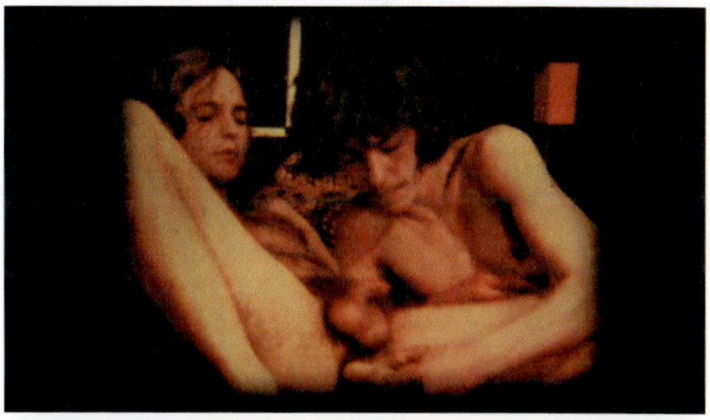

00:13:15

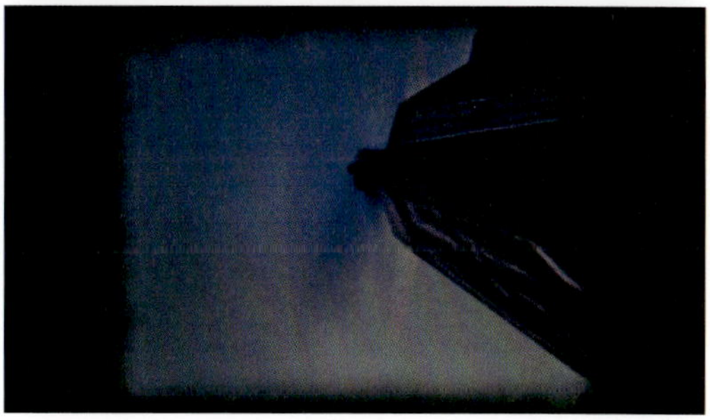

You'll learn that there is only one biography,
the biography of a tormented character that usually,
at the very latest during the second act of a film,
meets one of many tragic ends.

You'll learn that you're doing well when they tell you:

00:15:36 PR-2 LY

"It's funny but it always sounds like
the exact same story...
But when you see the people
you just know it's true."

00:15:52 VO VK

You'll learn how to pass
from one box right into the next.
And you'll promise to stay there,
phrase the clichés eloquently,
and repeat,
and hide.
You'll learn not to say
that you are actually fine,
and sometimes even proud of yourself.
Because if it's pleasure
it can't be real.
You'll learn that you're supposed to be
in deep emotional debt,
and that you'll now pay it off
with a mental loan.
You'll learn to press the right buttons,
to invent and remodel.
You'll learn that this isn't about you.
And unnoticed, almost casually,
you will learn to hate yourself,
and mistrust everyone
who doesn't.

And eventually you'll forget that you're just
like a rat leaving a sinking ship.

Rats are glorious deserters,
and we must admire them.
"You'll sink, I won't... But thanks for everything!" they say;
and jump right into the ocean.
Rats don't want to be captains
trying to keep the cause afloat,
but swim on open water.

00:17:52 VO VK

One of the few things I remember clearly from my childhood is family Christmas. My Aunt Solveig would always bring her girlfriends along. Us kids were told that her friends didn't have the money to travel across the entire country to see their own families, so it was very nice of Solveig to bring them along so they wouldn't be alone. No one ever spoke a word about them being lovers.

00:14:05

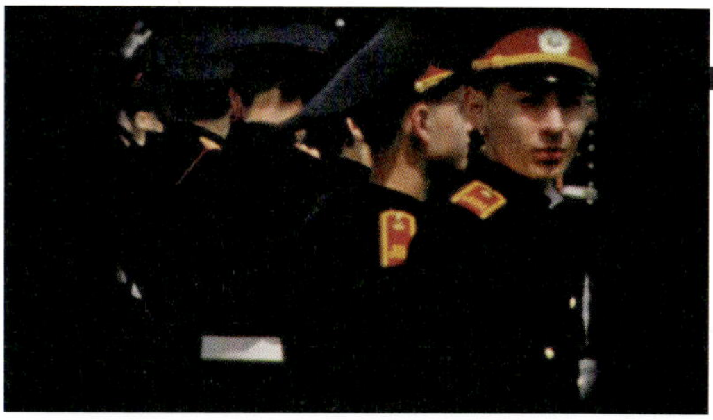

00:15:28

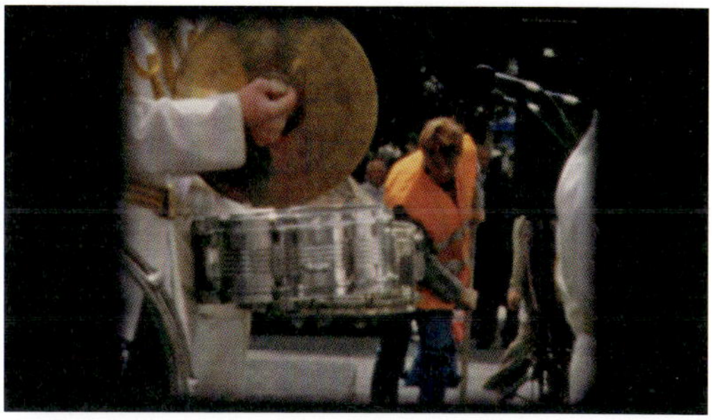

00:15:46

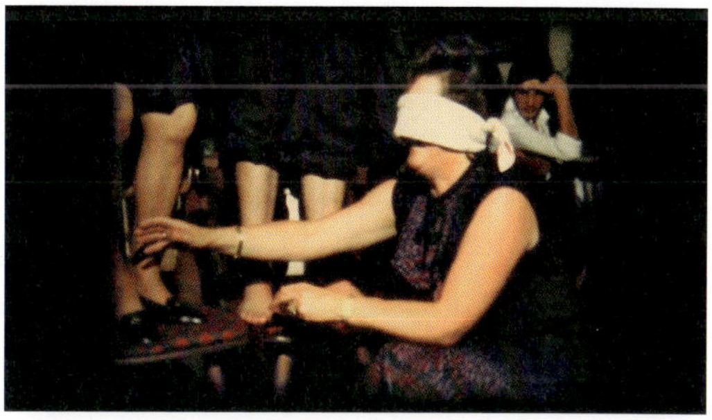

00:16:48

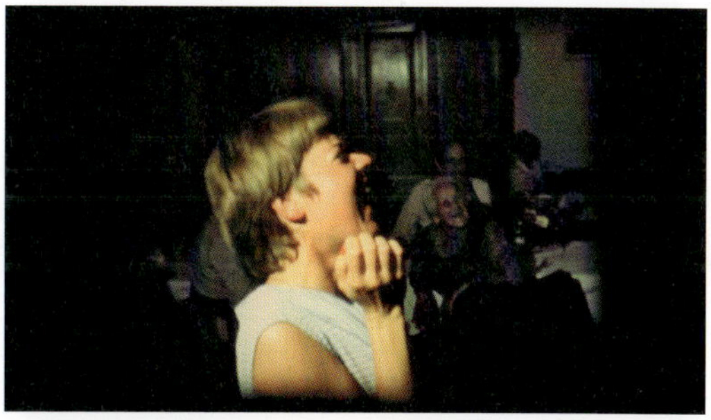

00:17:40

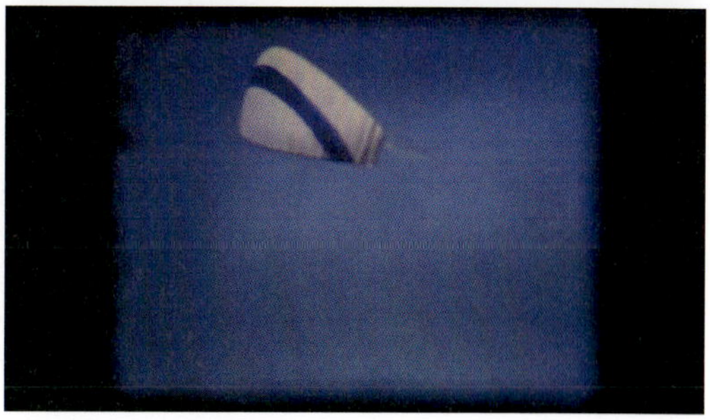

00:17:58

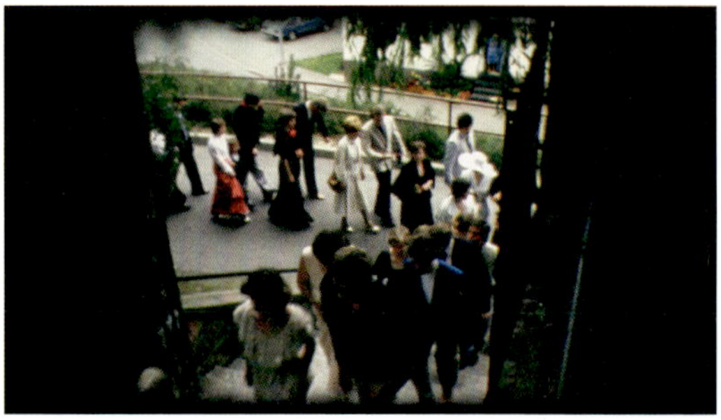

00:20:17

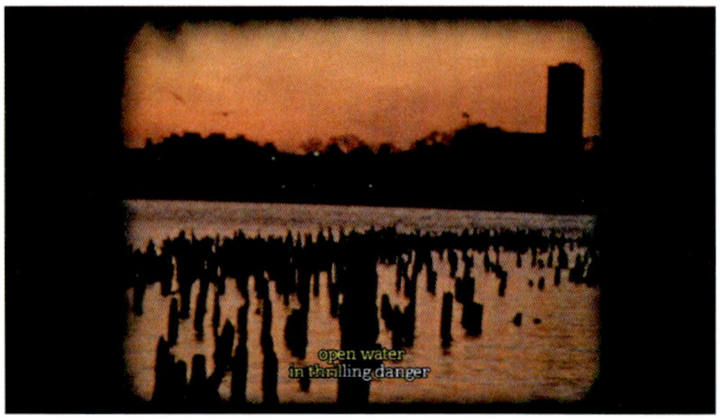

00:20:33

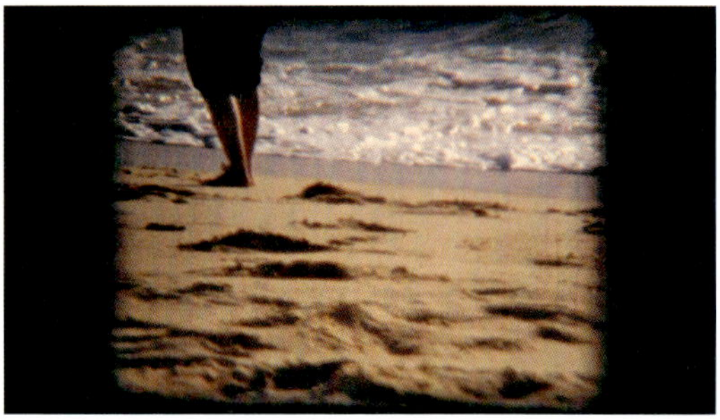

00:22:10

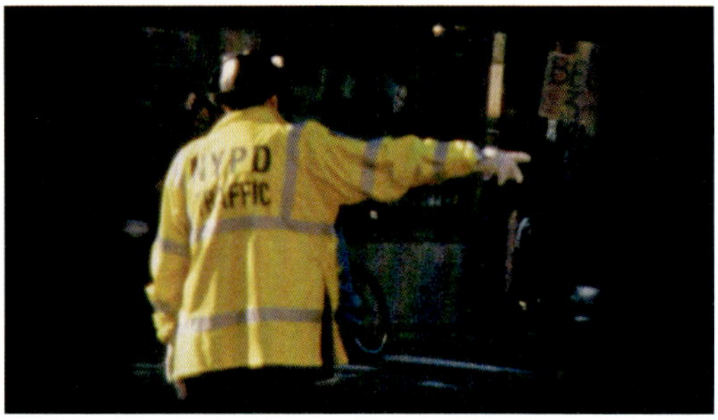

00:22:15

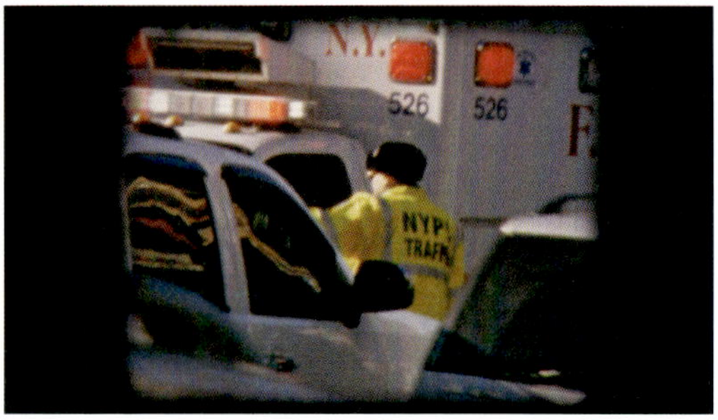

Until Solveig died at the age of 38, and my sister diagnosed that she only got cancer because she was a lesbian. The very last time I saw Solveig was in hospital. She said she was sorry for her hairdo. I assured her that I saw worse at the supermarket every day. And when we said good-bye I didn't kiss her. But I should have.

00:19:32 VO VK

People keep asking me if my voice is "breaking back" from the hormones ...
No, once it's broken it's broken.

00:19:49 SONG VO VK

karaoke-style subs included in video

"dare no-one tell me
what's gonna be
dare no-one tell me
what's gonna be

and we'll run the streets
in thrilling danger

on open water
in thrilling danger"

00:20:23 VO VK

I could practice every day...
But that would just make me feel sick.

00:20:48 PR-2 LY

Since early childhood, the applicant has exhibited behaviour which corresponds to the female stereotype.

00:20:57 PR-1 RS

A latent homosexuality can be excluded, nor is it a pure transvestism, by which is meant purely the need to wear feminine clothing without any desire for gender change, nor is it a fetishistic transvestism (the wearing of feminine clothing for the purpose of sexual arousal).

00:21:39 PR-2 LY

Results of the self-assessment of the body still reveal a below-average sense of attractiveness and self-confidence as well as an above-average physical and sexual discomfort.

00:22:03 PR-1 RS

This physical discomfort is to be considered a disease. The applicant is diagnosed with a case of transidentity (transsexuality) that is not curable.

00:22:53 VO VK

A day thoroughly enjoyed:
This morning I woke up and the day was beautiful. One of those rare sunny and hot days where crowds of people fill the streets ... Everyone's outside, like people were inverted vampires. I decided not to leave the bed and to open the window just a bit, letting the smells and the sounds enter my room. I enjoyed the luxury of that, and spent the day in bed thinking: "Fuck you world, I owe you nothing!"

00:22:24

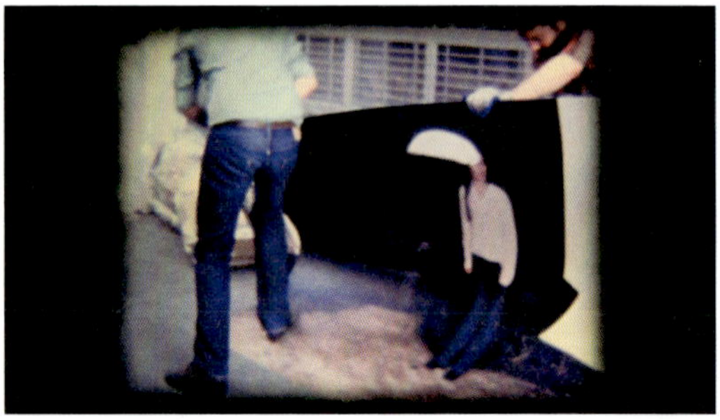

00:23:33

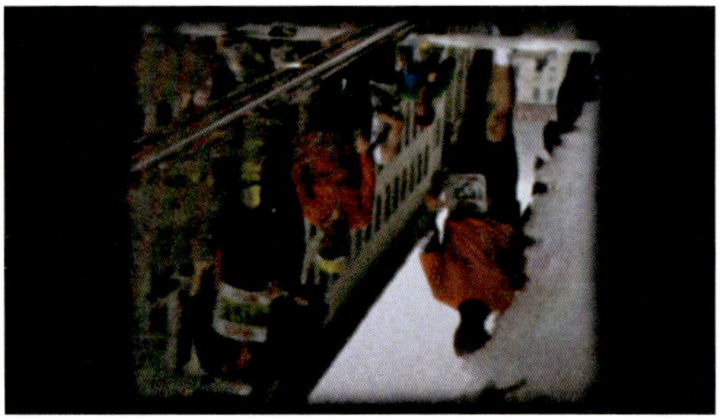

COMPOSER	NIGEL FARRELLY
POST-PRODUCTION CONSULTANT	MARTIN SULZER
ADDITIONAL SOUND RECORDING	PAULA SELL
STUDIO RECORDING	HANS UNSTERN

UNTITLED SEQUENCE OF GAPS

VIKA KIRCHENBAUER · SINGLE-CHANNEL VIDEO · 12:31 · 2020

VO VK VOICE-OVER: VIKA KIRCHENBAUER

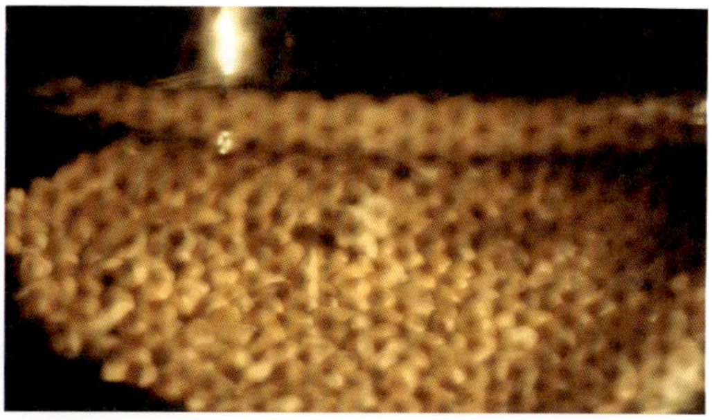

00:00:18 VO VK

Tapping around the black hole of a childhood unremembered,
fearful of being sucked into a place
where not even light can escape.

Childhood is mostly a fantasy for adults,
not a reality many people experience at that stage of life.

A broken collar bone, as seen in an X-ray decades later...
Nothing unusual apparently.
A child cries and something might be broken.
Who would know at the time?
Only later will she wonder what might have happened.
But detecting a crack doesn't offer many clues as to its cause.

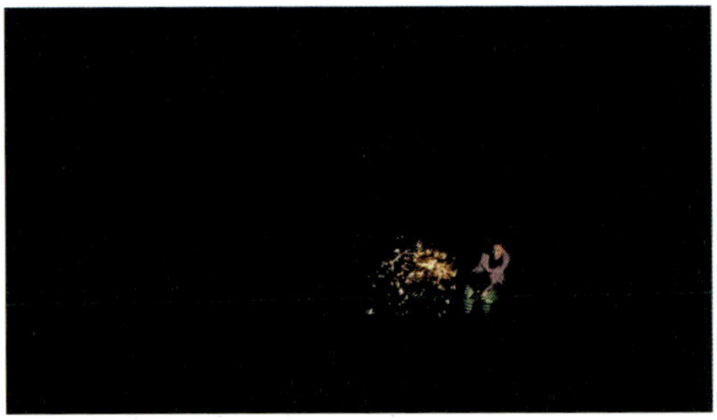

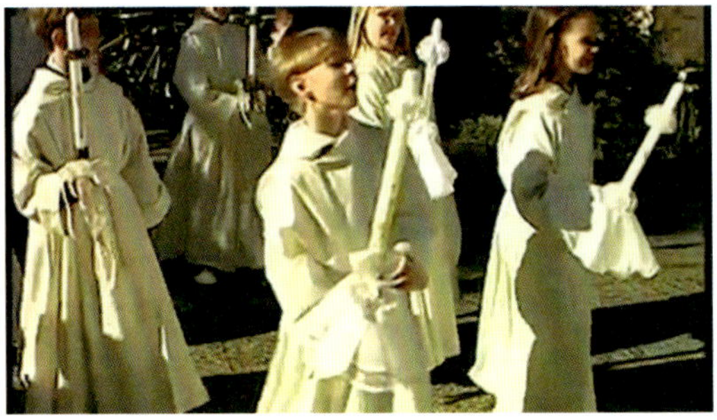

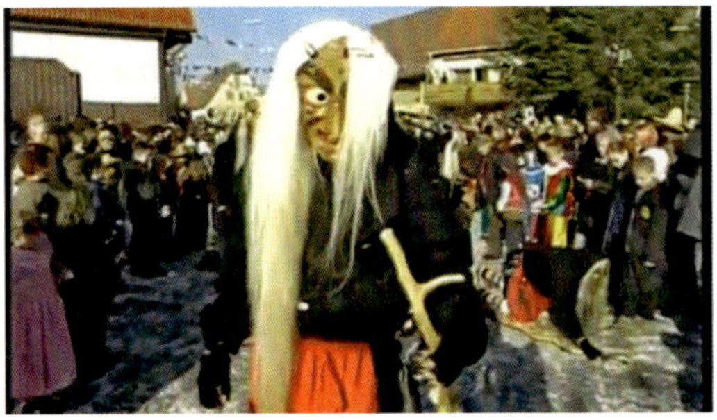

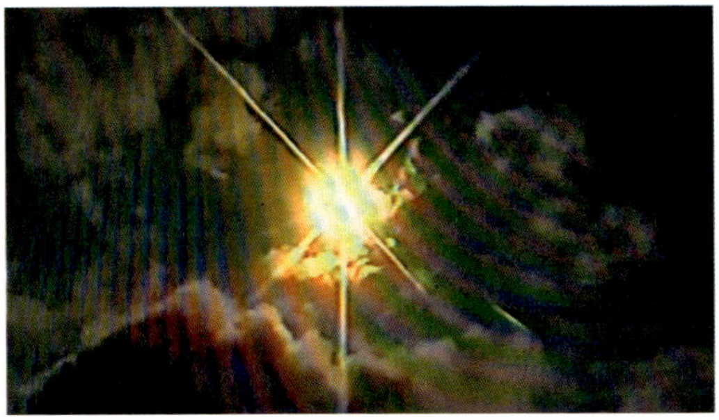

00:02:06 VO VK

Human eyes see only the colours the sun emits most strongly, with retinas designed to perceive sunlight's most abundant energies and nothing else.

A person will be seen in the light
that most structures her reality.
Whatever light is most powerfully thrown upon her,
she will likely also learn to see herself in that light.

Human eyes see only the colours the sun emits most strongly,
and it is simply too tempting to let the sun shine in.

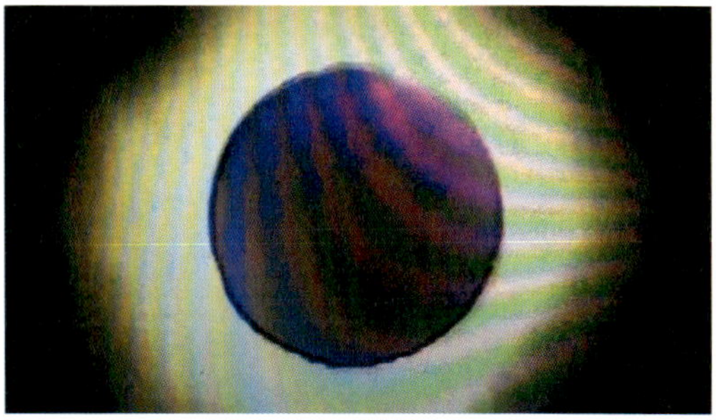

00:02:57 VO VK

Her memory sets in at age 7, around the time she starts attending school.
Before that: no images.
After that: mostly isolated memories that seem distant and detached.

At the age of 12 she got her first summer job,
at a wheelchair factory.
She didn't know one was permitted short breaks—to pee, for instance.
And naturally, she presumed one was expected to run when called to a different section of the workshop.

Three years later, at 15, when working in construction
she was too shy to leave the site to get a sip of water.

Looking back, she wonders what instills in a person
such fear of being seen as lazy.
It was the summer of a full solar eclipse.

At a later job in a car radio factory her coworkers point out to her that
she is betraying them if she moves too quickly.

She is beginning to understand.

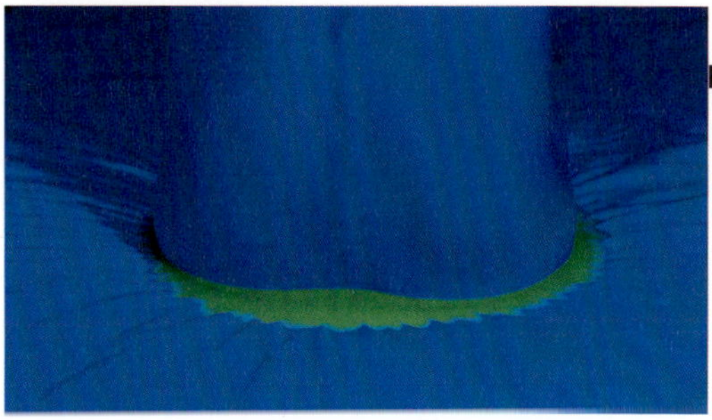

00:04:21 VO VK

That person is almost no longer visible
if one sees her now

since, in changing, one rarely adds on
but overwrites.

And what is erased occasionally returns
as a ghost.

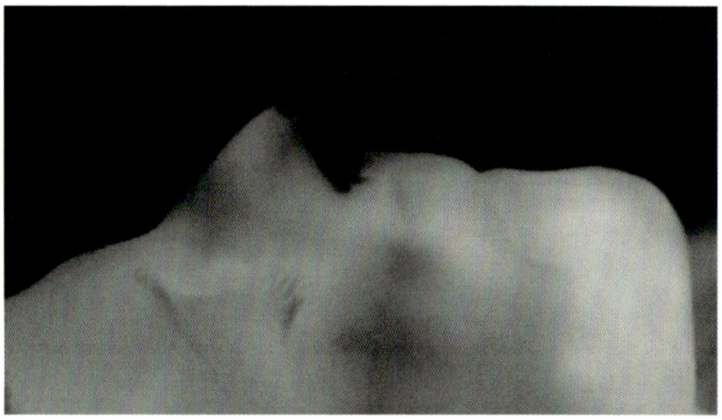

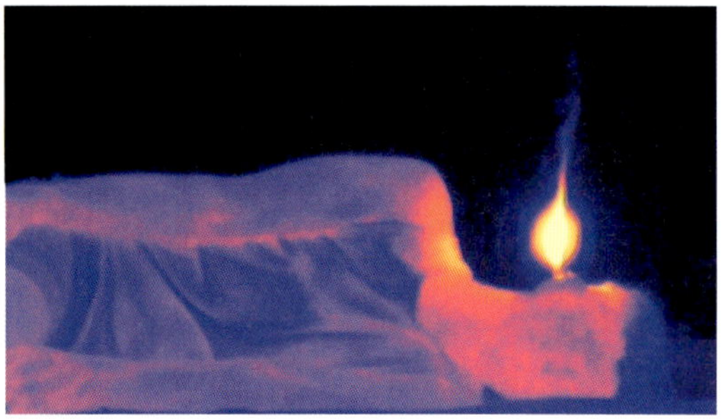

00:05:04 VO VK

Infrared lies just before red as humans see it,
its waves just a bit too long to be visually perceived,
measurable but invisible.
It makes atoms and molecules move, creating heat ...
It is constantly felt but never seen.

When watching the night sky, one is observing a past,
one is witnessing memories of stars.

What I'm talking about is rather different.
It is a violent celestial event that is moving away.
As it moves away its light waves stretch,
and its visible light shifts into infrared,
leaving no visible trace.

It is present but nameless,
vaguely felt yet inaccessible.

If only an observed phenomenon is a real phenomenon,
what becomes of an event once experienced
but later erased?

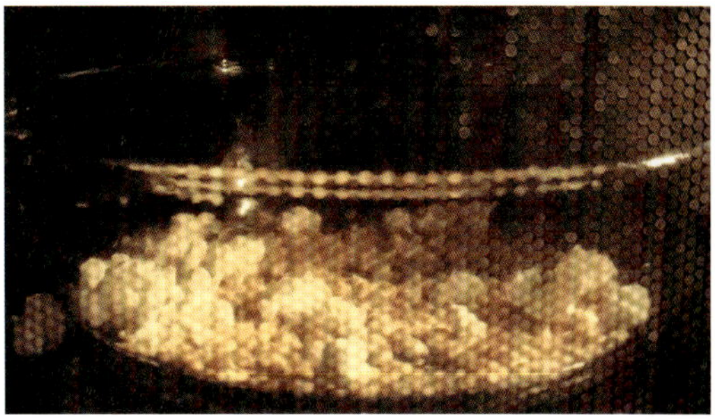

00:06:45 VO VK

She observes popcorn as microwaves penetrate it.
Microwaves are trapped in the oven
since they are too wide to escape through the holes
that she is observing them through.

It is argued in academic articles
that when the microwave oven entered the market
it was somewhat less clearly gendered
than other appliances,
allowing men to enter the kitchen
without appearing gay.

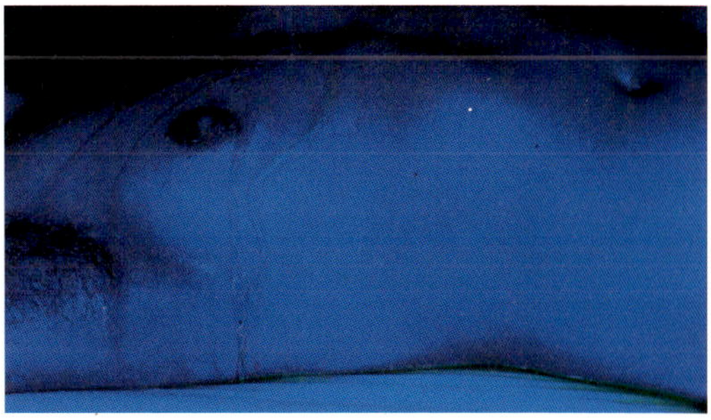

00:07:54 VO VK

Ultraviolet lies just after violet as humans see it,
its waves slightly too short to be visually perceived.
I imagine it like violet, but more radical.
Animals perceptive of it can see
the sky's true violet colour.
Birds detect the glow of mouse urine in fields far below,
the pee giving the mouse away.
The mouse sits in the grass erect,
certain of her invisibility to others.
A preying bird will detect the mouse's weakness
in what she herself would never consider remarkable.

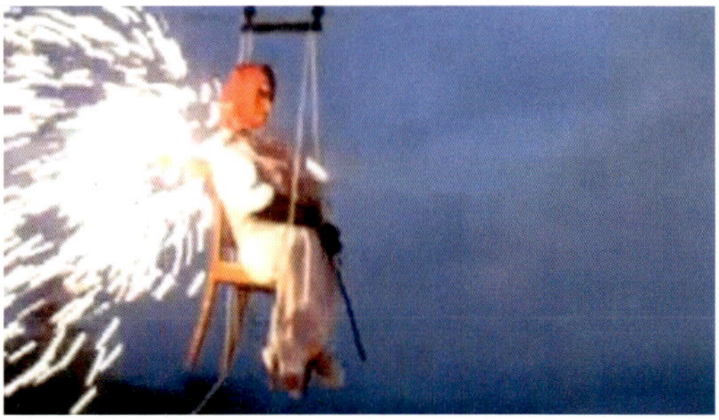

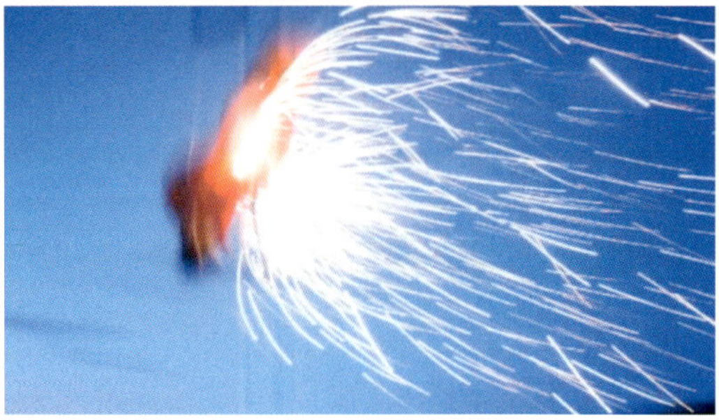

00:08:57 VO VK

She grew up in a small village where every year for solstice
a straw witch came sliding down a metal rope right
into the bonfire.
First, children with torches would walk around the woods
in the early evening to then light the big bonfire
and later cheer as the witch crashes in and is set aflame.

Her queer aunt Solveig was part of the carnival
club of witches.
They dressed in elaborate costumes and scared children
and adults
as viciously as they could.
She suspected Solveig was aware
that she was commonly considered a witch in any case;
so it was better for her to own that image of herself.

When for a person there is no hiding in the shadows,
one finds ways not to feel passive, but dangerous.

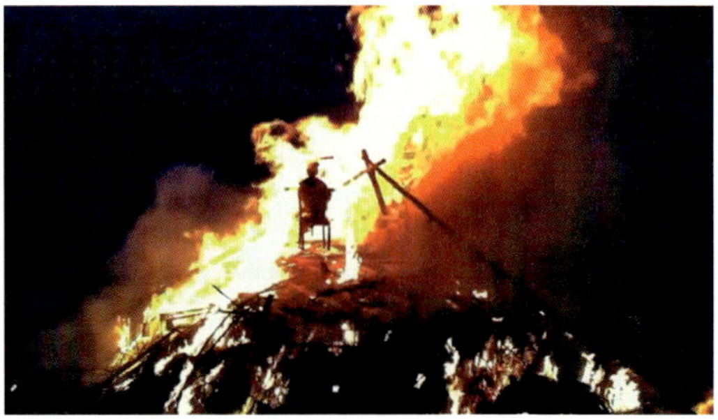

00:10:18 VO VK

The village stopped burning the straw witch a few years ago.
It appears to have concluded

that it is no longer appropriate to burn women or their images.
The fire remains and people gather.

I wonder whether violence decreases
once its image is removed
or if it does its work even better, invisibly.

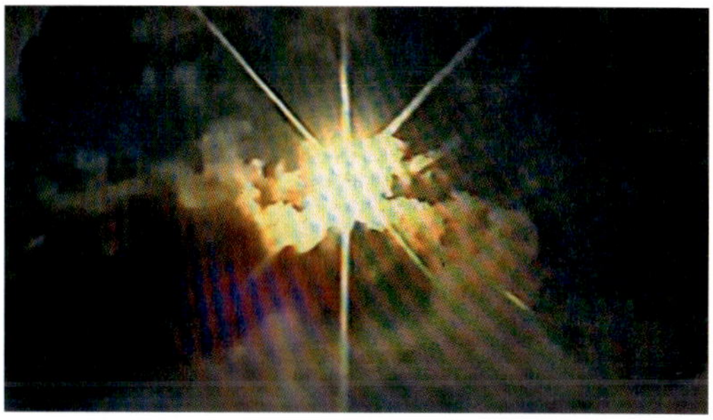

CAMERA	VIKA KIRCHENBAUER
	RITA MACEDO
ARTISTIC ADVISER	JUDITH SIEBER
SCRIPT ADVISER	PHILIP HUCKNALL
MUSIC	COOL FOR YOU

THE CAPACITY FOR ADEQUATE ANGER

VIKA KIRCHENBAUER · SINGLE-CHANNEL VIDEO · 15:08 · 2021

	VO VK	VOICE-OVER: VIKA KIRCHENBAUER
00:00:31	VO VK	The last time I was on the phone with my grandmother—some years before she died—she asked me how I'd earn money with my education in film, and if I thought I could find work at a TV station. I explained to her that what I did meant more or less doing what I wanted in the hope that people liked it enough that I could make some money from it, and that I could continue working. She asked if I did that so that I could one day work in television. I said no, that what I did was more like something one would see in a museum. I said that knowing she had never been to one, and neither had I ever exhibited anything in a museum at that time. She replied: "Ah, so you work for the museum, okay!"
00:01:37	VO VK	When I was 8 years old, I sat in her kitchen, shocked as I watched the news that Freddie Mercury had passed away. For the years to come I posed like him in all family photos, and I learned to perform all of his moves from watching videotapes. When Freddie's song with Montserrat Caballé was removed as the official song for the '92 Barcelona Olympics I asked my parents why. They said he was sick and that sports and sickness don't go together.
00:02:25	VO VK	Magic Johnson joined the US basketball Dream Team at the same Olympics. At that point he had already stopped playing in the NBA ... He wished to come back permanently again,

00:00:57

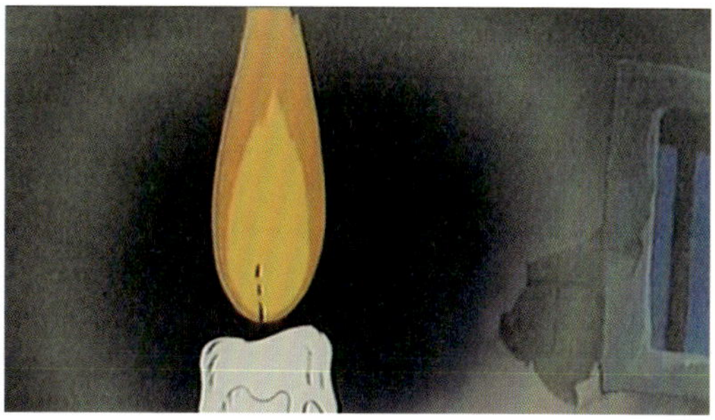

00:01:35

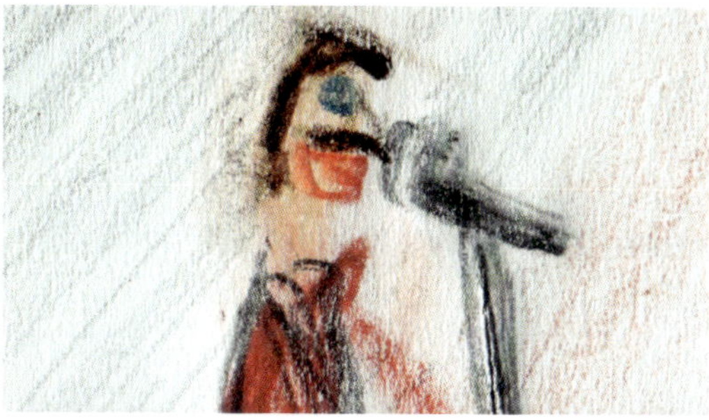

00:01:59

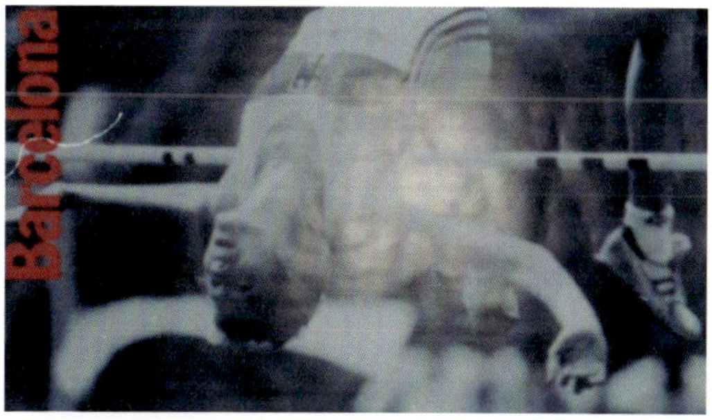

00:02:20

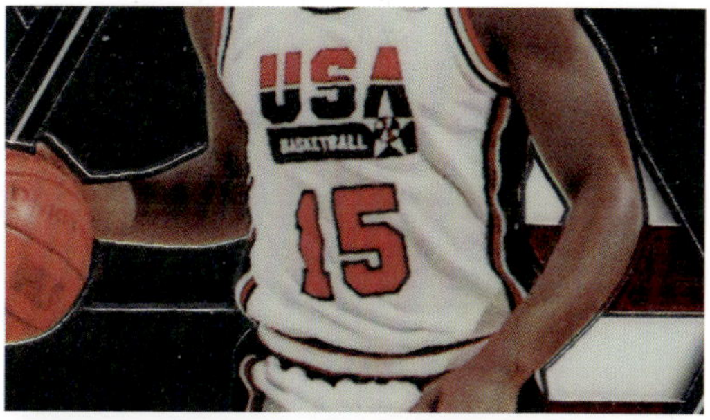

00:03:45

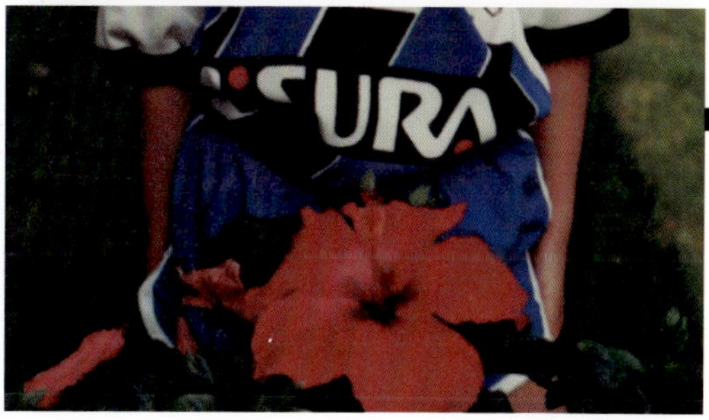

00:05:21

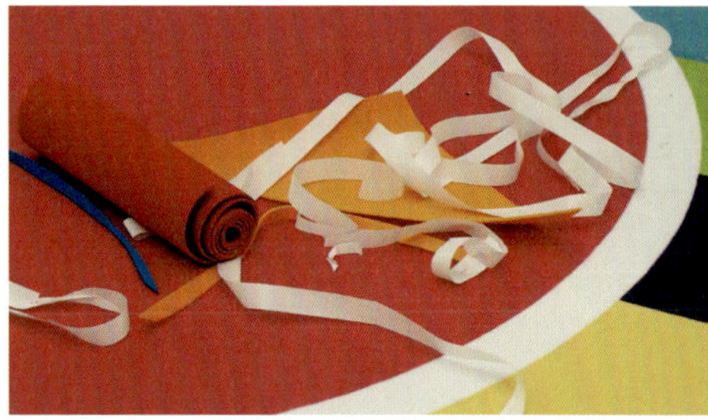

00:06:15

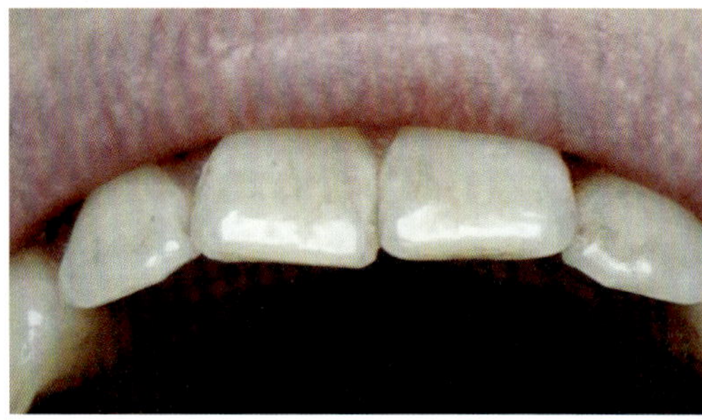

00:07:04

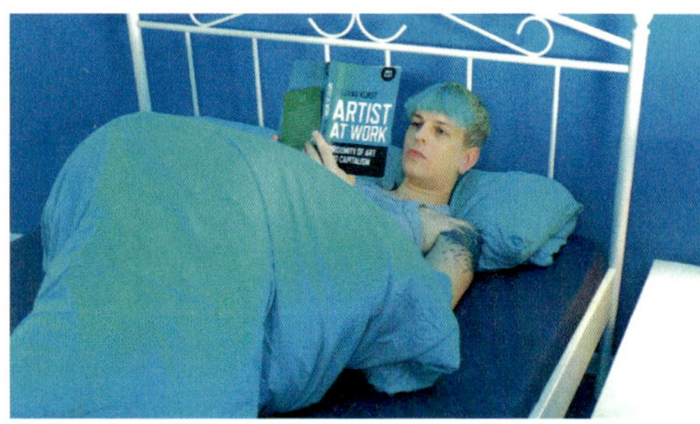

00:07:37

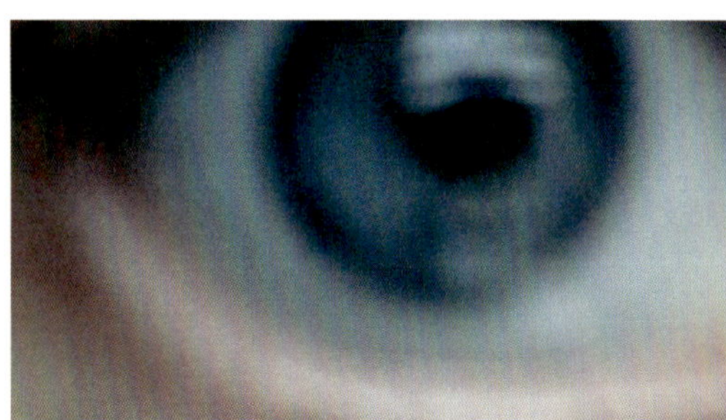

00:08:05

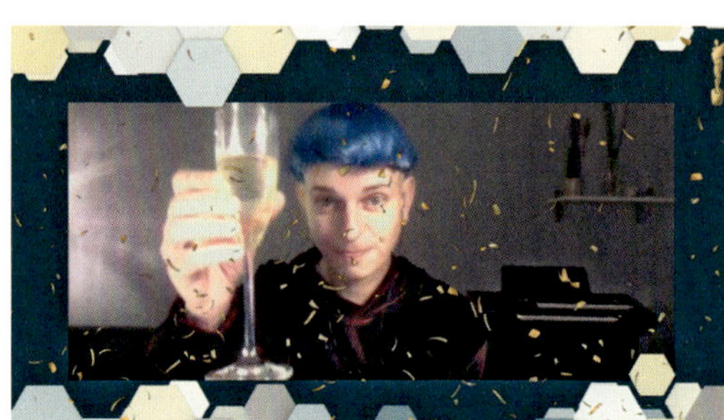

but other players expressed concern that he could bleed on them ...

00:02:58 VO VK

On the playground in the village there were big debates about Magic's brief return for the Olympic Games; amidst children routinely accusing other children of "giving them AIDS". I was often the one the others thought would "give them AIDS". I didn't understand why.

00:03:25 VO VK

I trained daily in pursuit of a professional sports career, the most promising chance to escape and find recognition. In case I failed, my backup escape plan was to become a fashion designer when I grew up. I spent many afternoons designing sports outfits for my favourite teams. I sent my designs to sports magazines hoping they would print them, which they didn't. When I became a teenager, I confessed to a friend that I wouldn't be able to become a fashion designer, because you'd have to be gay for that. Queerness occasionally surfaced on TV, but seemed to me like a qualification I was probably also lacking.

00:04:26 VO VK

In my early thirties, already in Berlin, I went to get my teeth cleaned professionally for the first time. Before starting the procedure, the dentist asked me if I was HIV positive. I said no, quietly and politely. I wish I possessed the capacity for adequate anger.

The dentist complained about the state of my teeth and later convinced me that I should really start flossing. That thought was new to me. All my life I had only ever thought of flossing as a useless thing rich people do to feel fancy.

00:05:27 VO VK

This piece is produced for my first institutional solo exhibition, at Kunstverein Düsseldorf. I am somewhat embarrassed to be offering this slide show interspersed with excerpts from children's television as a newly produced work. I am relieved that there probably won't be a preview dinner this year, or a big opening, or any kind of larger networking situation. A few years ago, when I attended my first professional preview dinner, I sat at a table full of art people for several hours not saying a word. The place cards seemed haunting, and I was afraid I would give away that I didn't really belong, so silence seemed preferable.

00:06:43 VO VK

Social realities first enter the human body through emotions, and sometimes settle. How can shame be communicated when all it demands is to hide?

00:07:01 VO VK

I feel an urgency to address issues of work and class, but the absurdity is that once one achieves a significant platform as an artist one can only reflect on a past one no longer occupies, though that past may still occupy oneself. What if it was possible to speak and be heard without the prerequisite of social ascent?

00:07:41 VO VK I look at the past as through a fog. What once was real now seems like a painted set.

00:07:53 VO VK In search of images, I returned to the place in which I grew up for the first time in over ten years. I returned as somebody who flosses her teeth, and as somebody who "works for the museum"—or rather, as somebody who exhibits at spaces that may look like museums to the outsider, and where the unseen labour of others suddenly bears my name. Undeniably a boss of sorts ... yet it continues to feel strange to me that someone would write a funding application on my behalf, or cut a circle into a carpet or glue turquoise translucent film onto a window just because that's what I want. Isn't that what I was supposed to do?

00:09:47 VO VK My return to the village gave me considerable anxiety. I dreamt about my father shooting me down with a rifle. I avoided seeing him while I was there. I came to find traces of violence in the landscape but could only find them in my stomach. I wish I possessed the capacity for adequate anger. Irritatedness, shame, unsettlement and disgust? Ugly feelings that move nowhere? Yes. But anger or rage? Almost never.

00:10:51 VO VK People in the village were generally envious of those who owned. Not necessarily from a sense of lacking, but simply because wealth itself seemed unjust. The factory owners I worked for never understood how lucky they were—for envy is the most generous of responses to perceived injustice. It was their good fortune that anger felt shameful to the villagers ...

00:11:37 VO VK In the late 18th century, the 'simple life' became fashionable among the French aristocracy. They loved acting like shepherds and shepherdesses, while still enjoying the comforts of their social position.

00:11:56 VO VK In 1783, by her Trianon Castle in the park of Versailles, Marie Antoinette had a hamlet built, the Hameau de la Reine. A rustic little village was constructed, including a mill and a farm, that she could look at from her castle; like a spectator yearning for immersion.

00:12:26 VO VK Her children were supposed to be raised in proximity to an image and enactment of such a 'simple life'. So the court contracted selected peasants to inhabit the village, performing full-time a variety of roles and tasks amidst fabricated decay. The casting priorities included bodily strength and pleasant appearance. When peasants turn actors of peasants in a durational performance, then what do they become?

00:13:11 VO VK Marie Antoinette wasn't particularly interested in politics as such, but still she engaged aesthetically with the political topics of the day in the form of elaborate hairstyles. When a bakery was looted during a famine, she would reference

00:08:19

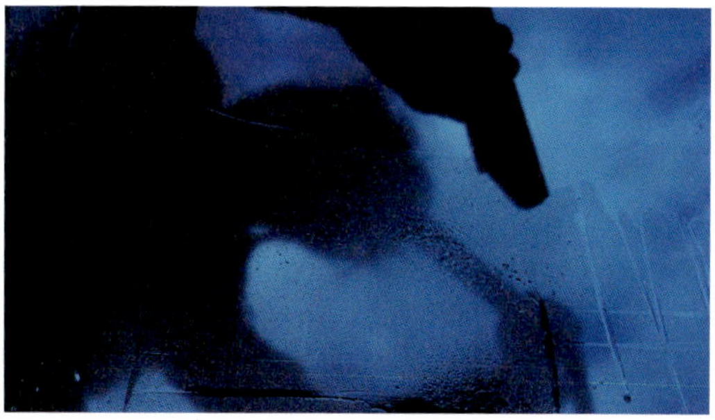

00:08:31

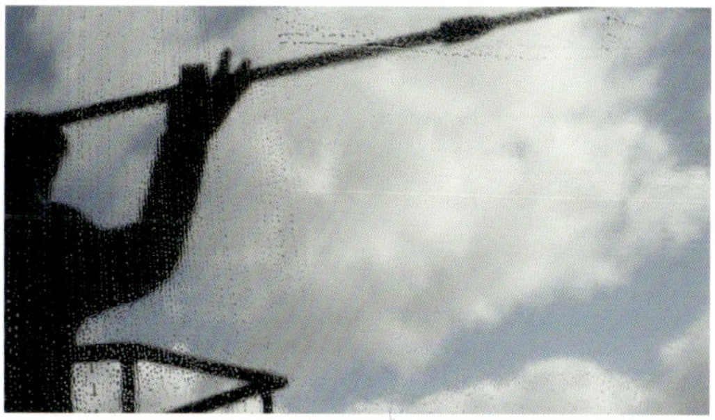

00:09:03

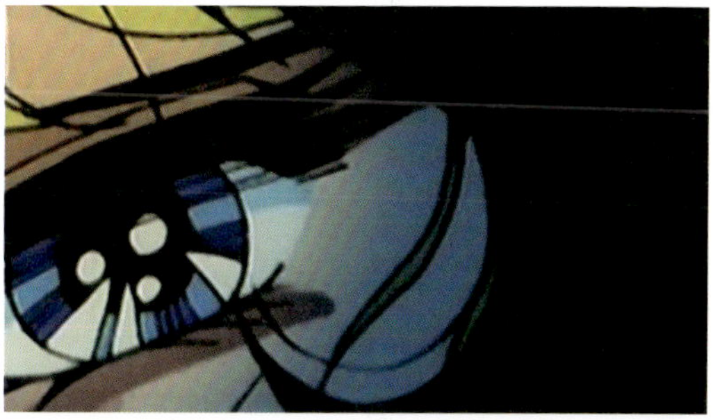

00:10:07

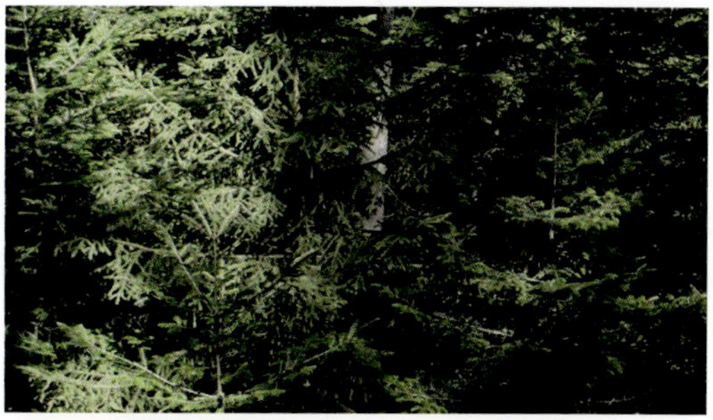

00:11:07

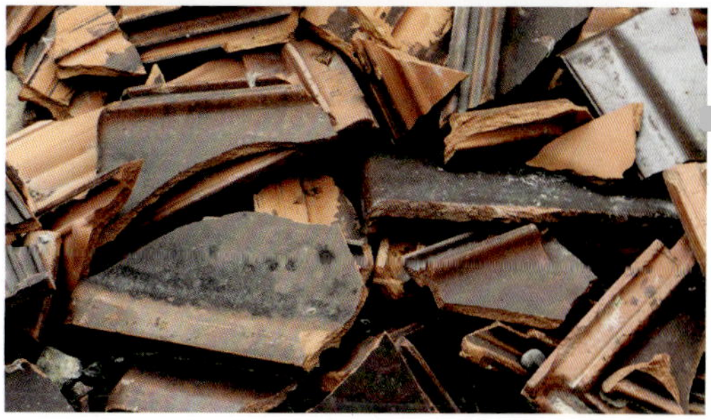

00:11:31

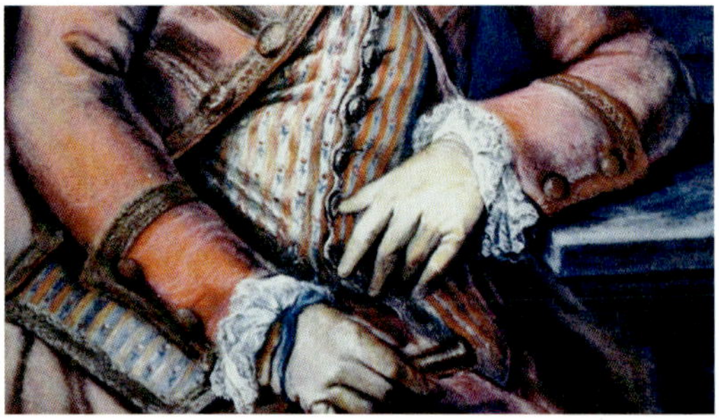

00:12:29

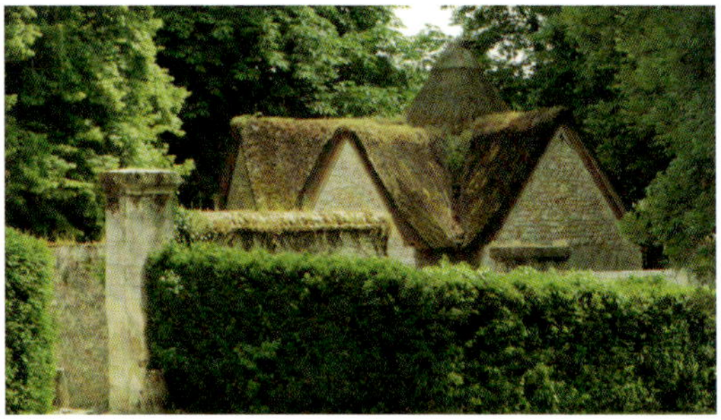

00:12:52

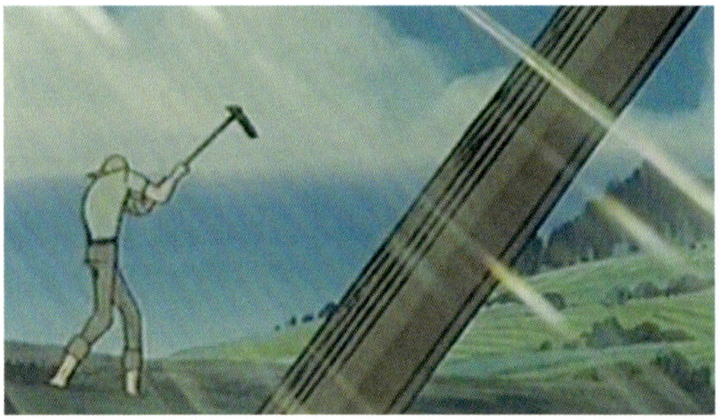

00:13:06

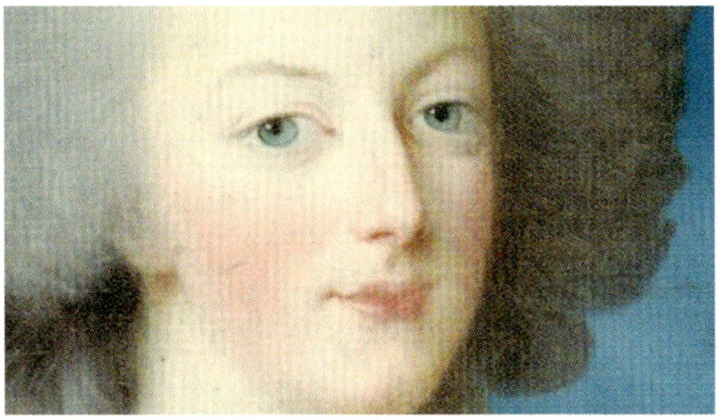

00:14:28

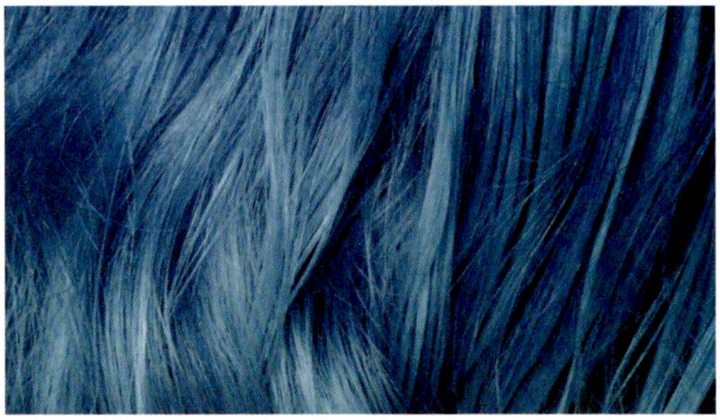

the event by having bread woven into her extravagantly arranged hair.

00:13:43	VO VK	By contemporary standards we might perhaps consider her an artist. Because in art, I learned, it is only ever possible to look at things from a distance, even—or especially—when feeling immersed. Critique is presumed to require distance; reflection is presumed to require distance. But distance is a resource administered unequally.
00:14:37	VO VK	I wear my past in my hair, and carry it as stains on my teeth. I look at it from a vantage point far away, and feel it tickling under my skin.

SCRIPT AND RESEARCH ADVISER — JUDITH SIEBER
MUSIC — COOL FOR YOU

SPECTRAL SENSITIVITY

VIKA KIRCHENBAUER · TRANSLUCENT FILM & UV FLUORESCENT TUBES · DIMENSIONS VARIABLE · 2021

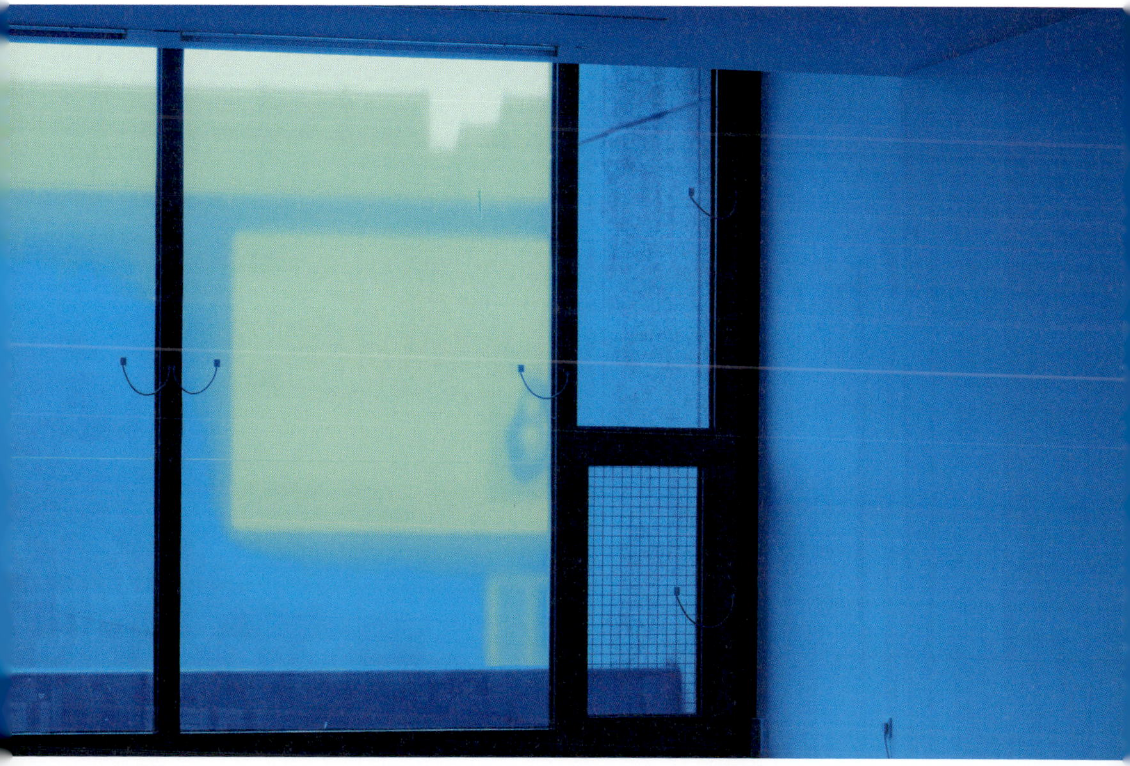

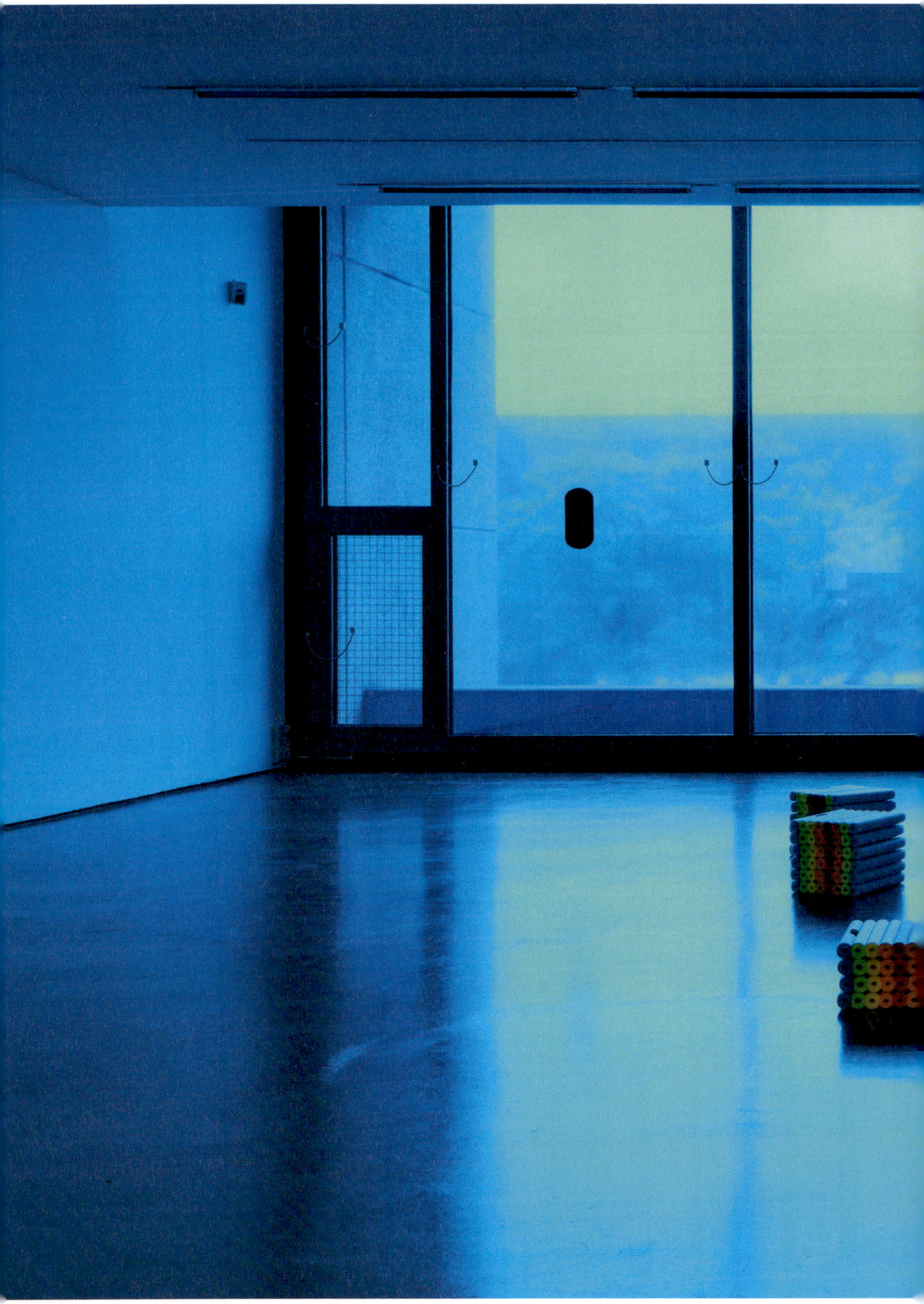

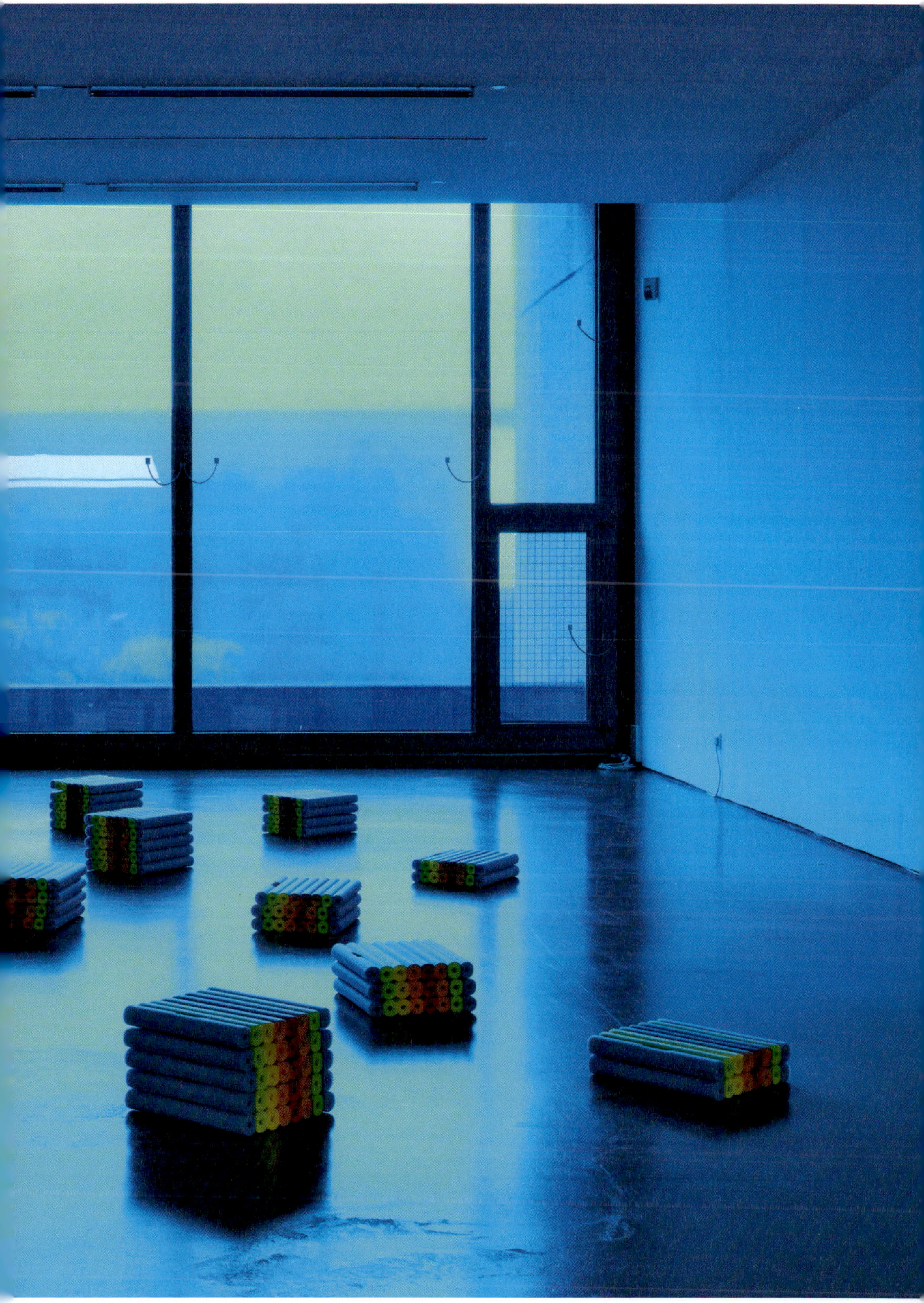

PLAYING FIELD

VIKA KIRCHENBAUER · CARPET · DIMENSIONS VARIABLE · 2021

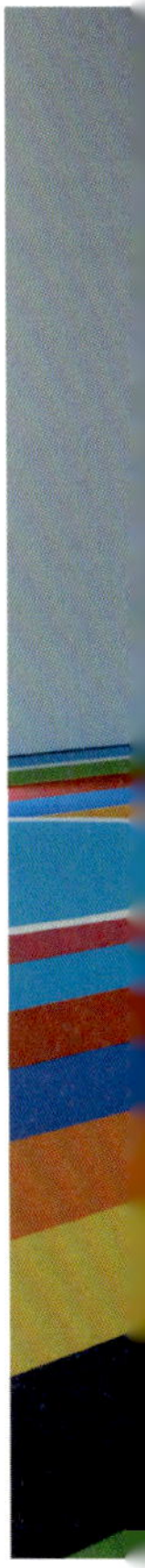

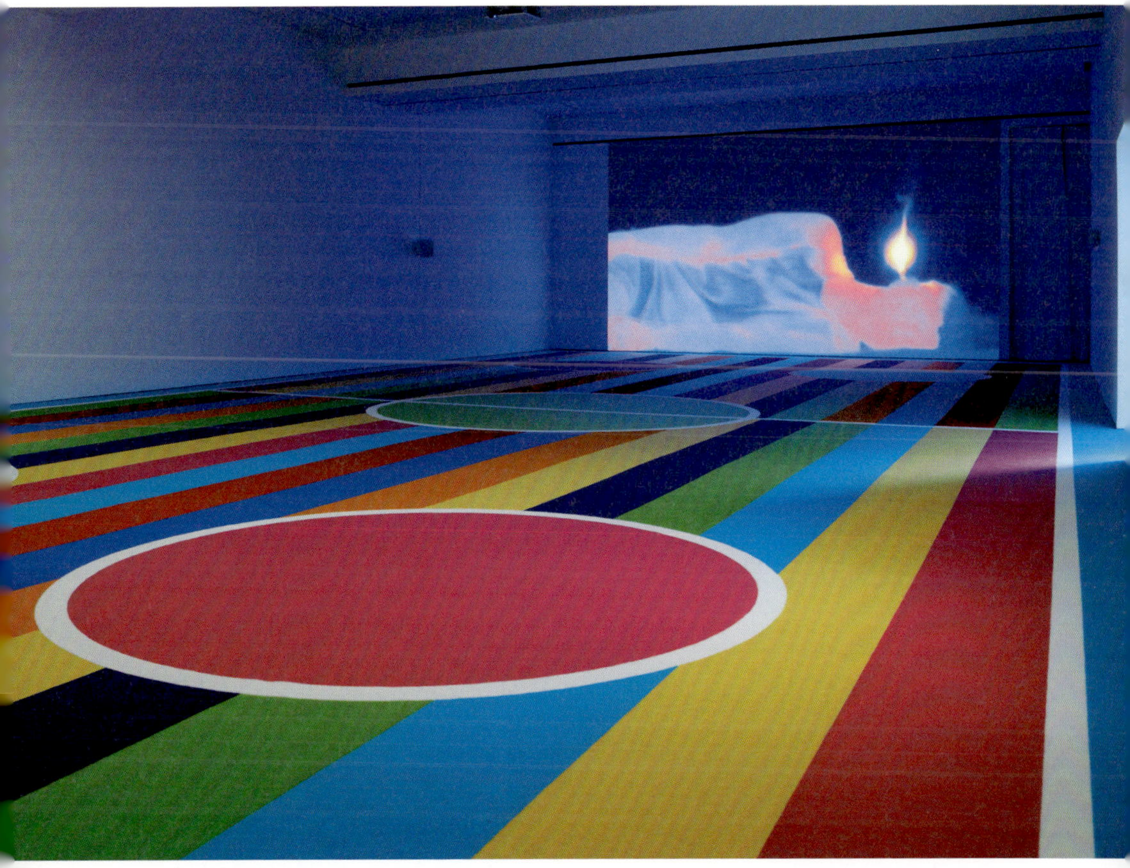

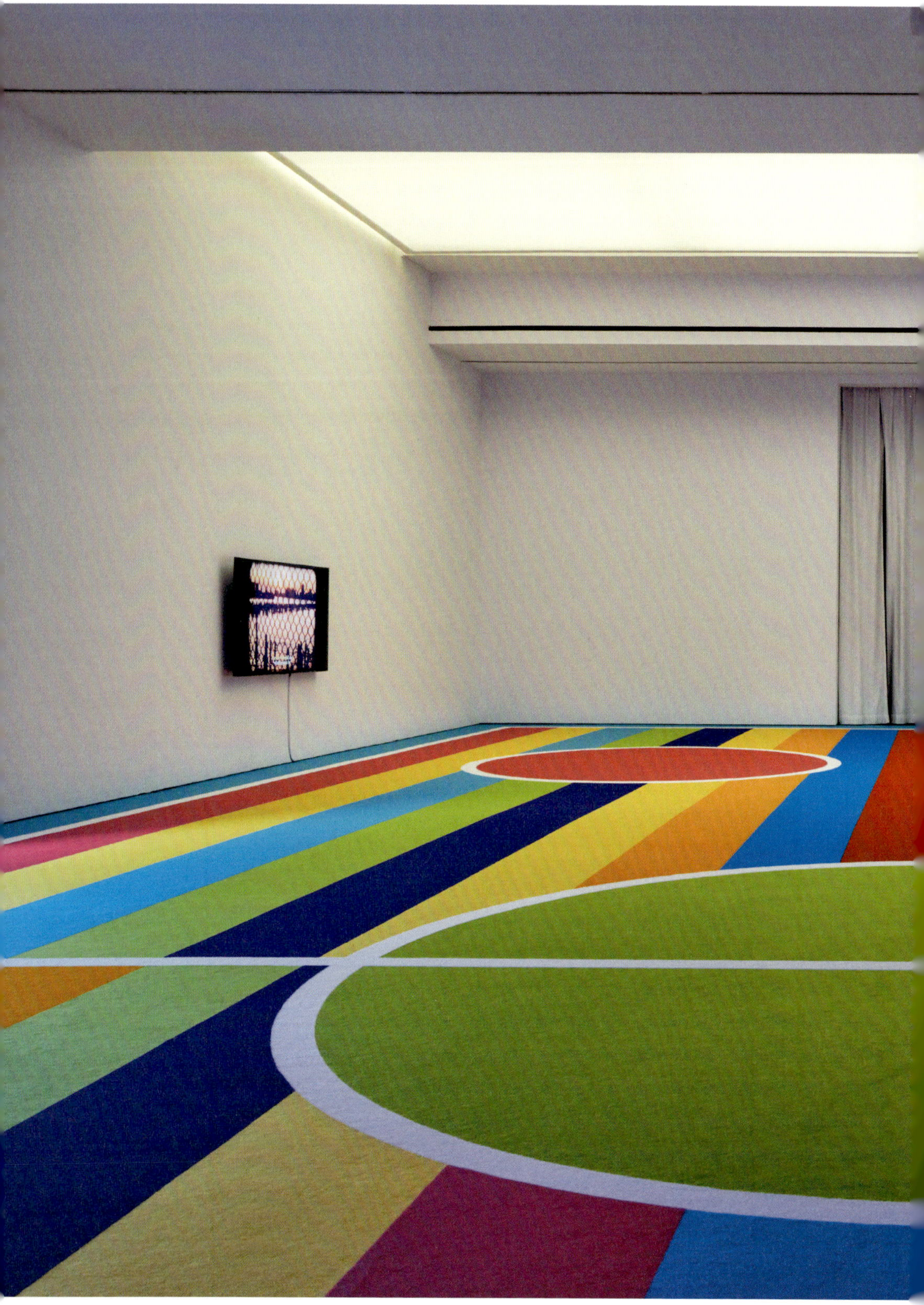

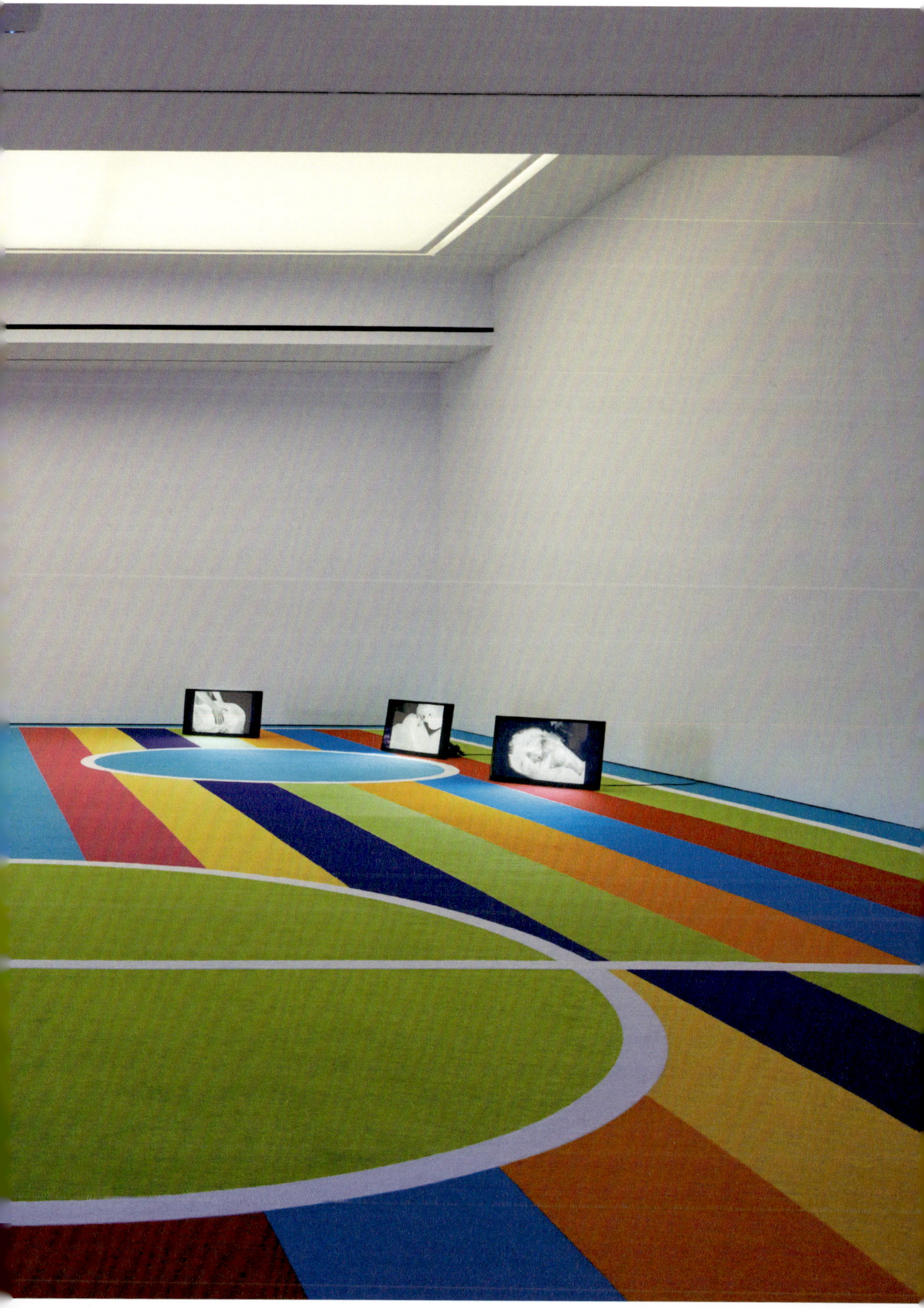

FEELING DIFFERENCE

VIKA KIRCHENBAUER · 2019

FOR THE EXPERIENCE OF OTHERS: WORK AS PERFORMANCE

Cook authentic Portuguese recipes with the drag queens of Lisbon! Explore Paris's African fashion scene with knowledgeable designers! Eat like a Russian! Discover Berlin's unique techno underground! Learn dance moves from urban hip-hop artists in the South Bronx! Play football with local street players in Barcelona! / Airbnb introduced its Experiences programme in 2016. In addition to its ongoing service of brokering lodging and homestays, it is now trying to meet travellers' demand for "authentic, experientially oriented opportunities with more meaningful interactions with locals."[1] People's casual realities are turned into marketable experiences for visitors to dip into, while those rebranding their lives as experiences become dependent on positive reviews and ratings from their paying guests. Providing access to worlds that would otherwise remain closed to the standard traveller has become a lucrative endeavour. / Given their leap from gig economy platform to immersive activities broker, Airbnb serves as a prime example to observe the transition from the service

1 Dominyka Paulauskaite et al, 'Living like a local: Authentic tourism experiences and the sharing economy', *International Journal of Tourism Research* 19 (2017), p. 619.

economy to the experience economy, the latter considered the natural successor of the former by economists B. Joseph Pine II and James H. Gilmore in their 1999 book *The Experience Economy*. With the slogan "Work is Theatre & Every Business a Stage", their theory suggests that goods will be used as props and services as a stage to create experiences that engage customers—or "guests"—in an inherently personal way.[2] Airbnb CEO Brian Chesky sees an "Amazon-sized opportunity" in selling people experiences.[3] By aiming to create lifelong memories, the experience economy surpasses the mere comfort and convenience provided by the service industry; it seeks to orchestrate experiences beyond entertainment, to instead immerse the customers. Customers are understood to pay for an activity in the hope that their future selves will look back happily at what they once experienced. Pine and Gilmore's verdict is that any experience people are not willing to spend money on is plainly not good enough, concluding that "the history of economic progress consists of charging a fee for what once was free."[4] / The organisation of labour within the experience economy is divided into "off-stage" and "on-stage" work. When "on stage", the experience providers perform under the eye of customers (and potentially co-workers); only while "off stage" would they be allowed to leave their role without risking the collapse of the previously crafted sense of authenticity and realness. The *performance mode* demanded from people in order to deliver these memorable and monetisable experiences requires the worker-as-actor to use her affective capacities to enhance the richness and detail, turning one person's regular life (or a service, or a product) into someone else's unique experience. While work was previously understood as the execution of a particular professional skill set that could be acquired through training and study, the experience providers now exploit the totality of their emotional selves as soft skills in order to evoke authentic feelings.

OWNING EMOTIONS: ECONOMIC SHIFTS IN THE SHAPES ART TAKES

Due to the increasing inclusion of audience-engaging, durational, multi-performer performance art in museums, biennials, and quinquennials, artists—in addition to museum and gallery personnel—have become actors and providers of experiences. The experiences offered to their audiences trigger affects and create value within the spectator's memory of *having been there* and the personal feelings felt through it—these subjective feelings being exactly what cannot be shared, what belongs

2 B. Joseph Pine II and James H. Gilmore, *The Experience Economy* (Boston: Harvard Business School Press, 1999), pp. 2-4, 11-12, 172.

3 Elizabeth Weise, 'Airbnb CEO says there's an 'Amazon-sized' market for selling experiences', *USA Today*, 26 February 2018. ›https://eu.usatoday.com/story/tech/news/2018/02/26/airbnb-ceo-amazon-sized-market-selling-travelers-experiences/365554002‹ [last accessed on 31 January 2022].

4 Pine and Gilmore, p. 67.

only to oneself. This is an important economic shift: Rather than being related to tradable objects, economic value is now created through the inherent untradability of the personal experience. When evidenced by means of social media, preferably in real time, the value of the personal experience is only heightened, since lifelong memory is considered to derive only from the pre-mediated event. Against widespread suspicion, social media does not necessarily bar people from being present in a given moment, quite to the contrary, image sharing platforms especially rely on physical presence and exclamations of *being-in-the-moment* as their raw material. They depend on first idealising and then mediatising the now. Social images and live videos are meant to be ephemeral, they are means of communication, an extension of language, rather than items in an old-fashioned photo book or home video archive where memories were meant to be stabilised and kept forever.[5] Social media platforms are therefore not in competition with an experiential turn in art, but are rather the medium buttressing that shift by widening an event's reach and by securing for those physically present an online audience's envy or praise.

/ So, after the production of goods (unique objects like paintings, etc.) and the offering of services (i.e., site-specific installations), we are now entering an era in which artists again mirror economic developments in terms of the forms their art takes. After commodified images, objects, and actions, we now have commodified experiences. Thus, it can be stated that not only in politics and economy, but also in art, affects have become the most promising currency that stakeholders deal in. /

Coinciding with museums' shift towards the visitors' experience as their main value is the relatively recent inclusion of art made from minoritised social positions within larger, more professionalised and institutionalised contexts. While this development is owed in large part to dedicated and long-standing activism, the marginalised body and the way it is institutionally displayed remain questions of concern, especially when considering modes of observation and reception that cannot be discussed independently from commercialised culture and socio-political hierarchies. While some institutions may have made certain progress in the sense of representation, the deeper structural imbalance of who is looking at whom remains largely untouched. If—within an experiential shift in economy and culture—the experience provider inhibits a minoritised position, a set of troublesome circumstances emerges that needs to be taken into consideration. /

The state of being constantly looked at is already a familiar day-to-day experience for people differing from cultural norms—in terms of gender expression, race, ability, etc. To be visibly "different" in this society is to never be "off guard," to never be "off stage," if you will. Hence, within an exhibition space, a doubling of that mechanism occurs. I have previously suggested

5 See Nathan Jurgenson, *The Social Image: On Photography and Social Media* (London: Verso, 2019).

that within hegemonic spaces value can be created by an ostensibly immersive presentation of difference out of context: institutions providing safe positions from which to cast unmet gazes that are lastly directed inwards with self-satisfactory fulfilment. This ethnographic principle of *exhibiting* and making legible, of stabilising the fantasy of a unidirectional gaze, runs through the centuries. Yet when regarded in terms of affect, the experiential value of encounters with the Other might, in fact, even transgress closeness and the clear distinction between the observer and the observed. Those encounters might give a forum to the fantasy of crawling into someone else's skin without the risk of getting stuck in it. When artists Zackary Drucker and Rhys Ernst exhibited their photographic series "Relationship" at Luis De Jesus Gallery in Los Angeles 2014, the *LA Times* tellingly stated in their review:

> *Further complicating 'Relationship' is its status as a record of a transgender couple. Their bodies are transitioning in opposite directions (for Drucker from male to female, and for Ernst from female to male). The relationship triples. It encompasses each person's physical interaction with him- and herself; the one between the protagonists; and, finally, the relationship of the photographs to a viewer. [...] There is something almost Pre-Raphaelite about the tone and feeling of the Drucker-Ernst display. Both noble and, in the best sense, moralizing, it offers the self-reflective pleasures of a secret society unveiled.*[6]

The review's final sentence stays with me: "It offers the self-reflective pleasures of a secret society unveiled." The—connotatively violent—unveiling of a previously "unseen" group apparently gives cause for "self-reflective pleasures" to those spectators enjoying this newly unobstructed vista.

CRITICAL FEELINGS AND THE SYMBOLIC FIELD OF ART

Having grown up not just *with* sports but very much *within* them, I have gained an understanding of arenas and stadiums as disorienting places where people—mostly straight men—find access to and outlets for emotions they struggle to encounter or express in regular life. Otherwise emotionally detached family fathers cry in each other's arms as their team gets relegated. *We* lost! Although in a more individualised manner and within different class customs concerning the publicness of feeling, in art spaces audiences similarly find access to otherwise concealed emotions triggered by watching actions carried

6 Christopher Knight, 'Review: Zackary Drucker and Rhys Ernst, from many angles', *Los Angeles Times*, 10 October 2014, ›https://www.latimes.com/entertainment/arts/culture/la-et-cm-review-zackary-drucker-rhys-ernst-luis-de-jesus-gallery-20141006-column.html‹ [last accessed on 31 January 2022].

out by others, accessing parts of themselves without having to live (or being able to live) the totality of that *other* "experience". The presence of *potential* interactivity with the Other provides a space for passivity, for delegated actions. While affects within the spectator might be plentiful when witnessing critical approaches towards social injustices on a video screen, they are rarely followed by actions outside the symbolic field that art represents to many. /
Particularly the affect world of critique itself is frequently bargained as a currency between different players on art's competitive pitch. To stay within the context of sports analogies, one could look at "critique" in art as "the ball" in team sports: as an object that instigates movement from different players playing different positions—as artists, curators, funders, donors, etc.—while remaining in agreement not to leave the shared field and to loosely follow a certain set of rules. If, as during the 2019 Whitney Biennial, critique *does* in fact materialise outside the symbolic, and teargas manufacturer and Whitney Museum board member Warren B. Kanders *is* sent off the field after artists' and activists' dedicated organising, it marks a resounding success that at the same time highlights how rarely this usually happens. And perhaps even more importantly, one must note that Kanders was merely suspended from the art field; when he returns home, he will still be on his way to becoming a billionaire. / In her 2015 book *Artist at Work*, Bojana Kunst asserts that even the rich and powerful seem to expect or even enjoy being critiqued and shamed. This makes it possible to understand art as a playing field of actions relatively devoid of real consequences. It could be that the (relatively) powerful simply learn that they do not die from shame, since only their symbolic double is shamed without affecting the remaining social order and, within it, their positioning.

> *But what happens with capitalists who donate their wealth to art and receive tickets to the performance art pieces of the rich, in which they not only participate, but are also critically addressed? Their pleasure lies in the critical attitude towards them; it is in the co-existence of their status as the rich and a parodic critique of their role. [...] these patrons are well aware that art will reveal this uneasiness without consequences.*[7]

Beyond the trade of symbolic shame, there are many more emotions on offer for any art spectator in possession of a critical amount of relative privilege. Particularly within socially engaged art, after gaining access to the Other's experiences of social oppression, exclusion, and difference, this spectator—perhaps even having been confronted with her unaffectedness—leaves the gallery knowing that her life will likely continue the way it was going to before she entered the art space. To be sure, it would be grossly reductive to measure art primarily

7 Bojana Kunst, *Artist at Work: Proximity of Art and Capitalism* (Winchester: Zero Books, 2015), p. 47.

in regard to its effects on the outside world, and it is beside the point. Social issues must be subjects of art, and communicating beyond differences is obviously essential, yet the self-centralising affective aspects of spectatorship allude to a relational dimension of these encounters that demands further thought.

MAPPING DIFFERENCE: COMPASSION AND EMPATHY

So how to consider the display of othered bodies within contemporary economies of affective and experiential gain? I propose to address *all* forms of identity not as stable but relational, and to approach empathy and compassion—as exemplary emotions of profound historic entanglements with the arts—as affects involved in shaping a Western hegemonic constitution of the world as such. /

Philosopher Édouard Glissant notes that encounters of humanities are marked by a very foundational, yet secret demand to place the recognition of difference as the prime element of any relation.[8] This becomes important when thinking about the relational nature of spectatorship. Following Glissant's thought, we understand and recognise the Other by mapping her difference from ourselves. We measure the Other against ourselves. I look at you and grasp you through what's different from me, rendering you same and Other simultaneously ... I split you into bits that I consider same and those that I declare different. I must *feel* and understand you in order to relate to your difference and troubles. There are of course those who reject the Other for being other, for not being fully same, those who cannot come to terms with the impossibility of fully grasping the Other. Yet, there are also those who overstate sameness, wanting to experience the Other's sadness and rage led by an urge to discover, to encompass and to feel good about oneself. That compassionate spectator says "I feel you!" yet wouldn't want to hear "No, you don't." /

What is important is that these two groups—for simplicity's sake I will call them the compassionate spectators and the non-empathic spectators—operate on shared assumptions and symptoms deriving from the same culture of transparency. Both are deeply connected to the idea of *understanding* or *grasping*, of making the Other transparent and legible. Both make it their principal condition to *understand the Other* in order to accept them and admit them to existence (or not); both measure the Other against themselves ... just with different, yet no less complicated, results of judgment. /

Now, it is difficult to approach empathy and compassion—which are both required for any kind of relation—without coming under suspicion of seeking to befoul one's object.[9] While I don't regard empathy and compassion to be altogether bad, I nonetheless consider it necessary to

8 Édouard Glissant, *Philosophie de la Relation: Poésie en étendue* (Paris: Gallimard, 2009), p. 29.

9 Lauren Berlant, *Compassion: The Culture and Politics of an Emotion* (New York: Routledge, 2004), p. 5.

complicate the relational dynamics of such affects within the socio-political hierarchies they are bound to. Compassion assumes a social relation between those experiencing difficulty and those *regarding* that suffering.[10] The emphasis lies on the spectator's experience of *feeling compassion* or—particularly when speaking about art made from a minoritised experience—on the spectator's relating to displays of more or less abstracted trauma. We have learned from Susan Sontag's theory of photography that empathic feelings do not guarantee any action to alleviate the Other's suffering, nor do these feelings necessarily signify the willingness to do so. For oneself to continue rendering empathic feelings, the Other must not leave their position of suffering. Compassion relies on maintaining the Other as a normative construct. Compassion might therefore be too dependent on hierarchies, as are all types of relations that place transparency and understanding at their root. / Compassion is successor to judgment, and thus also comes with awareness of the power to be cruel ... the awareness that compassion is a generosity, possible to be withheld at any time. Empathy and sadism as well as compassion and coldness, after all, might not be oppositional, "but two sides of a bargain that the subjects of modernity have struck with structural inequality."[11] / What if compassion did not rely on recognising or overstating partial sameness as a pre-condition for its own becoming? What if mapping the Other's difference from *ourselves* was not the principal requirement for relation? And speaking with Glissant again: What if the Other had the right not to be understood?

POLITICS OF SPECTATORSHIP AND THE CODED MATERIALITY OF VIDEO

Tying these thoughts and questions back to the politics of spectatorship, I want to consider an analogy within the immaterial aspects of video production and exhibition that might help illustrate people's habitual *efficiency* of mapping difference and desire for centred subjectivity. Looking at the most widely used video codec for compression of large files, the H.264 video stream, whilst keeping in the back of one's mind cultural ideas of dominance and relation ... / The H.264 codec is a form of video compression that reduces the amount of data in a stream significantly compared to full frame codecs such as Apple ProRes. While H.264 deploys a system of key frames and inter frames, in ProRes each video frame is rendered as a separate, self-contained image. The H.264 codec reduces the amount of data by rendering only the key frames as full frames, whilst the frames between the first key frame and the next key frame are encoded (and later decoded) only via their difference from the key frames.

10 See Susan Sontag, *Regarding the Pain of Others* (New York: Farrar, Straus & Giroux, 2003).

11 Berlant, p. 10.

It uses prediction models to determine where a certain colour pixel will move within the following image, how its shade of colour will change etc., by relating it to a similar pixel in the key frames, also called *reference frames*. Therefore, if there exist very few changes in a video, the amount of data is reduced significantly because only *difference from the reference frame* needs to be coded. In such a case, when there is much similarity among the individual pictures in a video, the risk of prediction error is much lower than in streams that show very diverse pictures. / Trying to relate this to the idea of relation and spectatorship: Who or what is the reference frame that all difference and motion needs to be linked back to? We might imagine the reference frame as that compassionate spectator or institution, noticing only what difference they perceive whilst declaring all the remaining bits as "same". And who are the inter frames encoded and decoded via their difference from that reference frame? We might imagine the inter frames as those reduced through transparency, those only *understood* through the reference system of normative measuring. / Metaphorically speaking: Would it be worth returning to the pursuit of the idea of full frames that need to be captured as full independent subjects, even at the risk of a higher, more overwhelming data rate to process? Or: What would it look like if the idea of a reference frame was abandoned altogether and *all* frames were understood only through their relation to each other, even at the risk of perhaps not being able to fully decode, reduce, and display all of the structure's individual components? / This would be an instance when dissolving the distinction between regarding subject and objectified subject would no longer be a temporary immersive thrill for the safe spectator, when relationality would become de-hierarchised, mutual projections acknowledged and intensified, yet at the same time destabilised. It might lead to a less fluid stream, but a disturbance both worthwhile and necessary to be experimented with.

PLEASE RELAX NOW

VIKA KIRCHENBAUER · SINGLE-CHANNEL VIDEO · 12:10 · 2014

VK VIKA KIRCHENBAUER

00:00:00 (white screen)

00:00:23 (image starts fading in)

00:00:26 VK Dear spectator,

Hello, I'm really happy you are here! It's a pleasure to see you!

As we are now together in this situation, let me briefly introduce myself: I am the artist behind this little video, you can call me Vika.
Okay, now that we've established that: why don't we assume our positions just for a moment?

Please relax now, dear spectator!
Make yourself comfortable ... The seat you sit in is designed for you to feel just right. Lean back!

This is going to be a memorable event, orchestrated by me for you. Believe me, you will never forget this. Isn't this great? Never to forget, forever to remember ... With your commitment, dear spectator, you will be transformed during this piece. Let me just guide you a little first!
The deal is: this is an immersive piece. And only through your thorough collaboration will it unfold in its full richness.

00:00:00

00:00:22

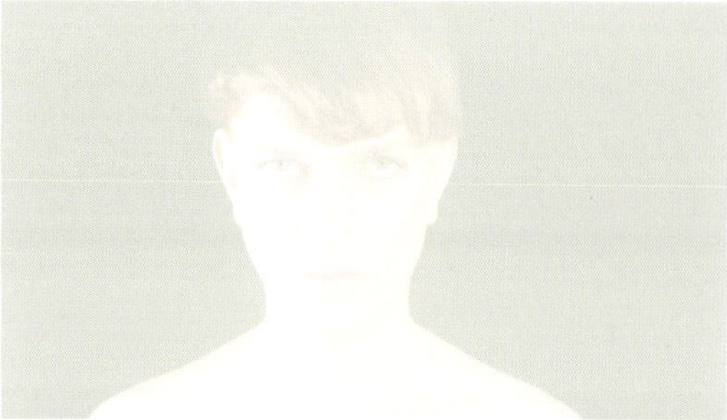

00:00:23

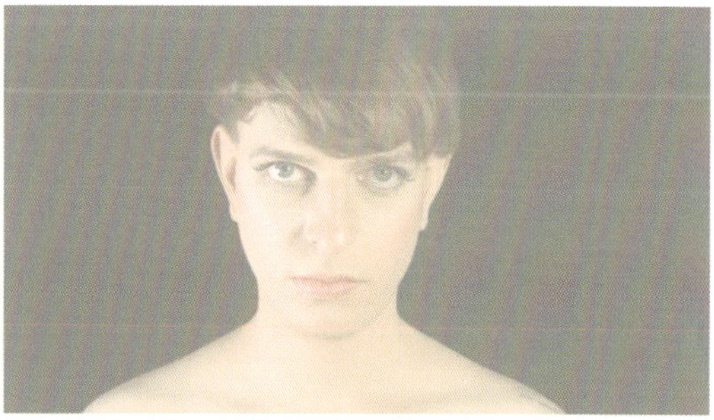

00:01:37

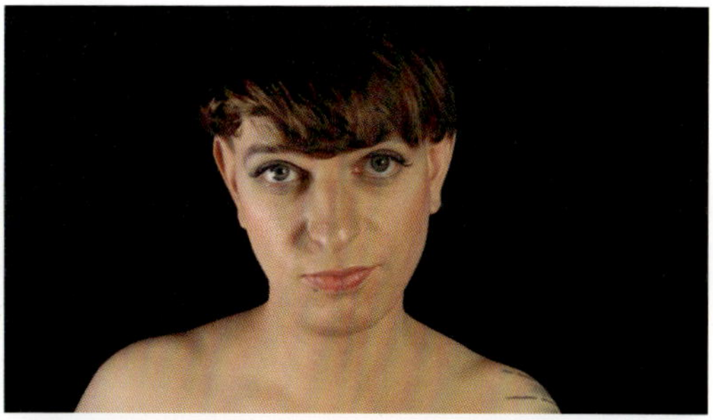

00:01:47

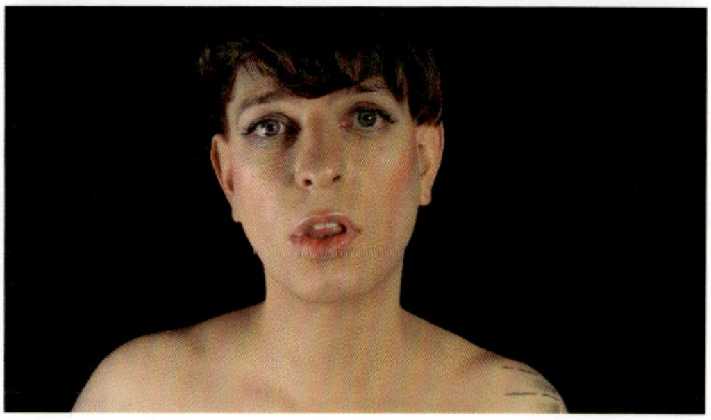

00:02:33

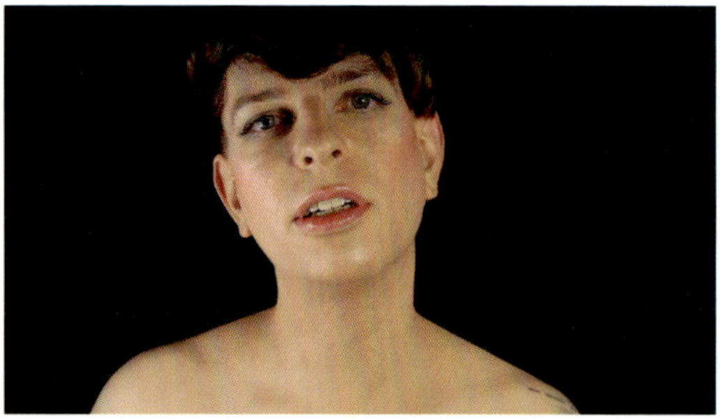

00:05:05

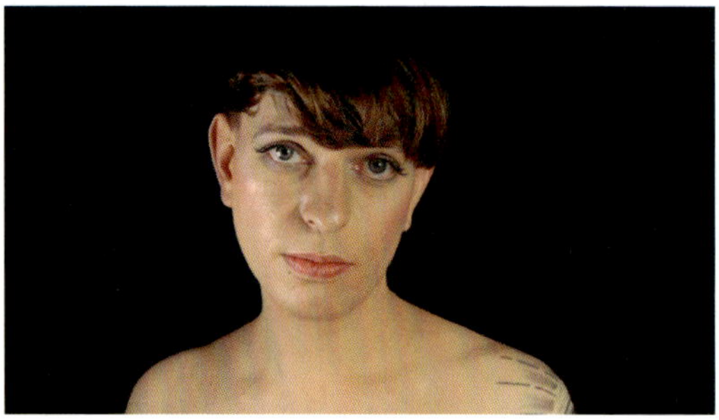

00:05:13

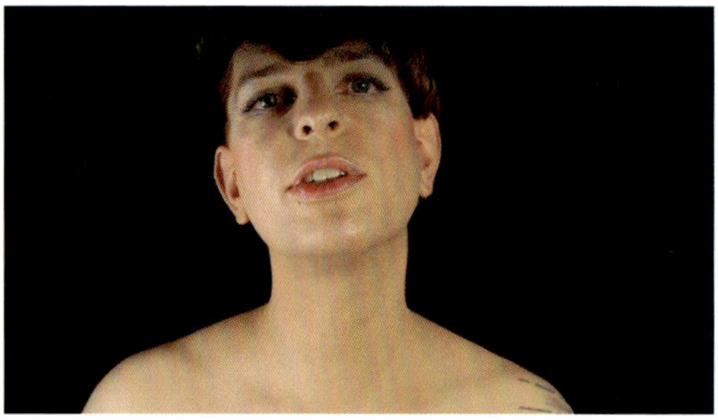

00:05:19

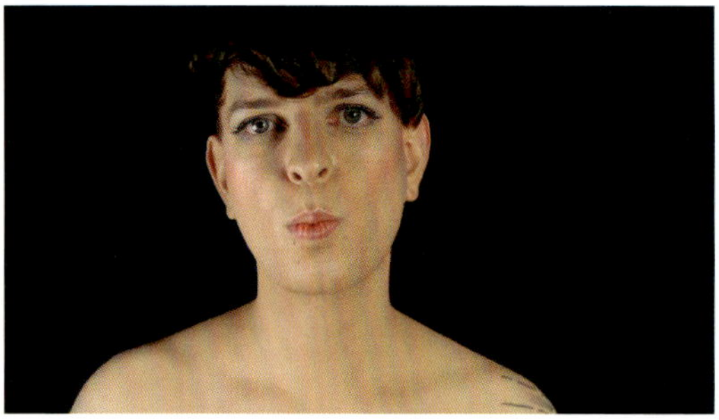

00:05:59

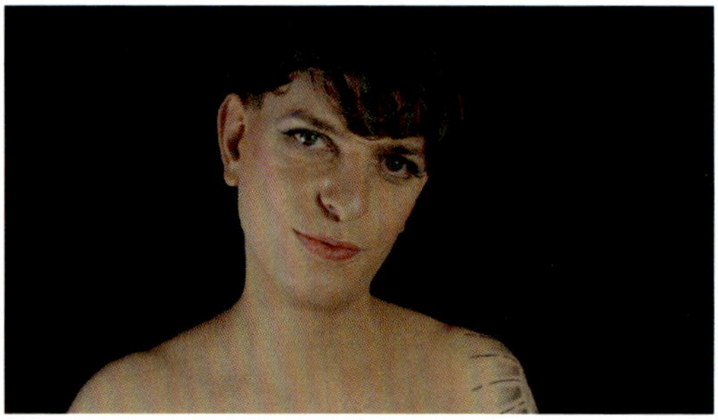

Only you can give life to the artwork. You will not be a spectator anymore. You'll become much more than that. You'll become an integral part of the piece. You will in fact become everything! You will become the artwork!

Whenever I walk through a museum, a gallery or any sort of art space really—some things might be interesting or thought-provoking, for sure—but primarily, I have to admit, I just get very horny. It just really turns me on. Do you know what I mean? Can you relate to that experience? Often the only thing I can think of is sex, whatever I look at really. On numerous occasions I went to the toilet to masturbate, but often wished this sort of reaction was possible within the art space. The reason why I'm talking about this here is because this is your chance to do just that. This space has been created for exactly this to happen. Masturbation! Isn't this special?

Have you ever come in an exhibition space? Or in a cinema even? No? Now you can just do it. It's part of the piece, no one will look at you strangely ...

You've got absolute permission to touch yourself now. For your comfort I've made completely sure that there is no institutional staff in this room policing you in any way.

You must understand that we can't be 'democratic' about obtaining our liberty. We must just take it! And that starts with desire ...

I installed this territory for you, and you are not merely a visitor, you are welcome here, this could be home for you, if you want to.

If it's helpful to you, you can think of this as a space that we've just privatised, it's simply no longer public. So you can just wank off in it. I guarantee you: it is absolutely fine ... you little naughty beast.

If you still perceive this space to be public, that's great, too. No problem. Because together we are right now establishing a new law: a new code of liberty. Together let us introduce something that breaks with all the conceptions that have been here before. Isn't that exciting?

I think it's better if I lower the light for you now. You'll see, it'll be much better then.

00:06:04 (screen fades to black)

00:06:16 VO VK It's much nicer, isn't it?

It's nice to take a break from all those images for a moment, right?

And you deserve that. A break ... an island for liberty and desire that can be your home ... You do deserve this. Don't be too modest.

Okay. Are you ready?

This is your opportunity to unleash your desire, your hidden fantasies. Please, let me be your slutty guide!

Gently place your hands on your genitals and feel them. Whatever name you find for them, just feel them.

Don't be shy, darling. The room is dark. No one's watching you. This is an intimate moment with yourself.

You do have your hands on your genitals, right?
I knew it. Excellent!

Touch them, caress them, stroke them softly and close your eyes now.

Imagine me sucking your pussy or licking your dick.

What does that feel like? Does it feel good? Imagine you're pressing yourself against my little ass ...

Hmm, that feels good! Thank you!

Don't stop. Keep it going. Enjoy your little sexy activity.

Are you having a good time? I bet you are!

Fuck me, I am at your service.

Are you getting there? Oh, I bet you are.

(heavy breathing)

I like having my face in your crotch. And I want you to come. I want to hear you lose control.

(moaning)

Hmm, the art piece is almost ready, isn't it?

(moaning)

Just rub it a bit more.

And let's come to the final step.

Oh, almost, you're almost there ...!

(moaning)

00:06:01

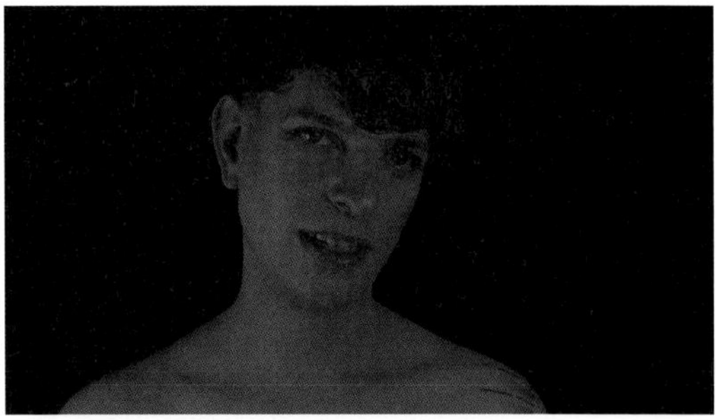

00:06:02

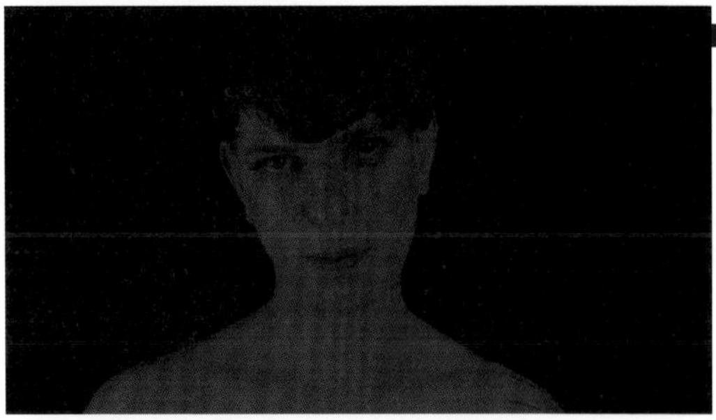

00:06:03

00:11:19

00:11:20

Ah, oh my god.

(heavy moaning)

And now: exhibit yourself to the others!

00:11:21 (screen suddenly goes white)

(continued heavy moaning)

00:11:21 VO VK Thank you.

CAMERA, COMPOSITING	MARTIN SULZER
MAKE-UP	MANU WOLF

YOU ARE BORING!

VIKA KIRCHENBAUER · 3D VIDEO INSTALLATION · 13:11 · 2015

LJJ	LAUREN JOHN JOSEPH
MG	MAX GÖRAN
M	MYSTI
N	NADIA BUYSE
VK	VIKA KIRCHENBAUER

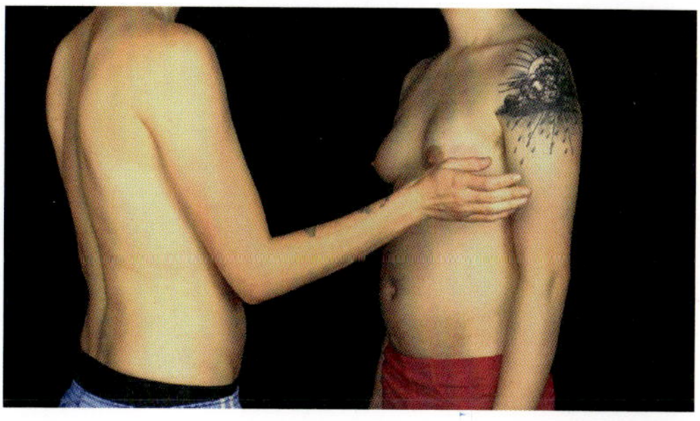

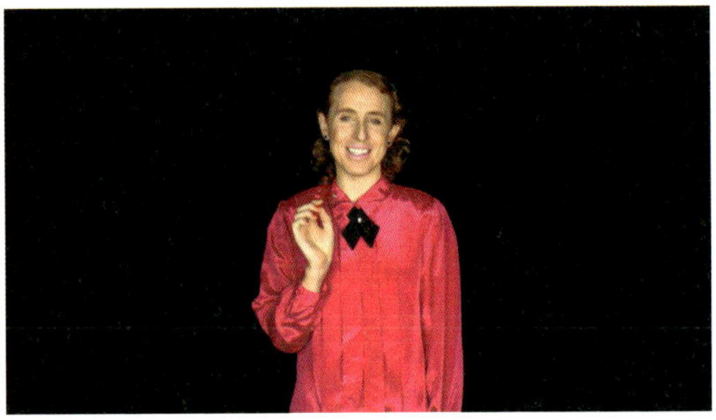

00:00:45 LLJ

Let me welcome you here in this world of experiences. This beautiful haven of experience heightened by the presence of the other. Here you can experience, here you can be part of us, here you will be truly engaged. Without the inconvenience of being spat upon on the street or the unpleasant smells of darkroom...

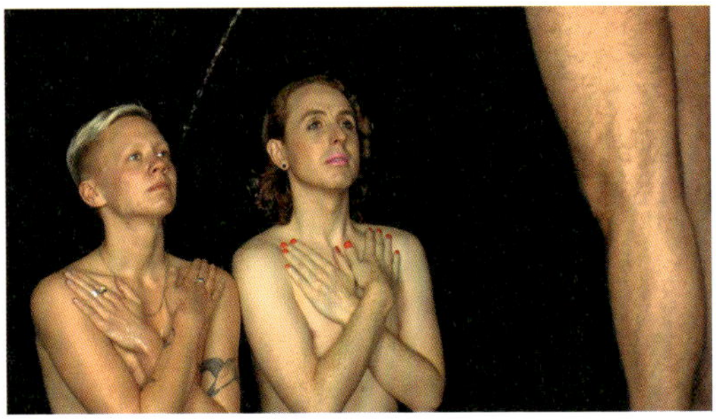

00:01:15 VO LLJ

The driving experience, the pumping experience, the reading experience, the grocery shopping experience, the appliance-delivering experience, the cooking experience, the eating experience, the wearing experience, the cleaning experience, the soap-dispensing experience, the washing experience, the drying experience, the sleeping experience, the life-scaping experience, the car-renting experience, the drawering experience, the briefcasing experience, the wastebasketing experience, the mask-taping experience, the drinking experience.[1]

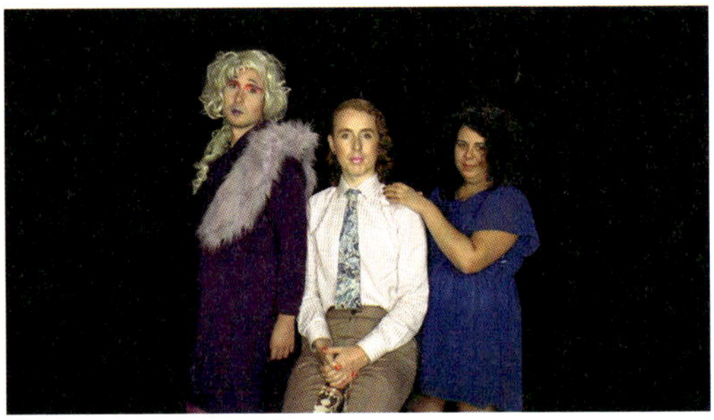

00:02:38 LLJ

We are interested in the transference from subcultural bedroom practice to legitimate public culture and further into bourgeois domestic culture.

00:02:49	M	A historic moment has been reached where our difference is now ripe for consumption.
00:02:55	NB	We are post-oppositional complexity-lovers. We are ready now to fully engage with the deterrence that held many of us away.
00:03:03	LLJ	This will lead to fundamental changes. We are neither too optimistic, nor too narcissistic when we just realistically estimate the potentials of our impact.
00:03:14	M	You, on the other hand, will also profit from this in your way. You can buy us, make us site-specific. We are ready-mades ready for your lust—crisp and refined.
00:03:27	NB	We are what you can't attain. Yet only you can make us free from time and change. You can jerk off to our images until you're totally dry, or you can have us decorate your dinner party.
00:03:38	LLJ	Whatever you want, darling. Because we know that you have either the economic or educational capital to consume us ... ideally both.

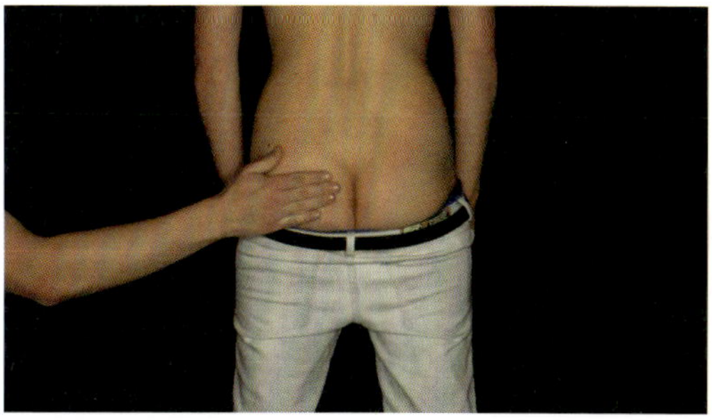

00:03:56	VO M	Your ass is out of character. I'm sorry, but it ruins the integrity of the performance. When on stage, engage with the guests, personalise their experience. Customise our offerings to meet their needs, don't ever drop out of character and let no part of yourself drop out of character. Not your ass, not your toe. You are who stages the experience. Eliminate all negative cues, make our aspirants experience less sacrifice. When period-costumed never talk the present-day talk of guests. All personal conversations with co-workers may only happen off stage. Keep off-stage work off stage, conduct on-stage work on stage. Period. We finally have to accept that our work is theatre and act accordingly.

1 A collection of marketable experiences suggested throughout the book: B. Joseph Pine II and James H. Gilmore, *The Experience Economy* (Boston: Harvard Business School Press, 1999).

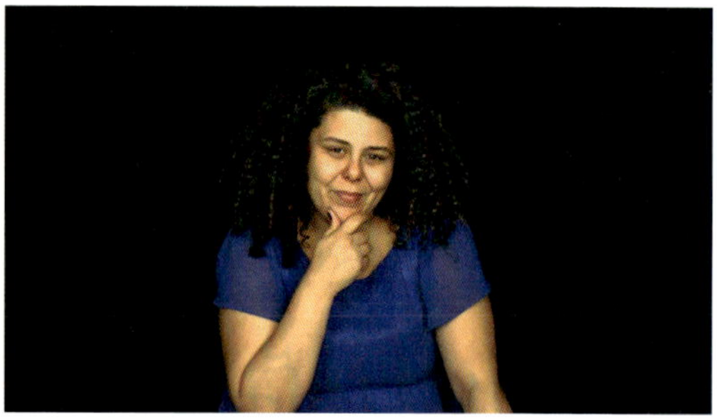

00:04:52 NB

As you might have noticed, I am making certain assumptions about you, and they might to some extent be my fantasy, but I have taken great efforts to get to know you; and to be able to offer you just exactly what you need. I've been to spaces like this myself before. So many times ... Who you are may be my fantasy, but nothing I imagine. I know you. And you know that ... you are cultured but stiff, "sexually liberated" yet somewhat deeply ashamed. So let me help you.

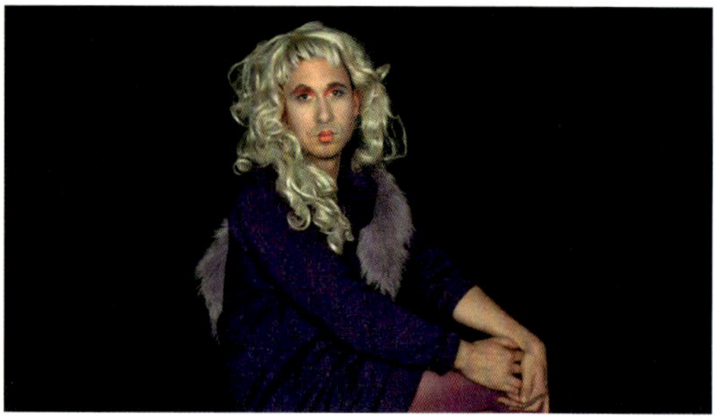

00:05:27 M

Let us agree that without us you are fundamentally boring, tedious. You can navigate your way through all of life's situations considerably well, but you need help for that special thing. Only when interacting with us do you gain the deepest understanding of certain parts of yourself. You desire is to be changed. Nothing's worse than being life-size: you want to be larger than life. You too, want to be a beautiful, extraordinary and wonderful person. And that's why you're here, right? Please take advantage of this little surplus we're offering you via our inherently exhibitionist nature. For our labour: pure pleasure and satisfaction to us ...

2 In reference to the subtitle and one of the central arguments of the book *The Experience Economy*, namely that "Work is Theater & Every Business is a Stage".

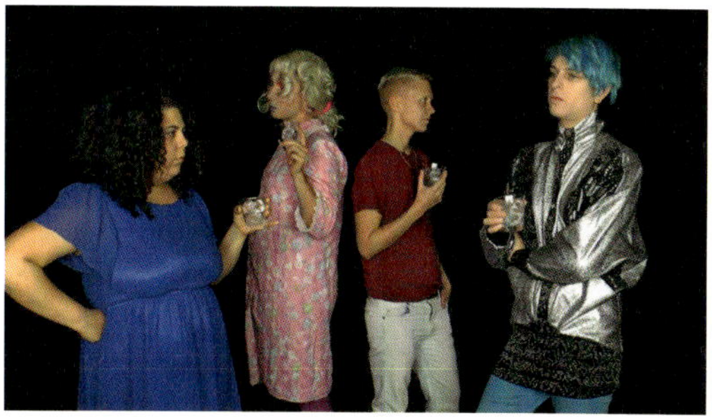

00:06:20 VO LLJ

Use goods as props and your gallery as a theatre to stage a memorable experience:[2]

The community-building experience, the contact-making experience, the taste-acquiring experience, the introducing experience, the small-talking experience, the social-climbing experience, the belonging experience, ...

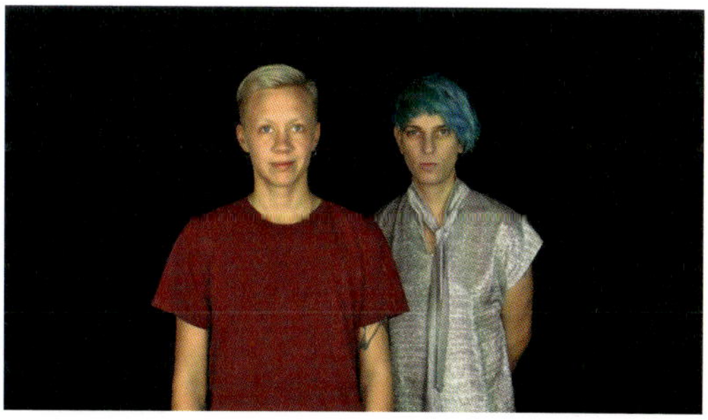

00:07:01 MG

We need to admit that sleeping with us is actually pretty weird, but a cool experience. We have all these crazy combinations of genitals and body parts... it's outrageous. We're totally unique, so being with us will not only be like the craziest thing you've ever done, it will also be very easy for you to do stuff that you couldn't even imagine. Like fucking that exotic asshole that is actually a cunt, or borrowing a dick from someone on whose tits you can come with it. I mean, who wouldn't want to fuck a work of conceptual art, abstraction become flesh!? I mean wow!

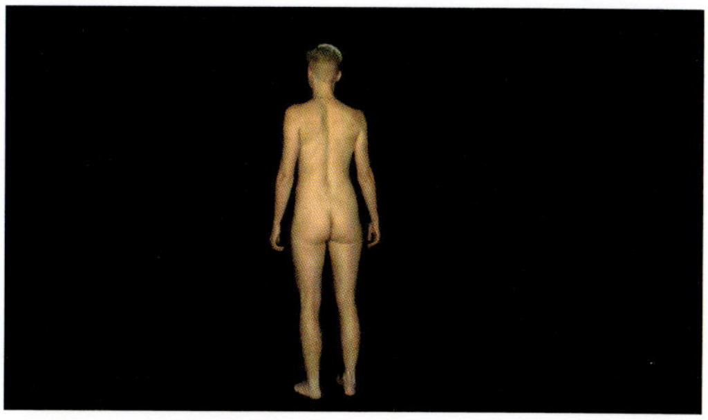

00:08:08 VO M

"The intention of mission statements, strategic plans, and action steps must be grounded in one's uniqueness, not in a fixation on the activity of competitors. This is not striving to be differentiated but seeking to discover the unexamined dimensions of oneself, with competitive differentiation resulting as a natural by-product. The corporate self-examination provides the wellspring of renewal (just as examining the uniqueness of one's audience opens the wellspring of unarticulated needs). The strategy of a business confers meaning only if those called on to execute it understand—ideally, viscerally—how the company plans to alter the very structure of the world through its industry. Every activity of the company must be performed in order to advance external change."[3]

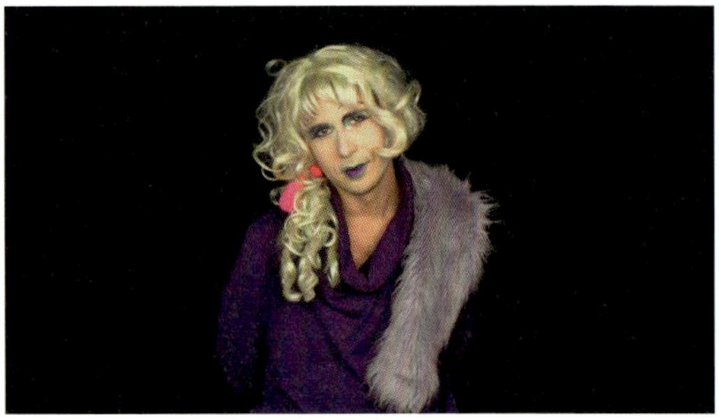

00:09:07 M

Darling, let me share with you my unresolved emotions. These issues are too great and intense for them to just be transferred within family structure. Besides, I won't procreate anyways. So this is where you come into play, my dear. I have distilled the finest problems, the ones you want to experience but can only do so through me ...

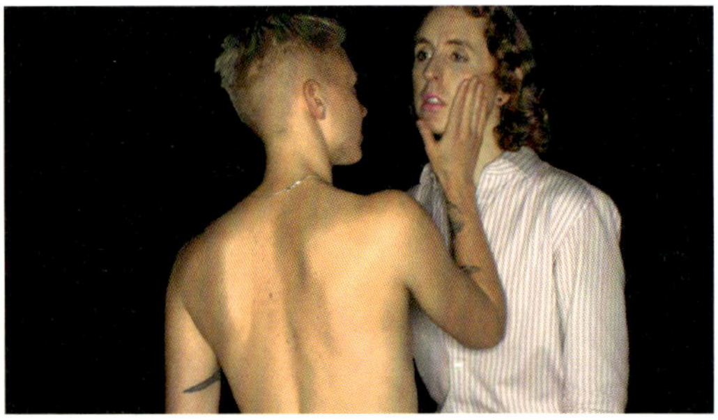

00:09:38 VO VK

It's not a stage I ever really choose. Every time I go outside people look ... Because of course they see something. It makes me quite ... I don't know. I just feel I can never really be off-guard ... I don't think I'm calling for the attention! Or yes and no ... if that makes sense. It's really not like I hate myself, it's something different ... I do think of myself as quite strong ... maybe ... I don't know ... I just know I'm some sort of prototype ... and I'm aware that prototypes can also just break down suddenly ...

3 Pine and Gilmore, p. 202.

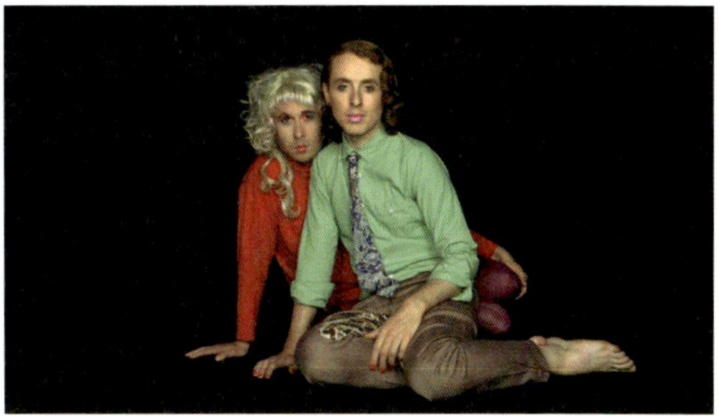

00:10:44 M

Only bloodless people can't be made to bleed, but we know you are a special and warm-hearted person. Your face looks so gentle. Please take all of this as a compliment. Your death will start from now.

00:10:59 LJJ

Don't be sad, death is the best thing that can happen to you ... Have you ever thought about how you might stage your own death? Discover the potentials of unique death, not some middle-class heart attack! Art history will teach you the most extravagant ways of dying. Death is your opportunity where concrete meaning can finally be achieved! Death is the means by which you can rewrite your entire life!

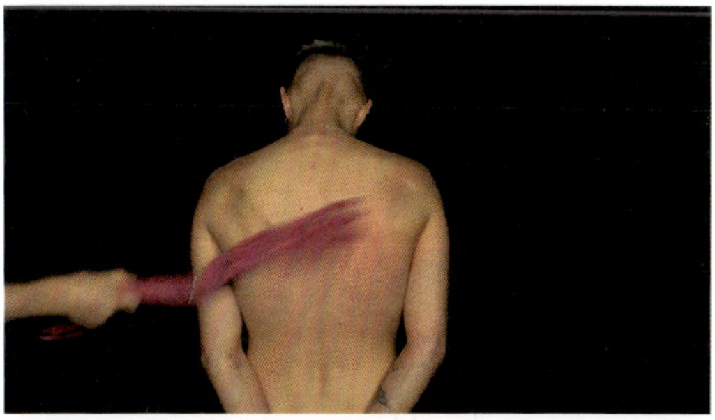

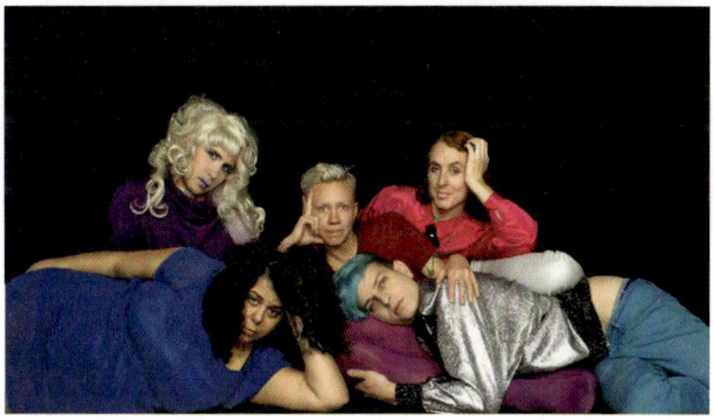

00:11:59 NB

Dear aspirant, not only will all of this will make you a better person ... We're also your access port to a magical place of possibilities. Let us take this path together ... We have given our bodies to your eye as a token of our authenticity and best intentions.

00:12:20	MG	Being close to us will always increase your chance of getting laid. After the opening, or even during the show ... anything is possible when we're around.
00:12:31	LJJ	This is owing to our ability to change the way an entire room functions. We can alter the atmosphere to the point where it would seem rude not to turn and start making out with the stranger standing next to you.
00:12:47	M	Considering approaching death, why not engage yourself, engage with the others in the room with you? Who cares anymore?

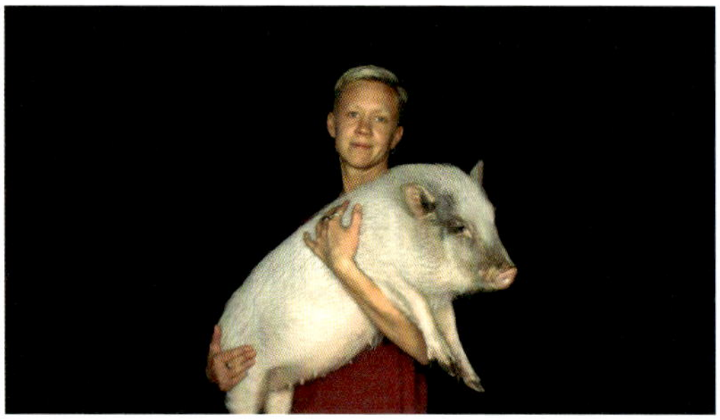

CAMERA, COMPOSITING	MARTIN SULZER
SOUND	RITA MACEDO
SOUND MIXING	DANIEL JOHN BOYLE
SET ASSISTANCE	CAIO AMADO SOARES
CATERING	FRAUKE BOGGASCH

WELCOME ADDRESS

VIKA KIRCHENBAUER · SINGLE-CHANNEL VIDEO · 12:00 · 2017

AS ASHKAN SEPAHVAND

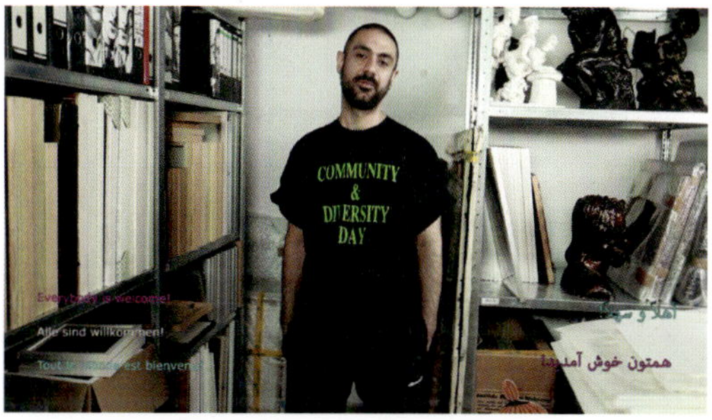

00:00:02 AS Hello, please let me welcome you! Everybody is welcome.

My name is Ashkan Sepahvand, and I am a research fellow here at the Schwules Museum*.[1] I responded to a call encouraging postcolonial perspectives on the institution, its practice and its archive. My position was made possible by a grant from the German Cultural Foundation, which I'm

1 The text uses excerpts from the institution's project funding application to the German Cultural Foundation, the call for applications for the curatorial fellowship "Postcolonial Perspectives on LBTIQ-Heritages", Ashkan Sepahvand's application letter for the position, as well as lines written by Vika Kirchenbauer. The distinction between the respective sources has deliberately been left blurry. Thus, citations are not marked.

very grateful for. This is the first time in the museum's existence that someone receives a fellowship to examine its collection and history under such a particular lens.

Again, welcome!

I am a queer person of colour and I identify primarily as an artistic researcher. In fact, I am flattered to be on display as well as to display.

I have worked for more than a year on this project. The resulting exhibition can be seen in this room that you have just entered.

The museum also features other exhibitions simultaneously. If you would like to know more about these, please feel free to ask the staff either inside the galleries or at the welcome desk.

Again, welcome! If I am welcome here, then so are you.

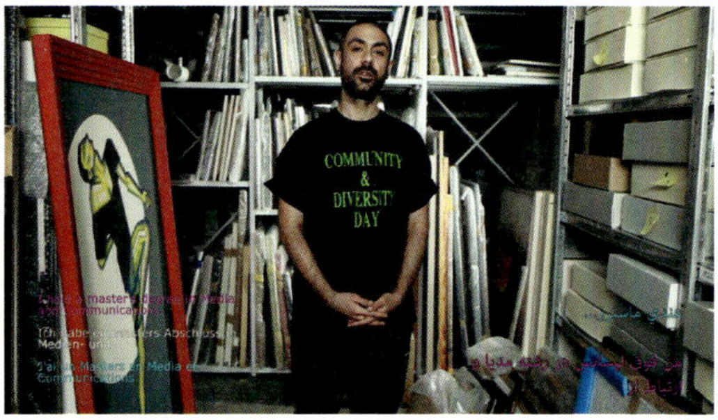

00:01:33 AS I hold a master's degree in Media and Communications from the European Graduate School. In the past, I have worked as a Research Fellow at the Haus der Kulturen der Welt in Berlin, as well as as an independent curator, artist, writer and lecturer at and with various institutions and publishing houses. I bring with me my personal network of contacts, collaborators, and institutional links, spread across the fields of contemporary art, speculative design, performance, feminist and queer activist circles, critical theory, experimental music, and nightlife undergrounds from Europe and the Middle East.

Even though English might come across as my first language, I've only spoken it since I was five. Ich spreche außerdem auch fließend Deutsch. Furthermore, I am fully fluent in written and spoken Farsi, with excellent French language skills as well as some basic Arabic knowledge. I recently applied for German citizenship – my application is currently being processed.

Welcome!

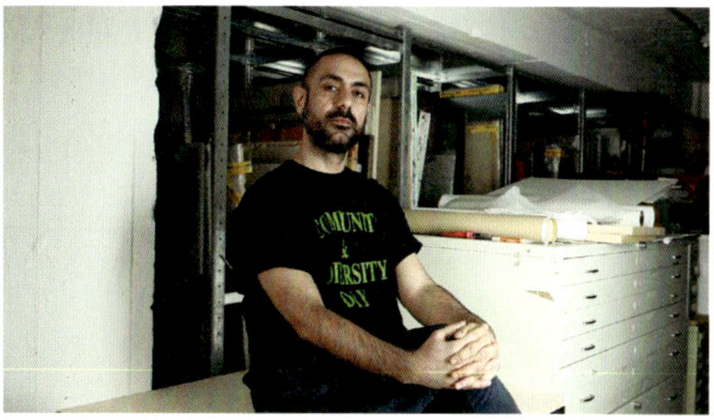

00:02:40 AS

Since its founding in 1985, the Schwules Museum* has grown into one of the world's largest and most significant institutions for archiving, collecting and communicating the history and culture of LGBTIQ communities. Changing exhibitions and events take *diverse* approaches to lesbian, gay, trans*, bisexual and queer biographies, themes and concepts in history, art and culture.

In over 150 special exhibitions shown over the past 30 years, the museum has presented a broad spectrum of perspectives on the history of homosexual cultures. Being over $500m^2$, the museum has at its disposal one of the world's largest archives, which includes more than 1,000 metres of archival material (files, newspaper cut outs, videos, posters, photographs, paintings, sculptures and so on).

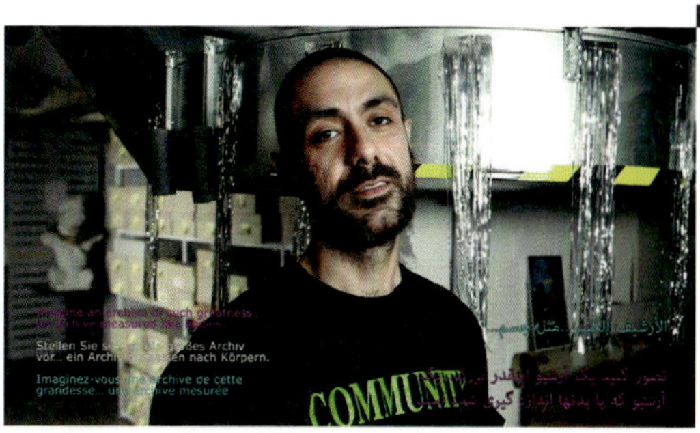

00:03:43 AS

Imagine an archive of such greatness ... an archive measured like bodies. More than a kilometre of bodies ... Imagine nearly 600 average bodies hung vertically on a wall. Such a wall would extend itself from here all the way up alongside the canal right up until the Neue Nationalgalerie. That's how big the archive is.

For this project, I was asked to question the ways in which European colonialism intersects with cultural discourses on homosexual emancipation. Of course, I'm more than happy to do this work on the museum's behalf, and I won't deny the security this position has temporarily provided me amidst a sea of precarity.

As an institution, we—if I may say so—believe that through practicing self-ethnography we will be able to embody the power we deserve. We believe that if we can put ourselves into vitrines, authorship over history will be more just.

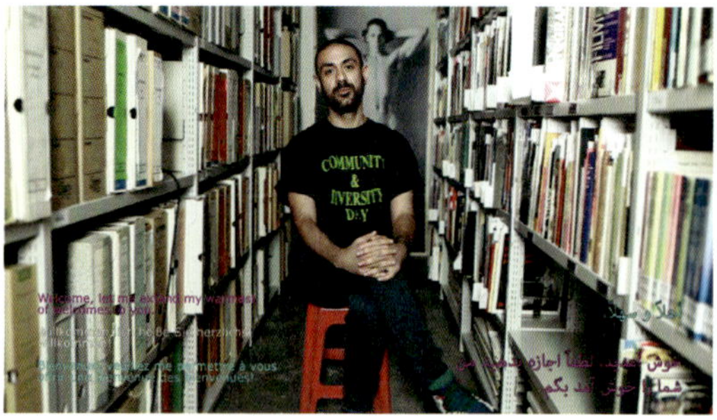

00:04:49 AS Welcome, let me extend my warmest of welcomes to you.

Welcome to Eldorado!

I feel truly privileged to have the opportunity to present this show to you. I admire the museum's courage to let me go through their holdings with my postcolonial set of eyes. Luckily, an institution does not die from shame.

This exhibition is happily part of a series of exhibitions that bring in diversity.

I have decided not to primarily display archival materials in this exhibition. Instead, I invited a series of contemporary positions in response to it.

On one of the walls of the "living room" environment just to your right, you will find my modest archival contribution to the exhibition. For instance, Magnus Hirschfeld arranged next to Leni Riefenstahl.

To find out more about my ideas and research questions, I would like to draw your attention, if I may, to the exhibition handout on the living room table—as well as to an extensive publication that will be released in September.

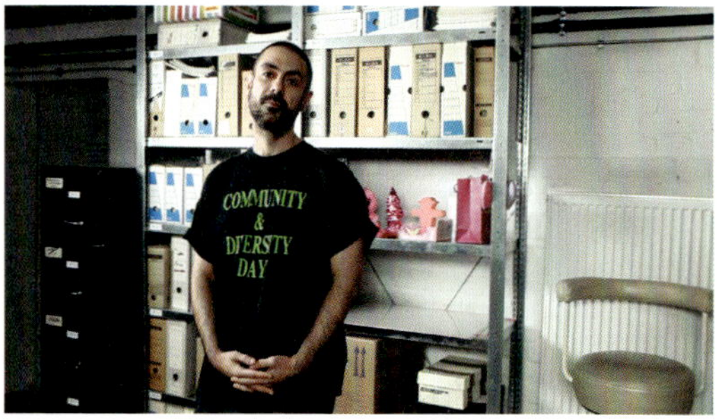

00:06:06 AS Again, I'm very glad to welcome you and it is my pleasure to welcome you with these words that have been compiled and written for me by one of the artists I have chosen to be in the show: Vika Kirchenbauer. I welcome her, too. Still.

I would also like to thank all the artists in the show for offering their work for display without compensation—in accordance with the museum's habits.

It is my honour to help you and the museum sail away, sail away, sail away.

"Let me sail, let me sail,

Let the Orinoco Flow,

Let me reach, let me beach

On the shores of Tripoli.

Let me sail, let me sail,

Let me crash upon your shore,

Let me reach, let me beach

Far beyond the Yellow Sea.

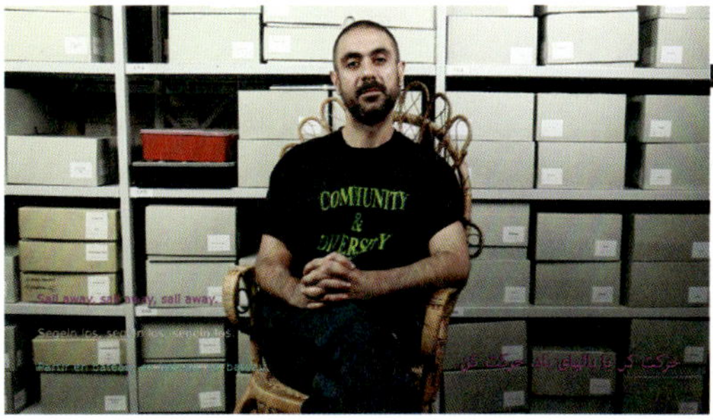

00:07:00 AS Sail away, sail away, sail away.

From Bissau to Palau, in the shade of Avalon,

From Fiji to Tiree and the Isles of Ebony,

From Peru to Cebu hear the power of Babylon,

From Bali to Cali, far beneath the Coral Sea.

Sail away, sail away, sail away.

From the North to the South, Ebudæ into Khartoum,

From the deep sea of clouds to the island of the moon,

Carry me on the waves to the lands I've never been,

We can sail, we can sail with the Orinoco Flow,

We can sail, we can sail.

Sail away, sail away, sail away."[2]

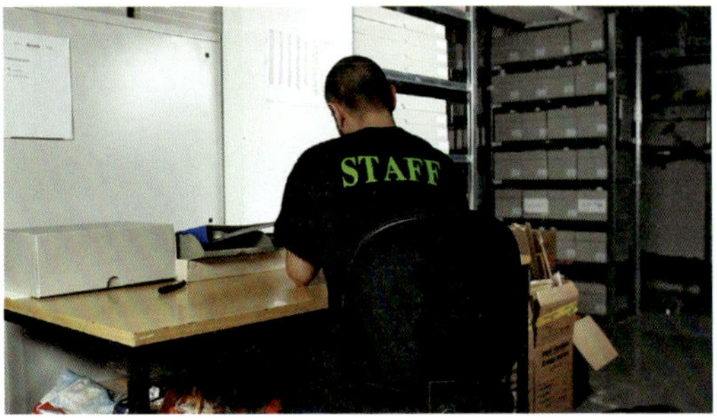

TRANSLATIONS ASHKAN SEPAHVAND
CAMERA, LIGHT RITA MACEDO

2 Lyrics from: Enya, "Orinoco Flow" (WEA Records, 1988).

WELCOME ADDRESS

VIKA KIRCHENBAUER · EMAIL TO ASHKAN SEPAHVAND · 2017

FROM VIKA KIRCHENBAUER
TO ASHKAN SEPAHVAND
DATE 8 APRIL 2017 AT 14:13
SUBJECT RE: VIKA TEXT

dear ashkan,

thanks for your revisions. at first, i wasn't completely sure how to work with them. i see your hesitations and take them seriously, but it is really a whole new text now; with a very different tonality and perspective and, frankly, quite little left of what i had written. it seems less risky and much more self-explanatory to me now. given that there's very little time now before we need to come to a final version, i think it's good we discuss the further process very soon.

after i sent you the text in late february i added that i think it's important we meet and talk about any insecurities and ambivalences we might have towards the text ... and to talk explicitly about your role and my role in it. i still think that. i am completely aware that it's a risky form of representation, so to talk about intentions and perspectives is more than necessary.

what i did now is to go back to the text that i had written trying to incorporate bits of what you have written into it. maybe we can work from there? if you have comments or remarks on why you didn't find certain parts of it relevant or felt the need to change them, would you please use the 'comment function' in word and send it back to me? would that work? find my revised script attached.

the questions you ask about the subject(s) of critique are very important. i'm not sure if formulating critique is completely what it's about ... i guess my aim would be to open up the institution, you and me as possible subjects of critique ... without formulating critique from a steady standpoint within the work, rather through trying to examine a structure and mechanism considering various aspects of it (with some fluidity in perspective).

my intention is neither to criticise you nor your 'cv self', but to examine how minoritised positions within this type of economy need to use their otherness as an asset to differentiate themselves from others, to differentiate themselves from competitors so to speak. and of course the institutional 'openness' towards otherness considering one aspect of identity (gender identity, ethnicity, etc.) needs to be compensated by other achievements that ensure some degree of privilege and access (often education or alternative forms of cultural capital). so this is not about you or me really, but about the structure one operates in.

to only point fingers at the institution or the museum would seem self-righteous to me. also, i'm thinking about my role in it of course. i want my decision to ask you to read a text that i wrote in a fictionalised first person voice for you to be somewhat visibly 'problematic', and to be transparent in its repetition of structural violence. if the text was flattened to a text that is closer to your actual subjectivity, that would falsely mask my strange role in all of this—that of a simultaneous observer and perpetrator within a complex set of power dynamics.

one of the things i was hoping to achieve with the video is to draw attention to one aspect that seems to plague all 'minority artists and curators' within contemporary art: however much 'we' try to resist and problematise 'representation', all readings will always be relinked and reduced to our identities. whatever you do, however critically, will still predominantly be seen as 'the brown person doing a show at schwules museum*'. when i perform, whatever i say, all that people will see is lipstick.

about the cue-cards: i think they make for bad performance, but i see the strong difficulties implied in doing one take of a relatively long text. i think breaking it up into segments would make a lot of sense. i will have to think whether or not different shots of just you in front a blue wall make sense (just on a technical editing level). so maybe we can meet at schwumu on thursday and re-consider perhaps shooting in the archive itself? that could make editing options for breaking up the script much easier perhaps. (i'm flexible time-wise... let me know what works best for you)

hope you're still recovering well!

xo

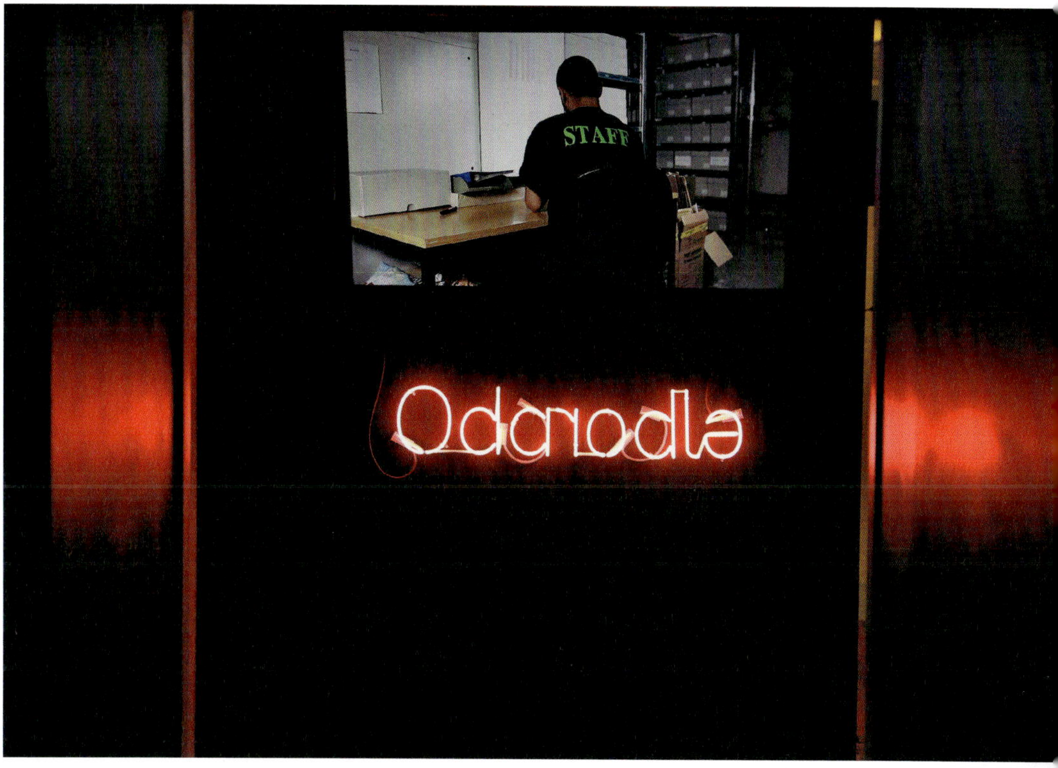
STAFF

THE ISLAND OF PERPETUAL TICKLING

VIKA KIRCHENBAUER · SINGLE-CHANNEL VIDEO / PERFORMANCE · 35:38 · 2018

AS ASHKAN SEPAHVAND
MG MAX GÖRAN
VK VIKA KIRCHENBAUER

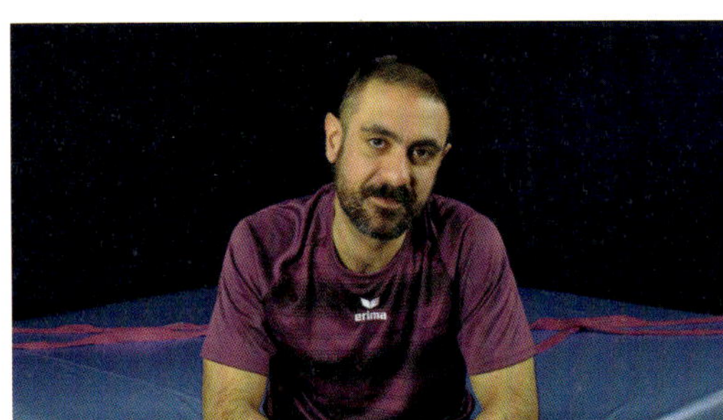

00:00:03 AS Hello. My name is Ashkan Sepahvand. I'm an artistic researcher, writer … and occasionally curator. I have worked with Vika in the past. And in a sense, I think, she has certainly tickled me with the piece she made for the exhibition I put together. I loved the piece though, don't get me wrong. She put me in a somewhat uncomfortable situation and I felt a bit exposed, but at the same it was an important contribution to my larger project. So am I ticklish? Yes, I am quite ticklish … and overall, I'd say I dislike being tickled. Just the thought of getting tickled here has filled me with a fair amount of anxiety. It's definitely something I am not looking forward to … In my personal life I even remember punching people really hard because there'd be no other way to make them stop … When I think about it though, it is also a form of attention somehow ... it always puts a smile to my face—whether I want it or not. My dad, he used to have this thing called "the claw", and every time I'd do something bad or talk back, he would use "the claw" and grab my knee or my ribs and just go crazy haywire and tickle me. I couldn't stand it, so I'd try and jump out of it. I'd squirm, I'd yell ... It obviously didn't work because he was so much bigger than me and could control everything I do. So that would be one experience. It was fun and all. Sometimes I think that, actually, if I could tickle myself, I would probably do it every now and then. The good thing here definitely is that I'm the first one being tickled. I believe that'll make the others know that they'll get it all back. And I am sure that'll make them go softer on me. And if it's soft enough, then perhaps I might even be able to enjoy the strange feeling it can give me. So yeah, let's go.

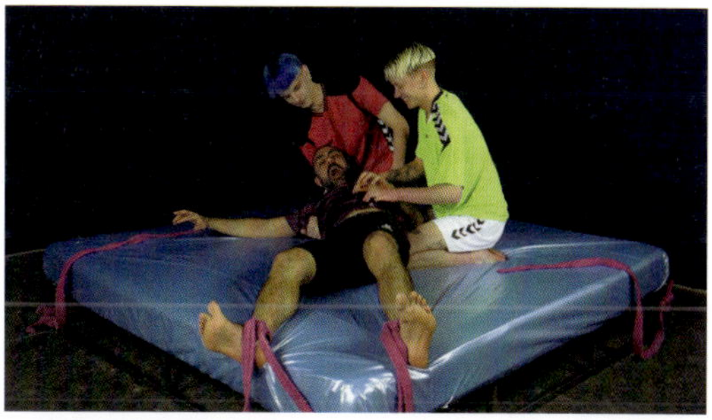

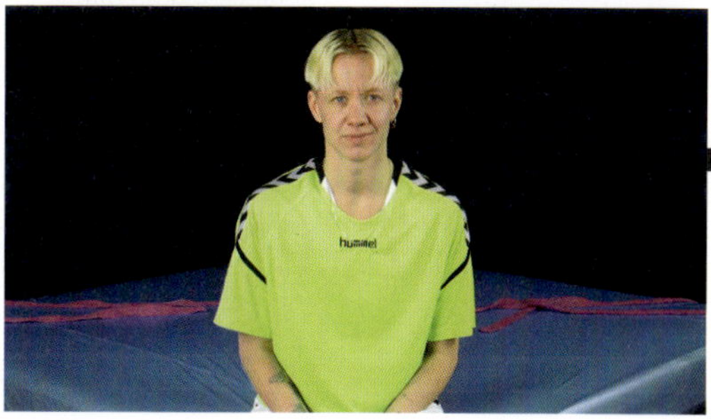

00:11:26 MG

My name is Max Göran, and I'm a bartender ... an artist and sometimes I also perform in other people's work. When people ask me if I'm ticklish, I usually say I'm the most ticklish person on earth. I'd say on a scale from 1 to 10, I'm probably a solid 20. I hate being tickled ... it's almost worse than pain. I mean, it makes you go crazy, it makes you lose your mind. My most sensitive area is definitely my neck ... like from the collarbone up to my ear, even air is enough; someone just blowing can already give me goosebumps and make all the hair stand up on my body. But maybe I'm also exaggerating because I think it's funny. Maybe I am not that ticklish? Because I think maybe I could make myself not be ticklish if I really wanted to. So I'm curious to see how ticklish I really am. But, anyways, I'd much rather tickle others ... that's something I can really enjoy ... I used to tickle this younger cousin of mine when he was a kid and force him to say that I was his favourite person on earth and stuff like that. He still remembers this very clearly. Now he's a huge man, probably double the size of me, but he was very small then. He laughs about it now though.

My fondest memory of tickling is when I was in bed with a former date of mine. I got on top of him and started caressing his navel, slowly working my way up towards his nipple, slightly touching his sides and biting his neck. Then all of a sudden I got on top of his arms and pinned him down. I knew he was quite sensitive to tickling, but anyways, so I set out to tickle him and while he first resisted, he then burst out into this extreme laughter. He was this big guy and to see him squealing ... I must say I found that really satisfying ... and to see him beg for mercy, yeah, that was nice ...

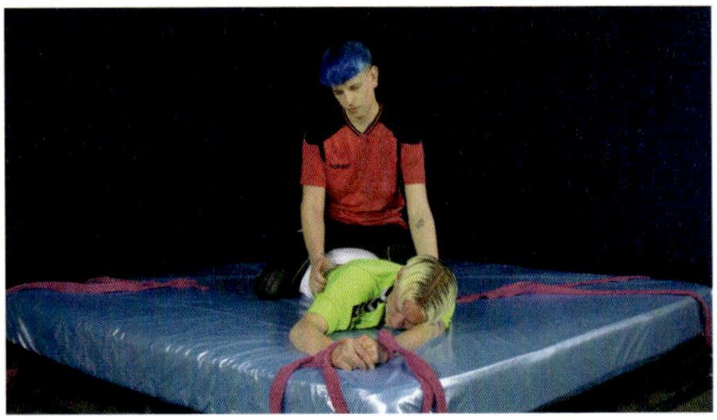

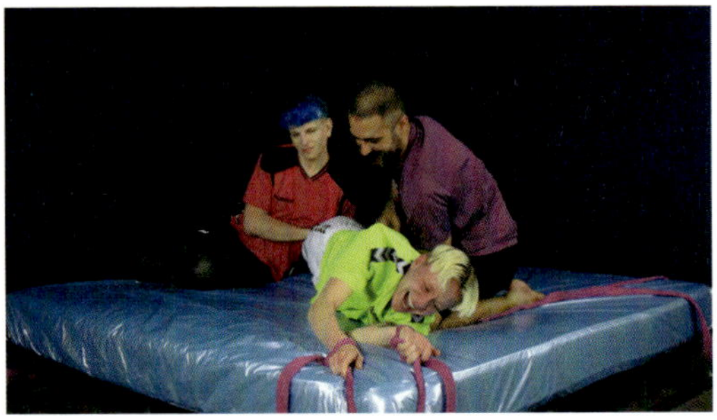

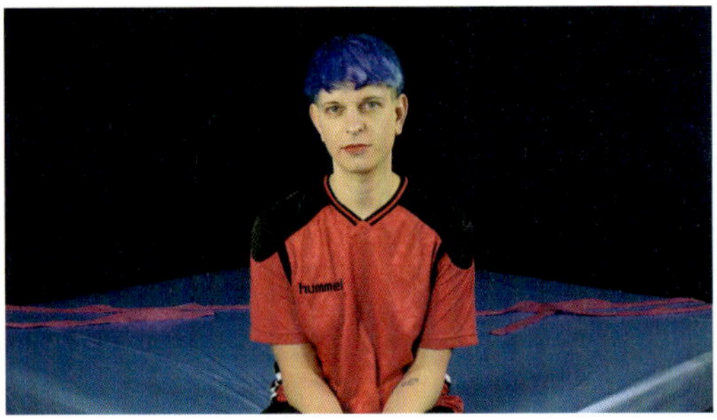

00:23:31 VK

I am Vika Kirchenbauer, I am an artist and the person responsible for this. Am I ticklish? Yes, incredibly so! I am ridiculously, ridiculously ticklish ... I can't even describe how sensitive to touch I am. Ever since I was a kid really. I thought

I'd grown out of it but clearly ... Being tickled is actually one of my first and most intense memories. I haven't got many recollections of my childhood, but I hold quite vivid memories of my sister—who is 13 years older than I am—tickling me quite heavily, mostly together with her husband-to-be. They really got a big kick out of it. I remember yelling and laughing and bursting into tears and also, I think I peed myself every now and then. In her bed actually ... which then of course usually meant she would get at me even harder the next time. And then the more you beg someone to stop, the more it encourages them to go on, so it can be quite a stupid situation. I hate having no control over myself. So yes, I hate being tickled, especially against my will. I've also learned to stand it quite okay though. I can usually pretend to not be ticklish at all for about 10 or 15 seconds, sometimes that is enough for the other person to just get bored, give up and let go of me, but of course, if they go on, then I'm totally lost. I can find myself in some sort of delirium then. Especially if it is more than one person and they're pinning me down ... It's a sudden feeling of fear, of being trapped, my blood would start rushing and I start to become hot, flustered. I'm a bit scared of what might come out now, but in a strange way I also really want it, which is why I am essentially employing people here to tickle me ... it'll be good! Okay ...

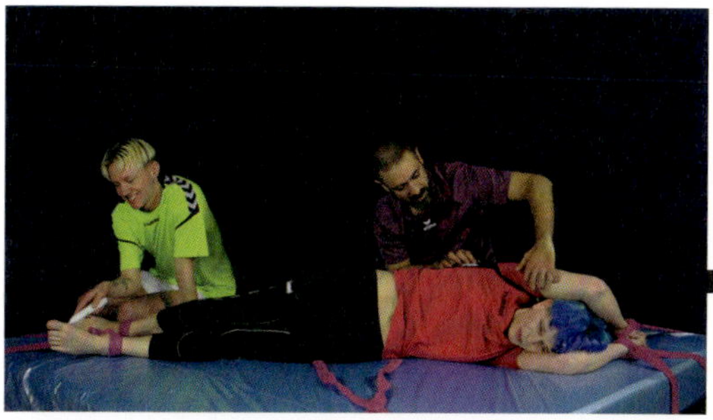

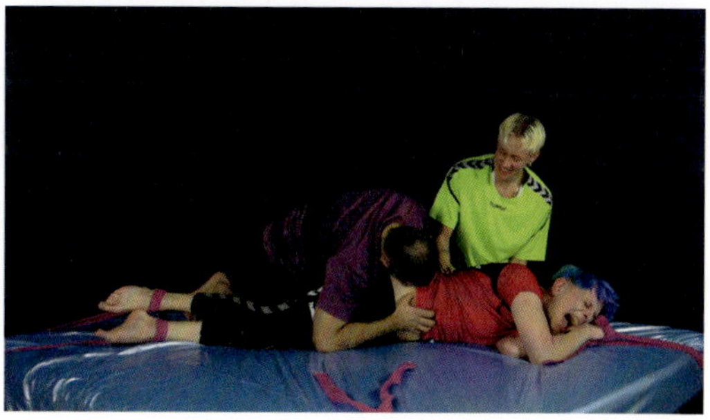

CAMERA, LIGHT — RITA MACEDO
SOUND — BIRTE GERSTENKORN

THE ISLAND OF PERPETUAL TICKLING

VIKA KIRCHENBAUER • PUZZLE SERIES • 2019

pp. 127-130	THE ISLAND OF PERPETUAL TICKLING (TOOTHBRUSH SCENE) VIKA KIRCHENBAUER • PUZZLE • 133cm × 48cm • 2019
p. 128	THE ISLAND OF PERPETUAL TICKLING (ASHKAN) VIKA KIRCHENBAUER • PUZZLE • 68.5cm × 48cm • 2019
p. 129	THE ISLAND OF PERPETUAL TICKLING (MAX) VIKA KIRCHENBAUER • PUZZLE • 68.5cm × 48cm • 2019

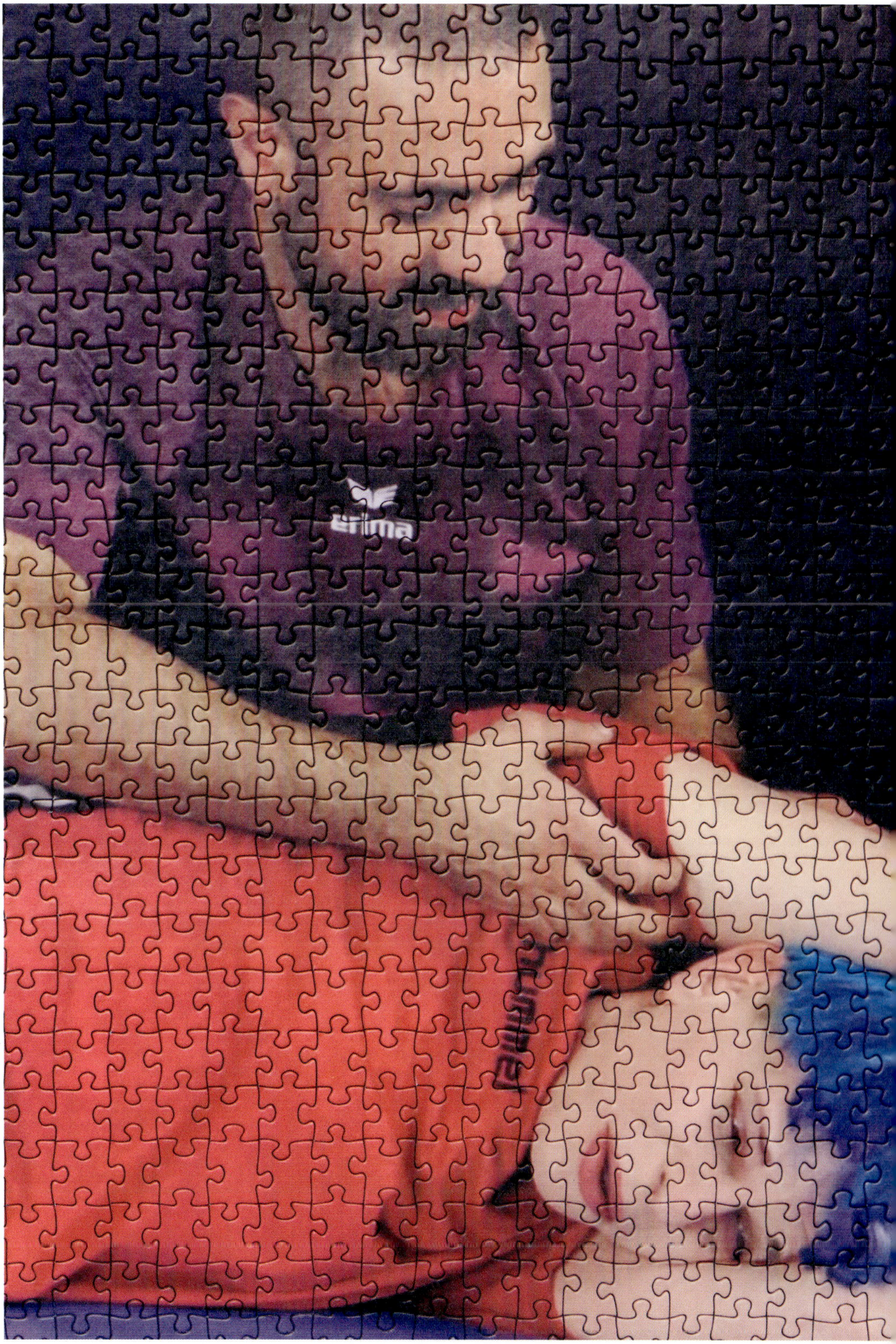
erima

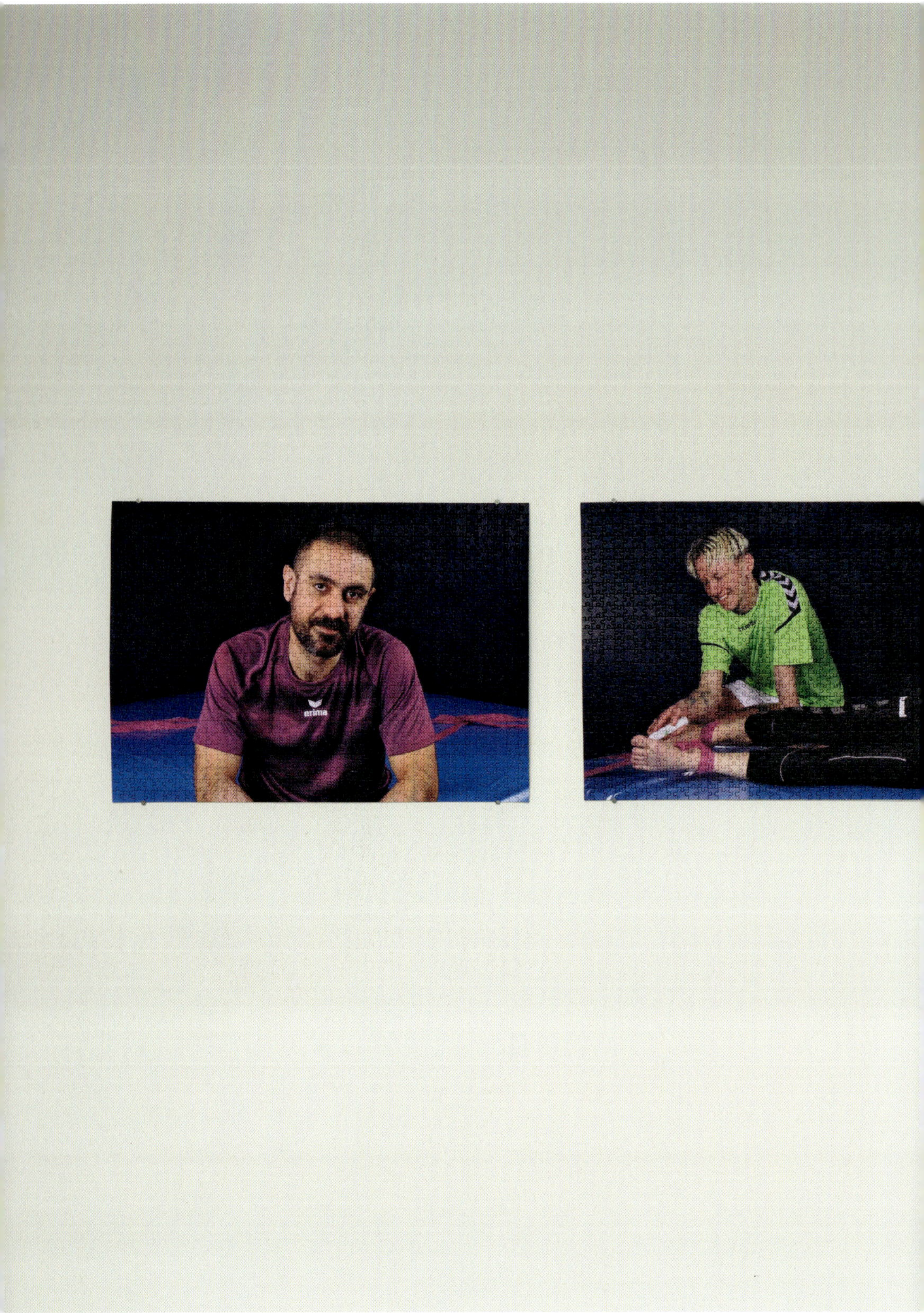
erima

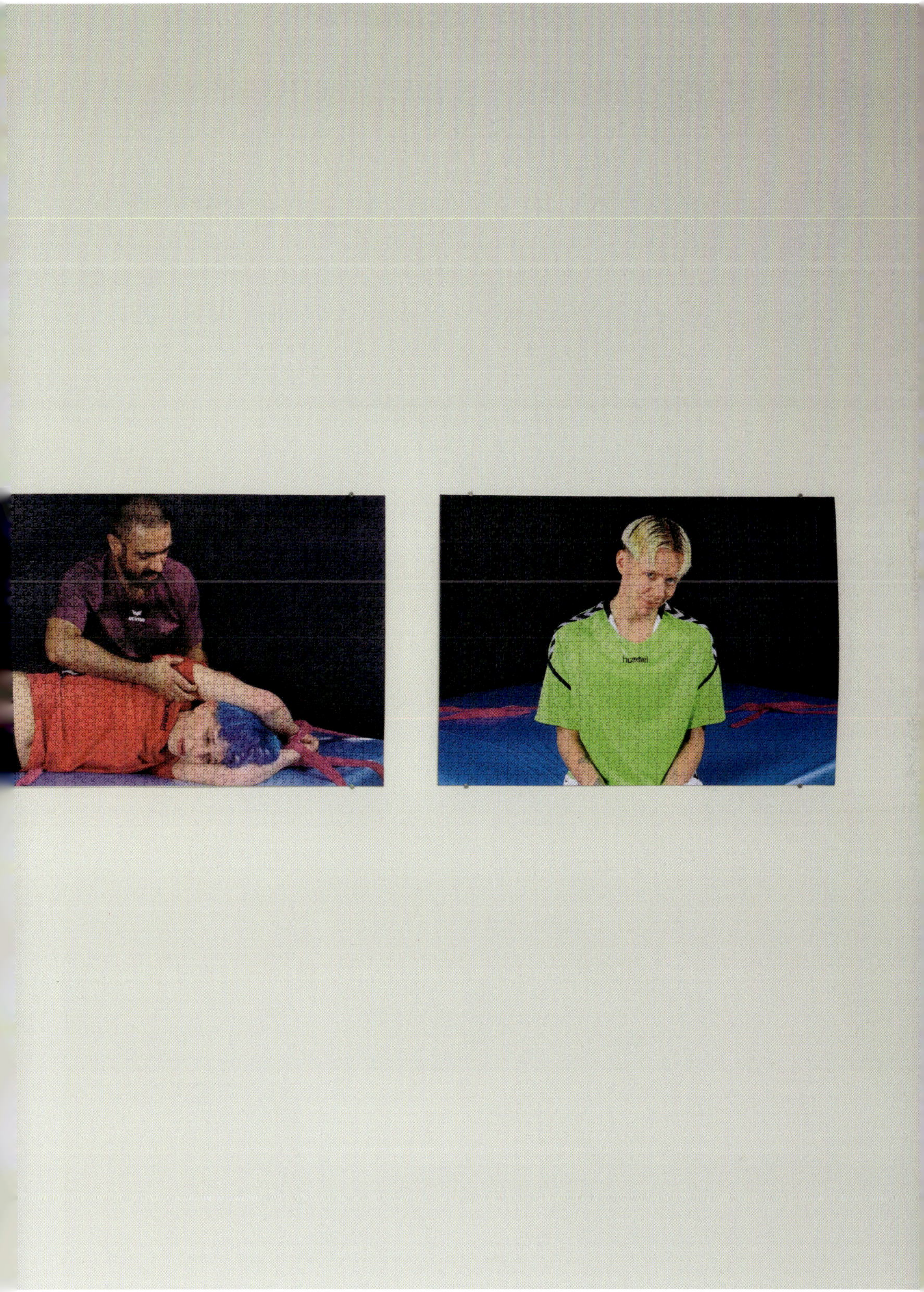

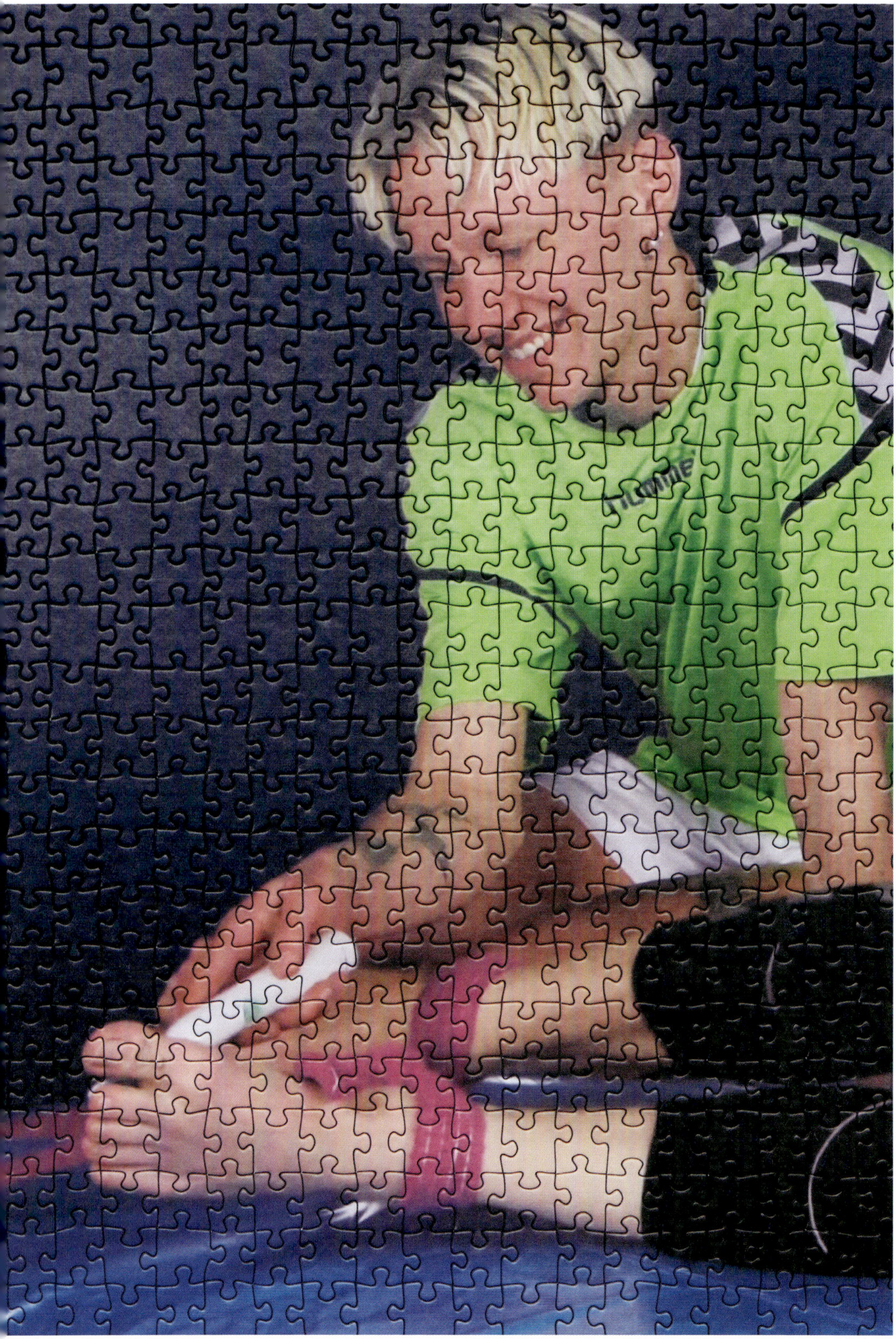
hummel

COMPLICATING CRITIQUE

VIKA KIRCHENBAUER · 2022

CULTURE AND COLONY

Almost since the very beginning of colonialism, European religious music served as a significant force in the Christianisation of Indigenous[1] people throughout the world. It aided missionaries as well as other church and secular officials in their attempts both to convert the colonised to Christian belief and ritual, and to establish European cultural practices as hegemony. Similar to the way that religious texts provided colonists and their supporters with a sense of justice and moral righteousness, religious music provided a sense of aesthetic and cultural authority. Religion and its cultural practices offered a model to frame expansionism as 'civilising', transforming imperial endeavours into moral allegories. As much as the violence of enslavement in fact profoundly shaped European theories of taste and notions of beauty,[2] music, in turn, must be understood as a tool that helped facilitate such colonial subjugation. Thus, far from being separate domains, colonialism and cultural practices were always closely connected, the traces of which can be found in creolised cultural forms around the globe. What is more difficult to examine is the influence the music of the colonised and enslaved had on European-based musical

1 In this publication *Indigenous* and *Black* are capitalised, while *white* is not when referring to groups in racial, ethnic, or cultural terms. To many people, *Indigenous* and *Black* reflect a shared sense of identity and community, while *white*, on the contrary, carries a different set of meanings.

2 See Simon Gikandi, *Slavery and the Culture of Taste* (Princeton: Princeton University Press, 2014).

traditions, owing to the circumstance that the processes of appropriation through which hegemony nurtures itself often remain deliberately unacknowledged and undocumented. This latter aspect becomes evident in the following when the exact makeup of particular harmonies remains unresolved.

/ Some of the history of the political entanglements of European-based music can be studied using the example of Sacred Harp, a religious choral tradition that developed in New England from the late 18th century onwards, and whose tunes were first formally compiled in book form in 1844.[3] Mostly popularised and perpetuated in the U.S. South throughout the 19th century, its origins can be traced back to the shape-note singing that was introduced to improve musical literacy in English parish churches in the 18th century,[4] the same century in which Britain rose to be the world's dominant colonial power, and also the century in which "slavery (...) replaced gold as the major commodity of trade."[5] British settlers brought shape-note singing to the American continent, first to the Congregationalist North. From there it travelled to the Anglican South, where in many colonial states the Church of England had already been established as the official state church, giving it political and social power over *all* subjects within those territories.[6] The spreading of Sacred Harp in the southern part of the United States corresponds with the expansion of white settlers towards the West—a movement fundamentally reliant on labour by enslaved people, and on violent land seizures from Indigenous nations.[7] During the Second Great Awakening,[8] white enslavers brought enslaved African Americans to camp meetings where Sacred Harp was practiced.[9] Even though there subsequently existed Black Sacred Harp music as practiced within African American congregations, the religious choral music remained labelled primarily as 'white spirituals'.[10] The extent to which *slave songs* and the mixing of Black and white congregants in New England churches and at camp meetings influenced Sacred Harp hymns' refrains and choruses in the tradition's formative phase remains a debated and unresolved issue. /

Continuously involved in various contexts of imperialism and colonialism since the 18th century, the Sacred Harp

3 Benjamin Franklin White and Elisha J. King, *The Sacred Harp* (Philadelphia: S. C. Collins, 1844).
4 Stephen A. Marini, *Sacred Song in America: Religion, Music, and Public Culture* (Urbana: University of Illinois Press, 2011), p. 77.
5 Gikandi, p. 10.
6 John A. Ragosta, *Wellspring of Liberty: How Virginia's Religious Dissenters Helped Win the American Revolution and Secured Religious Liberty* (Oxford: Oxford University Press, 2010), p. 3; Kimberly Pyszka, '"Built for the Publick Worship of God, According to the Church of England': Anglican Landscapes and Colonialism in South Carolina.' *Historical Archaeology*, vol. 47, no. 4, Society for Historical Archaeology (2013), p. 1; Beatriz Betancourt Hardy, '"The Papists... have shewn a laudable Care and Concern": Catholicism, Anglicanism, and Slave Religion in Colonial Maryland', *Maryland Historical Magazine*, vol. 98, no. 1 (2013), p. 6.
7 David Warren Steel and Richard H. Hulan, *The Makers of the Sacred Harp* (Urbana: The University of Illinois Press, 2010), pp. 14-16.
8 A Protestant religious revival in the United States from about 1795 to 1835, as part of which camp meetings were held in small towns and large cities throughout the country.
9 Derrick Fox, 'African American Practice of Shape-Note Singing in the United States', *Choral Journal*, vol. 56 no. 5. (2015), p. 40.
10 Kiri Miller, *Traveling Home: Sacred Harp Singing and American Pluralism* (Urbana: University of Illinois Press, 2010), pp. 9-11.

musical tradition is characterised by a harmonic structure that—with parallel fifths and deemphasised or altogether missing thirds—is significantly inconsistent with (western) European harmonic conventions.[11] In Sacred Harp, gapped scales[12] and at times heterophonic textures[13] are combined with dispersed harmonies,[14] the latter resulting from the circumstance that "each part except bass is sung by both men and women."[15] The liner notes to a 1977 vinyl release of material recorded at a Sacred Harp convention in 1959 open with the statement: "Many listeners will be surprised to learn that this fiery choral sound comes not from somewhere in eastern Europe but from a rural white singing convention in northern Alabama."[16] The listeners to the release addressed—expected to recognise as familiar the sounds produced by a white demographic in northern Alabama—are presumed to find the sounds of Sacred Harp unfamiliar, and ultimately, to consider them vaguely *other*.

CRITIQUE AS AN AFFECT WORLD

There have been musical releases of Sacred Harp singing since the 1920s,[17] yet they remain unusual in the sense that such recordings and releases stand in opposition to some of the tradition's core principles. Sacred Harp is a form of choral singing that does not normally admit or address an audience; it consists only of participants who arrange themselves in a square facing each other as they sing. It is not intended for performance or presentation, not as a display of musical skill, but as a form of communal worship that is practiced by non-professionals.[18] Taking its name from the idea that God unites the individuals into one single instrument by playing the singers' vocal cords like a harp,[19] within Sacred Harp to sing well is considered less significant than to sing passionately, to resonate heavily with God's invisible hand. This approach towards singing results in an astonishing amount of individual distinction among the choir's singers, something that is uncharacteristic in other forms of choral practice. /

11 Robert T. Kelley, *Sacred Harp Harmony: A Part-Writing Primer for Shape-Note Hymnody*. Paper presented at the Society for Music Theory Annual Meeting on 30 October 2009, in Montréal, Québec. ›http://www.robertkelleyphd.com/ShapeNoteMusic/SacredHarpHarmonyPresentation.pdf‹ [last accessed on 15 April 2022].

12 A "gapped scale" is a musical scale with fewer than seven notes. Sacred Harp often uses pentatonic scales, meaning that a scale contains only five notes.

13 Heterophony, which means that different variations of the same melody are being sung or played at the same time, is rare in Western music. Sacred Harp notes are sometimes homophonic, at other times polyphonic. But, due to individualistic singing styles and interpretations, the renditions often result in a heterophonic character.

14 A "dispersed harmony" is a harmony in which the tones composing the chord are widely separated, as by an octave or more.

15 Gage Averill, *Four Parts, No Waiting: A History of American Barbershop Harmony* (Oxford: Oxford University Press, 2010), p. 22.

16 Liner Notes by Alan Lomax, *White Spirituals from the Sacred Harp* (New York: New World Records, Cat. No. 80205, 1 January 1977).

17 Steven L. Sabol, 'Sacred Harp & related Shape-Note Music: Resources', Chapter 7: Older Recordings (Pre-1977), ›https://home.olemiss.edu/~mudws/resource/chap07.html‹ [last accessed on 15 April 2022].

18 Marini, p. 84.

19 Anonymous, Georgia: *A Guide to its Towns and Countryside. Compiled and Written by Workers of the Writers' Program of the Works Progress Administration* (Athens: University of Georgia Press, 1940), p. 127.

Within the context of my solo music project *COOL FOR YOU*, I have developed a body of work since 2015[20] based on Sacred Harp choral recordings, initially with the intention of exercising sampling as a critical practice. Out of small snippets of dissonances within the choirs, new compositions are arranged around beat patterns in various simple, complex or mixed time signatures.[21] In questioning music's ostensibly peaceful and unifying quality, and in approaching harmonies as colonisers, my artistic research interest originally centred on the ways in which music is implicated in the ongoingness of imperialism, the imprints of which do not always present themselves in an obvious manner. Rather than continuing, however, to take on the task of uncovering these traces, it may be generative to question one's own stakes in a critical theory or practice that places its faith in exposure. When considering the affect worlds that a critical practice offers to the critical practitioner, I follow Lauren Berlant, who describes affect worlds as "worlds to which people are bound (...) by affective projections of a constantly negotiated common interestedness",[22] and in which affect and emotion lead the way for belonging, ahead of the modes of rational or deliberative thought.

/ How is a critical stance generally characterised within different fields of Western academia and artistic creation? Almost self-evidently, critique is understood to be marked by dispassion and detachment, by disembodied analytical distance;[23] it presumes an idea of a suspicious critic of clear vision seeking to excavate hidden meaning from a position of level-headedness and unemotionality. Yet critical detachment is not an absence of mood, but rather a manifestation of it,[24] offering its own specific pleasures.[25] Oddly, the affect worlds provided to the critical practitioner through such self-understandings as rational, distant, and superior are themselves historically involved in shaping a Western hegemonic constitution of the world as such. They reflect values of European Enlightenment that, like music, were utilised as a cultural means within projects of subjugation. The affective dimensions of a critical stance are further complicated by additional, sometimes contradictory ties and attachments that the critic establishes to her object. This becomes particularly apparent during instances when a critical stance finds form through aesthetic engagement such as sampling.

/ As applies for any material a person works with artistically, a certain dependency upon that resource is established, and the continued artistic practice also requires the reproduction of that resource. If the relation to one's material or resource is a negative one, almost intuitively,

20 Consisting of one full-length release, two EP's, as well as related video works and performances.
21 Simple time signatures are duple or triple categories (e.g., 4/4 or 3/4); complex time signatures do not fit these usual duple or triple categories (e.g., 5/4 or 7/8); a mixed time signature does not have one consistent pattern (e.g., shifting between 3/4 & 7/4 in the same track).
22 Lauren Berlant, *Cruel Optimism* (Durham: Duke University Press, 2011) p. 226.
23 Rita Felski, *The Limits of Critique* (Chicago: University of Chicago Press, 2015) pp. 3, 18, 46.
24 Felski, 2015, p. 21.
25 Rita Felski, 'Suspicious Minds', *Poetics Today*, vol. 32, no. 2 (Durham: Duke University Press, 2011), p. 216.

a critical approach appears to lend itself most suitably for such a parasitic constellation. Critique is always parasitic in the sense that it "could not survive without the very object that it condemns."[26] So, there is a precarious yet sustaining connection to begin with. As is apparent in sampling, I work foremost *with* the material, and impossibly solely in opposition to it. However, there also emerges another complicated, twofold affective relationship with it. At the same time that I seek to engage musically as well as discursively with the original tune's entanglement within colonial and racialised violence, I want to turn it into something capable of satisfying my aesthetic sensibilities concerning the kind of contemporary electronic music I wish to produce. So, also on another level, there exists a simultaneously negative but also affirmative, almost needy relation to the material and what can be generated out of it. In the absence of any semantic elements in my finished tracks,[27] the critical aspects of the practice will certainly remain opaque to most listeners. Still, I place much weight on the discursive and conceptual components I surround my musical practice with. Thus, the attempt to create ambiguous musical affectscapes avoiding language is countered by a contradictory need to self-contextualise, to control and fix meaning. While approaching the material's strangely familiar internal dissonances, contradictions, and incoherencies, the question resurfaces as to what affectively binds a critical practitioner to her critical method of inquiry and engagement.

IMPLICATION AND CRITICAL DESIRES

My sample sources would not exist had a particular convention of singers not agreed to an ethnomusicologist's field recordings, preserving the material and making it accessible. It may be worthwhile to revisit the notion of Sacred Harp as a worship practice that does not usually admit an outside listener or observer, but only participants, independently of the dissonances their untrained voices may add to the choir. I ask myself if approaching an object through a critical stance speaks foremost of a desire to place oneself at a distance from a problem, to negate one's own implicatedness by wishing oneself outside the choir of participants. It may not be the critical position that provides an entry point through which an object can be analysed in a detached manner. Rather, the position the critic conceives for herself may be testament to her desire for detachment, her desire to be disassociated from her object. /

In his book *The Implicated Subject: Beyond Victims and Perpetrators*,[28] the Holocaust and memory scholar Michael Rothberg develops a theory of responsibility around the figure of the implicated subject, who "is neither a victim nor

26 Felski, 2015, p. 126.
27 Nor do the titles of the tracks highligh a criticial perspective or comment on the samping source and its context in any obvious manner.
28 Michael Rothberg, *The Implicated Subject: Beyond Victims and Perpetrators* (Stanford: Stanford University Press, 2019).

a perpetrator, but rather a participant in histories and social formations that generate the positions of victim and perpetrator, and yet in which most people do not occupy such clear-cut roles."[29] These forms of implication can reflect long distances, such as temporal or geographic distances, in instances in which actions and inactions of implicated subjects "help propagate the legacies of historical violence and prop up the structures of inequality that mar the present."[30] /

Implicated subjects such as white music producers in the West like myself structurally "occupy positions aligned with power and privilege (...); they contribute to, inhabit, inherit, or benefit from regimes of domination."[31] So evidently, I cannot possibly stand above or outside the sample in a critically detached manner; my subjectivity is inevitably deeply embedded and implicated in its violent musical history. The musical history of the Western world, quite obviously, cannot be faced without taking into consideration colonialism, music's role in supporting ideologies of supremacy through cultural means, and the relations of influence and appropriation it engaged in with non-Western kinds of musical expression during this centuries-long history. Yet methodologically, it has to be taken into account that critique does some things well, and others rather poorly. It makes certain thoughts and actions possible, while impeding others. So, it is necessary to develop practices and approaches that frame political and historical legacies not through a method that seeks distance, but one that questions implication, especially when exercised by those inhibiting perspectives and positions of relative privilege. Affect is important in this, since many kinds of inward-oriented negative affects like shame or guilt hinder or obstruct action, becoming unproductively self-centralising in their affective structure. A philosophy of implication and responsibility, in contrast, may offer a way to question the legacy positions a person holds within the continuities and hierarchies of imperial and colonial life. From there, it can be hoped that forms of active and self-decentralising long-distance solidarity could be fostered, "premised on difference rather than logics of sameness and identification."[32] The goal is not to abolish critique and its potentials, but to reckon with its limits and acknowledge its affective layers. Within artistic practices, what might be needed are different methods of engaging with objects one relates to negatively, that are resistant to the desire to write oneself outside the problem one is entangled with.

A first draft of this text originally appeared in *Sampling Politics Today (Norient Sound Series 1)*, edited by Hannes Liechti, Thomas Burkhalter, and Philipp Rhensius (Bern: Norient, 2020).

29 Rothberg, p. 1.
30 Rothberg, p. 1.
31 Rothberg, p. 1.
32 Rothberg, p. 12.

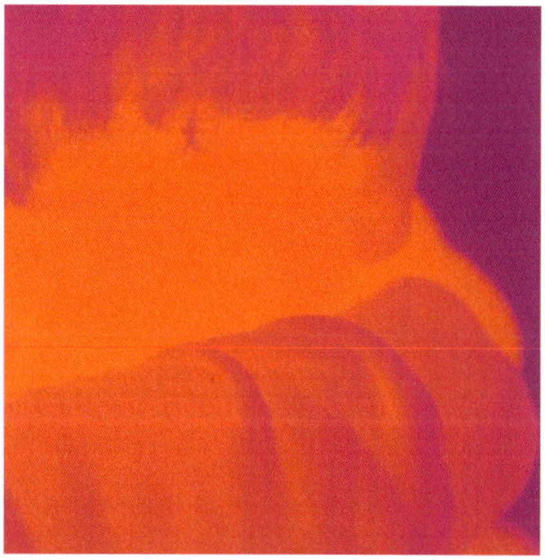

COOL FOR YOU: COMMUNAL MESS

11-TRACK ALBUM · 2019

RELEASED BY CREAMCAKE
MASTERING: DOUG HENDERSON
COVER IMAGE: VIKA KIRCHENBAUER

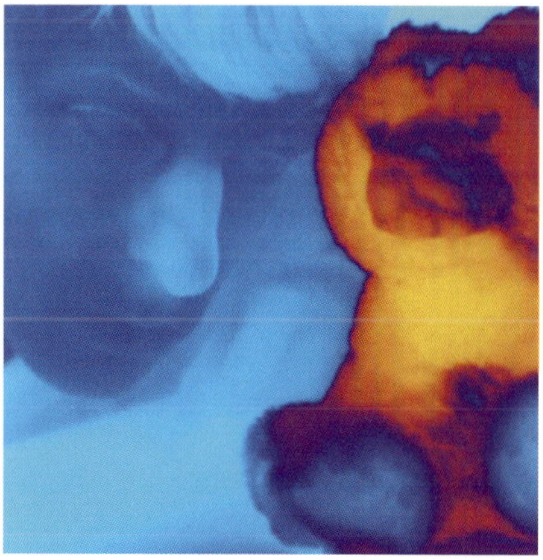

COOL FOR YOU: MOOD MANAGEMENT

5-TRACK EP · 2017

RELEASED BY CREAMCAKE
MASTERING: DOUG HENDERSON
COVER IMAGE: MARTIN SULZER, VIKA KIRCHENBAUER

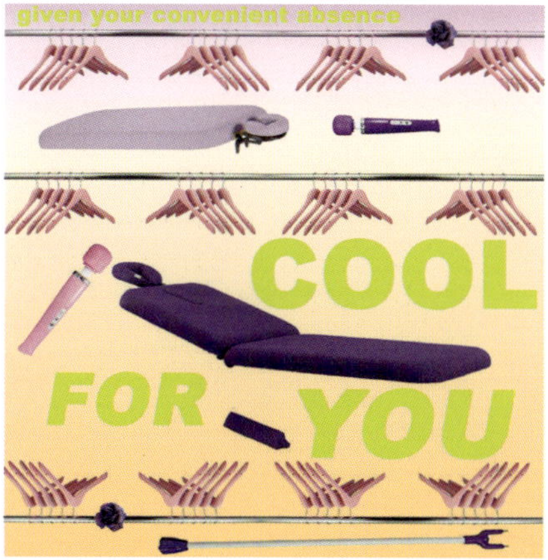

COOL FOR YOU: GIVEN YOUR CONVENIENT ABSENCE

5-TRACK EP · 2016

SELF-RELEASED
MASTERING: DOUG HENDERSON
COVER DESIGN: MYSTI

GIVEN YOUR CONVENIENT ABSENCE

VIKA KIRCHENBAUER • SINGLE-CHANNEL VIDEO • 2:21 • 2016

MUSIC	COOL FOR YOU

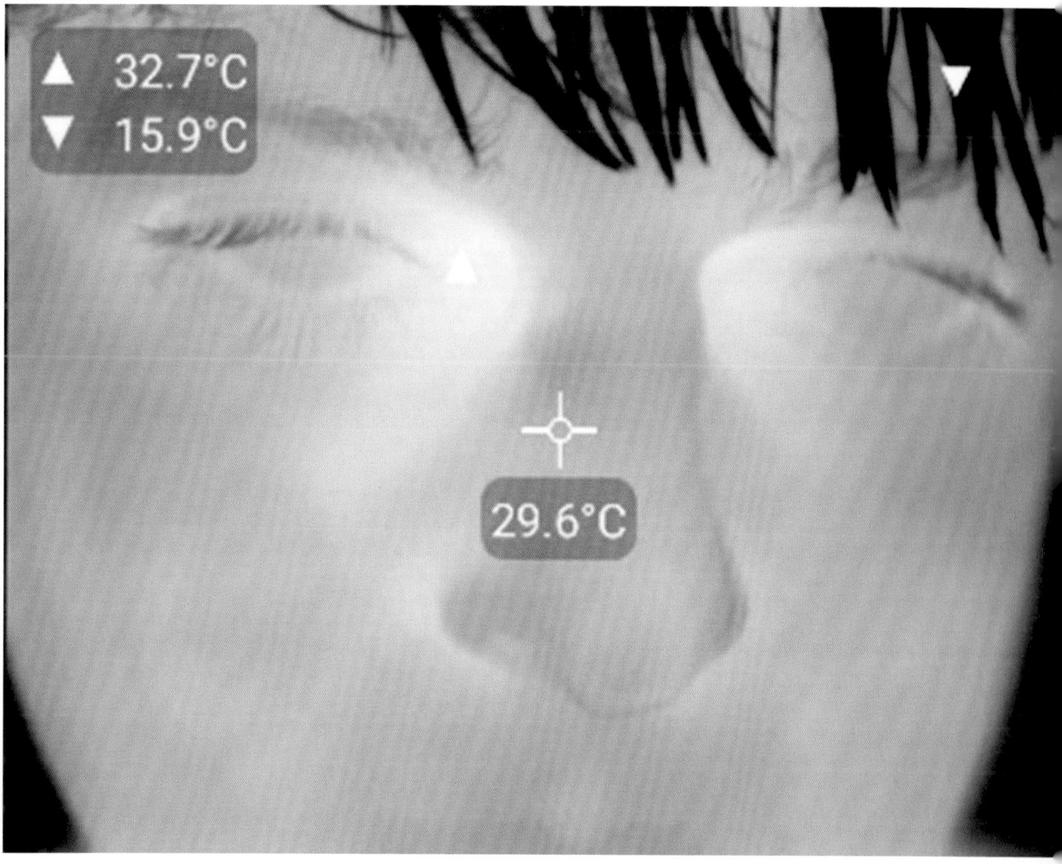
▲ 32.7°C
▼ 15.9°C
29.6°C

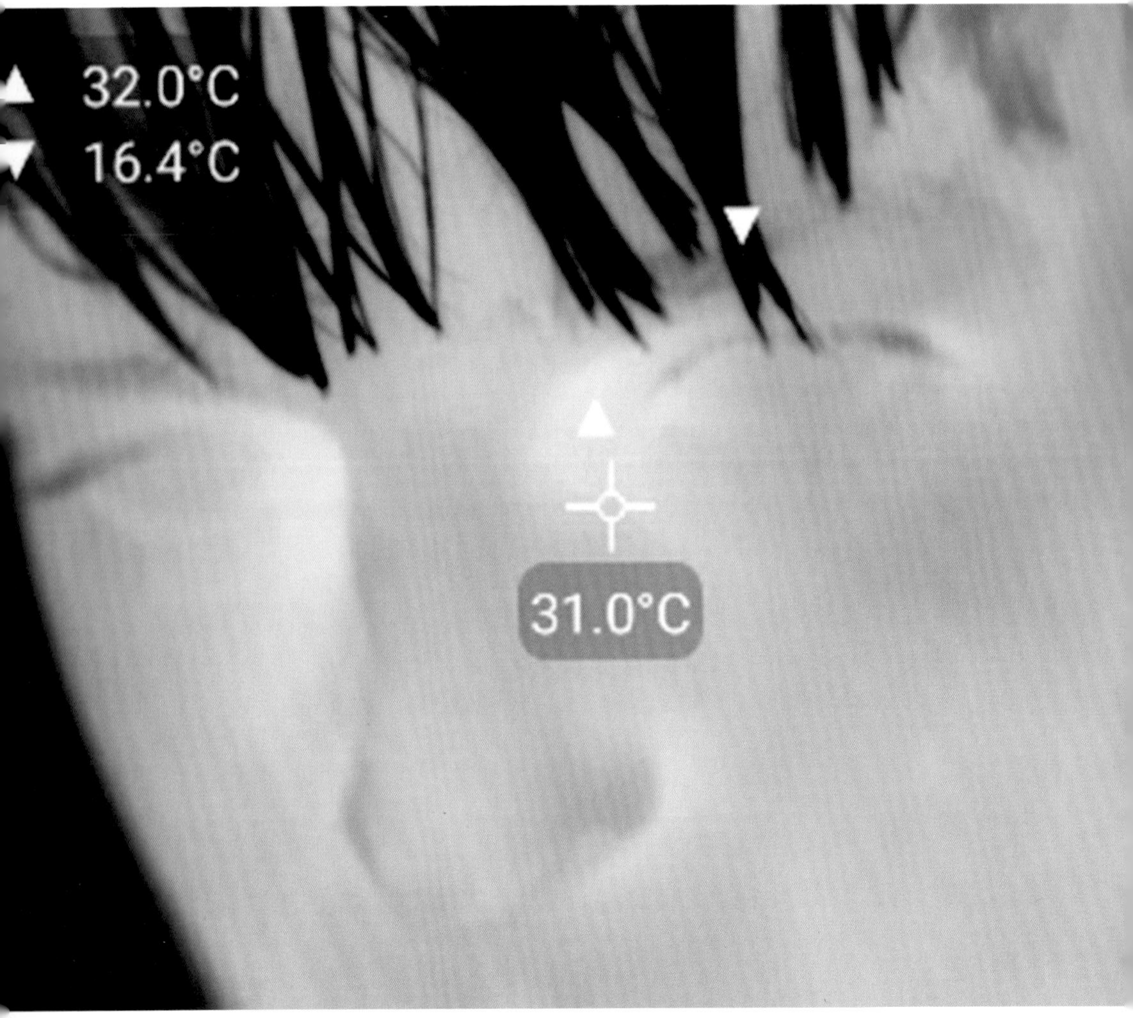
32.0°C
16.4°C
31.0°C

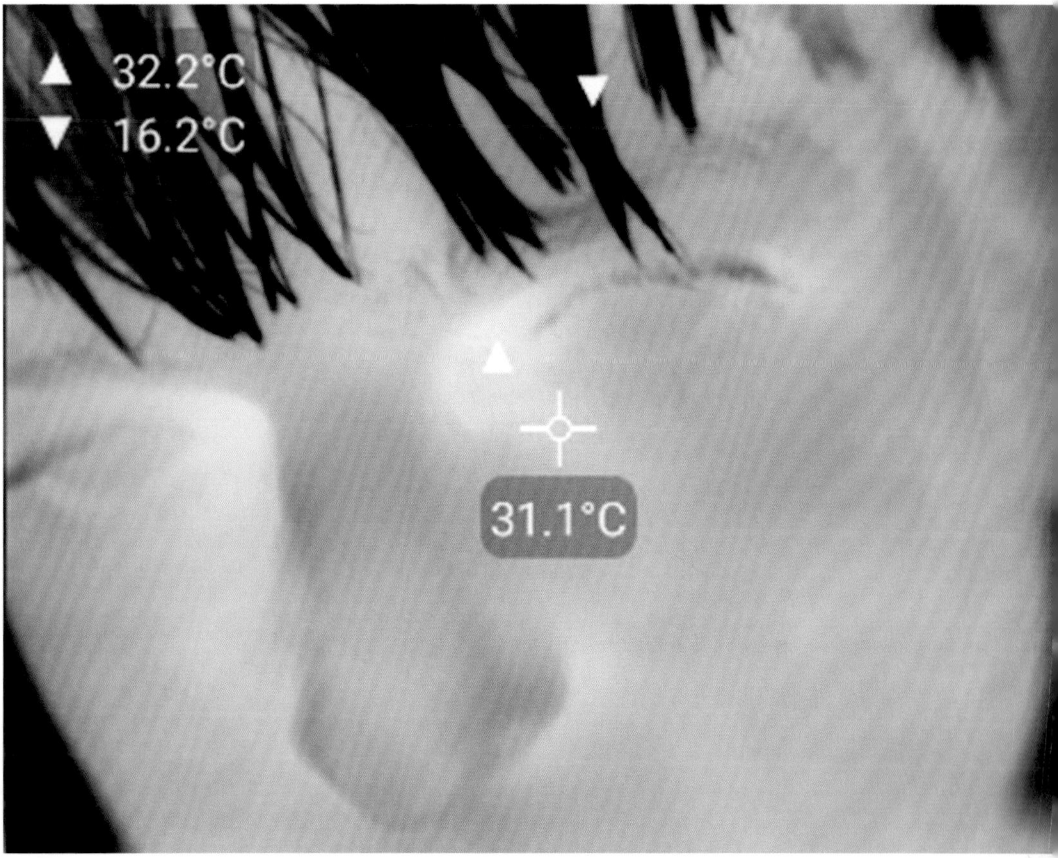

32.2°C
16.2°C
31.1°C

SHE WHOSE BLOOD IS CLOTTING IN MY UNDERWEAR

VIKA KIRCHENBAUER · SINGLE-CHANNEL VIDEO · 3:24 · 2016

PERFORMANCE	MAX GÖRAN VIKA KIRCHENBAUER
CAMERA	RITA MACEDO
MUSIC	COOL FOR YOU

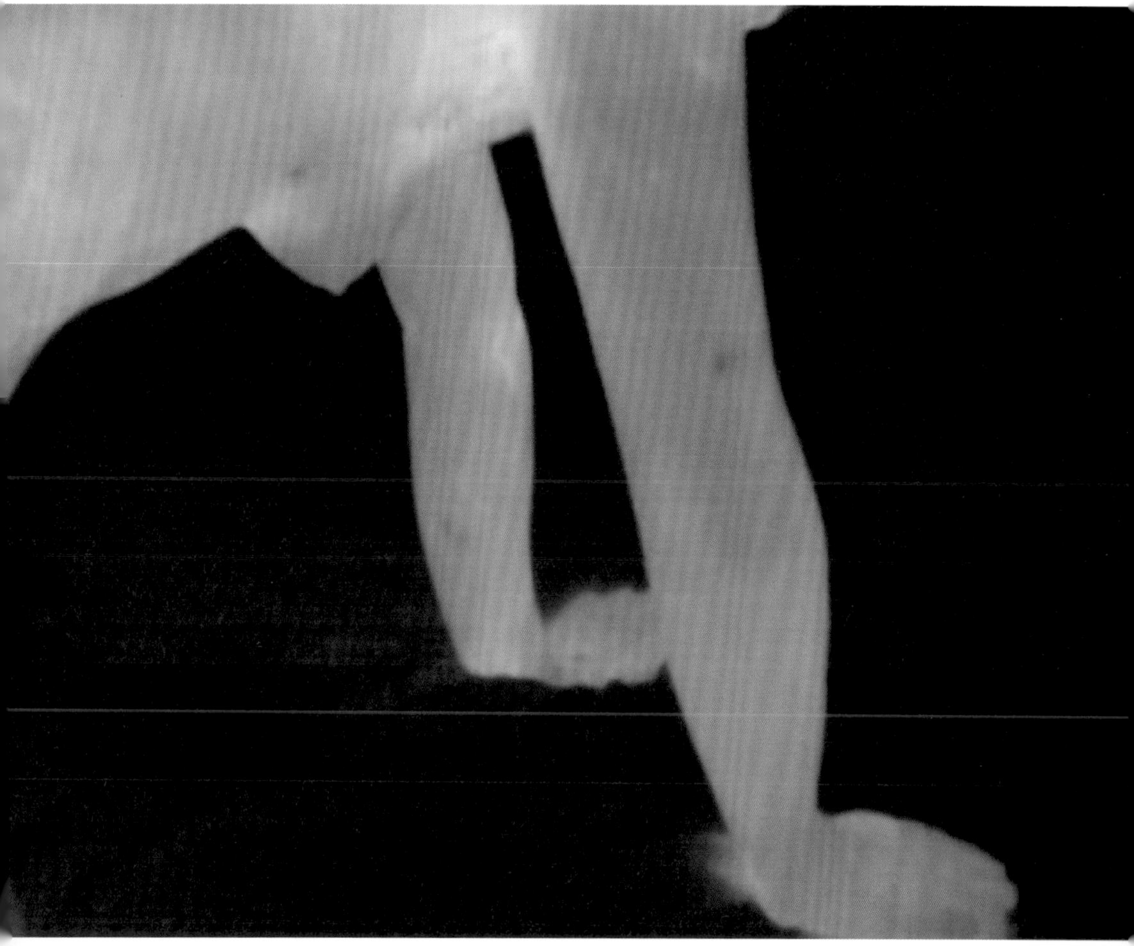

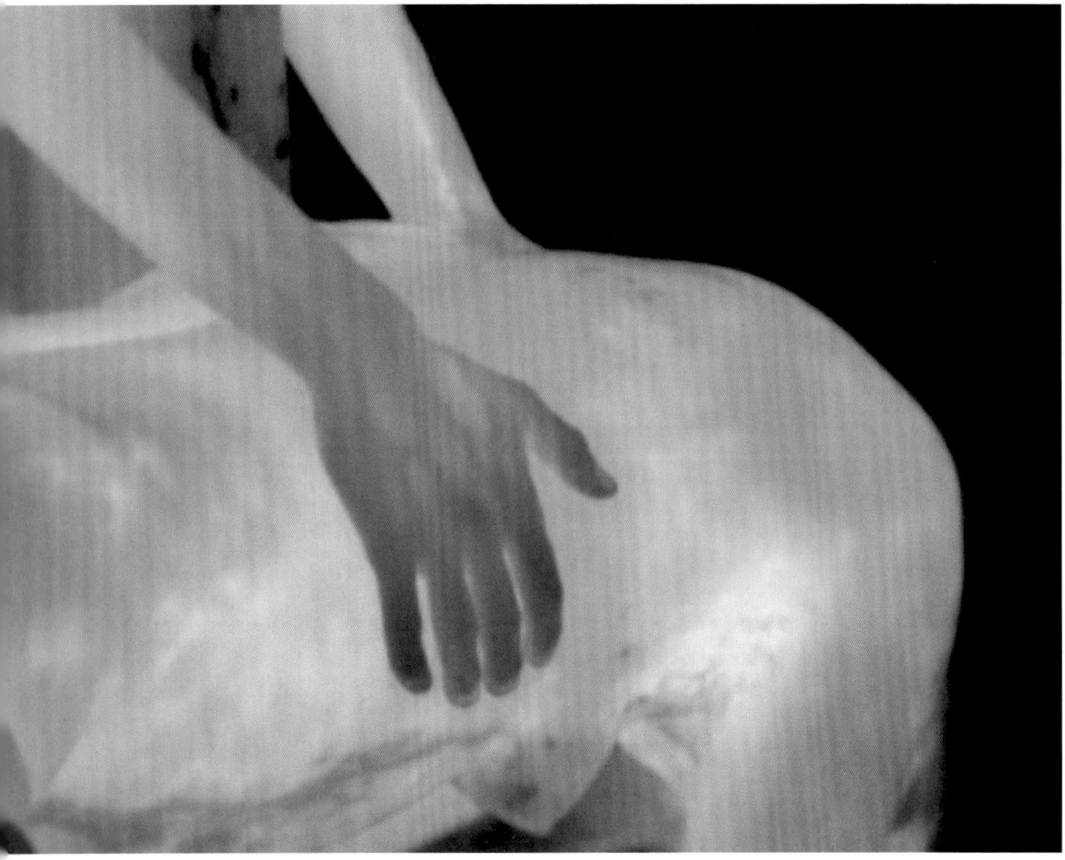

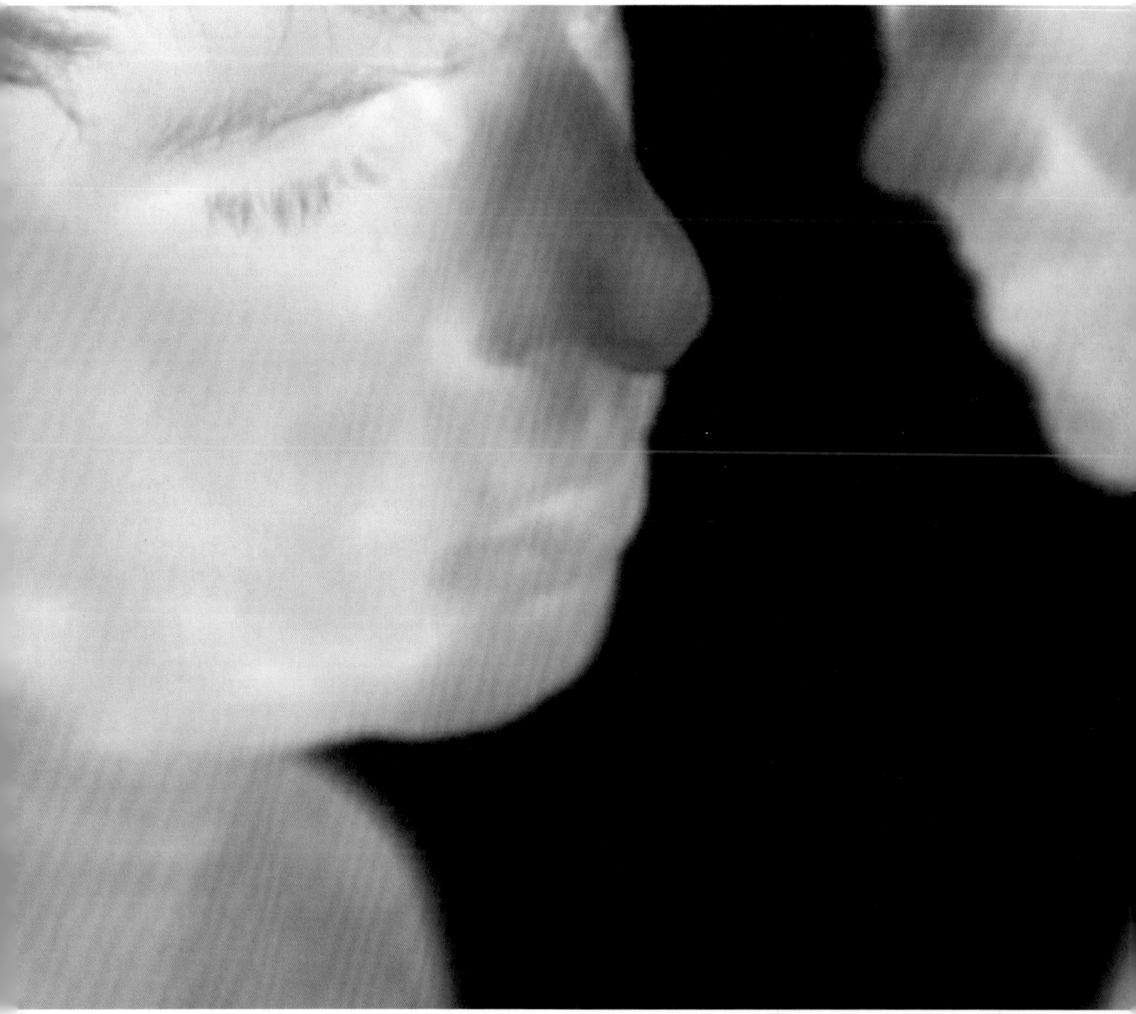

MOOD MANAGEMENT

VIKA KIRCHENBAUER • SINGLE-CHANNEL VIDEO • 1:53 • 2017

PERFORMANCE	JUDITH SIEBER VIKA KIRCHENBAUER
MUSIC	COOL FOR YOU

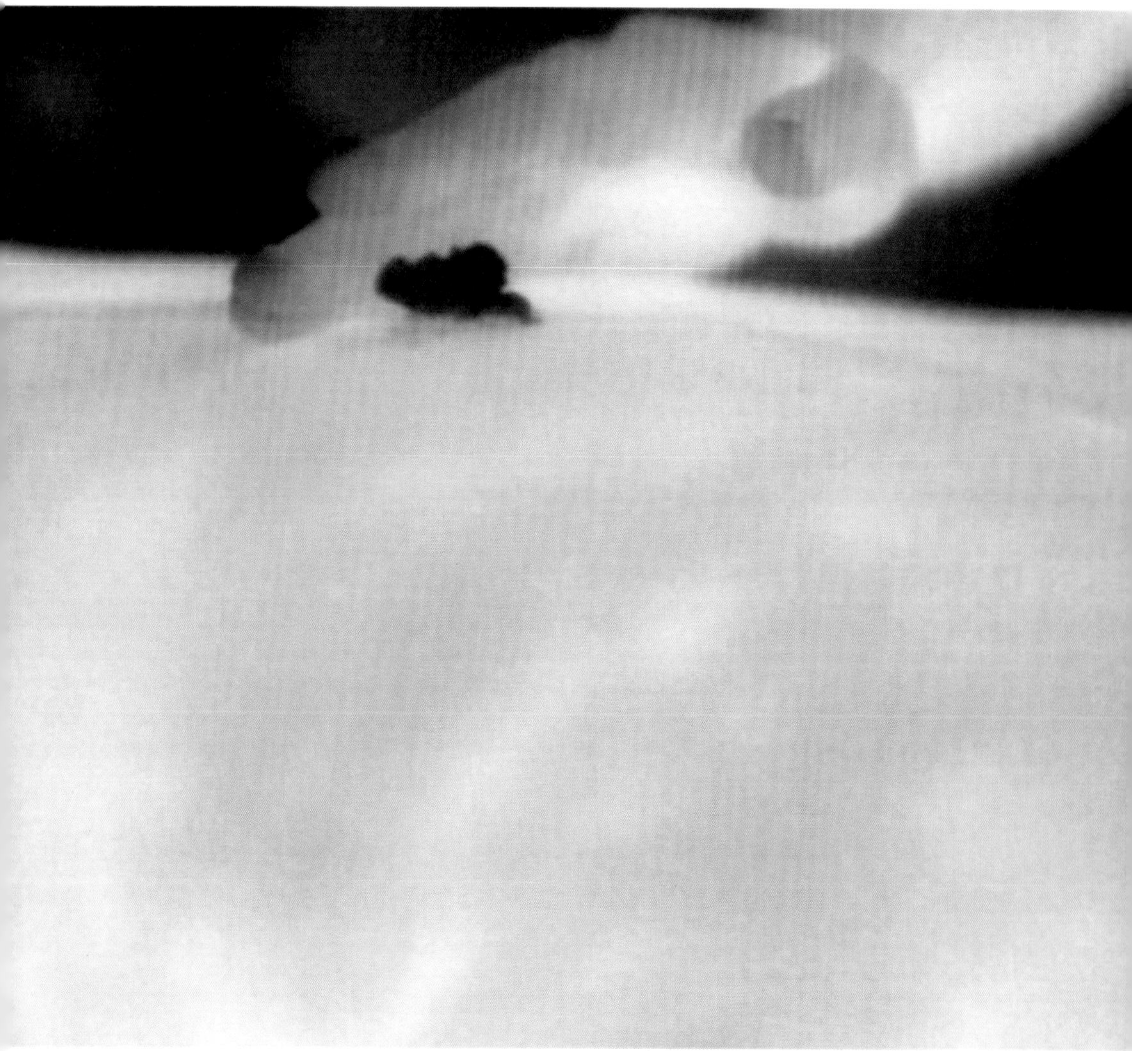

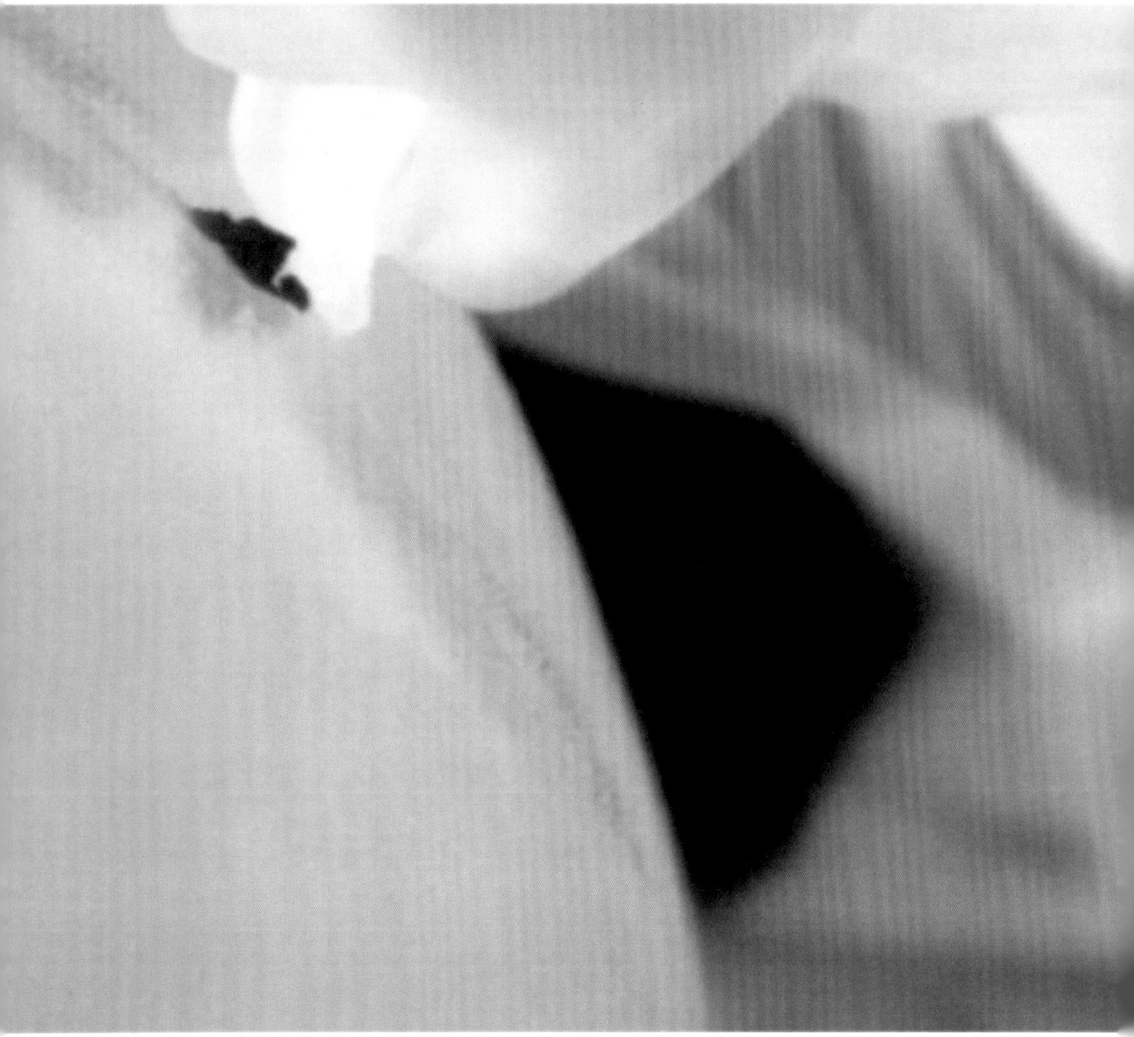

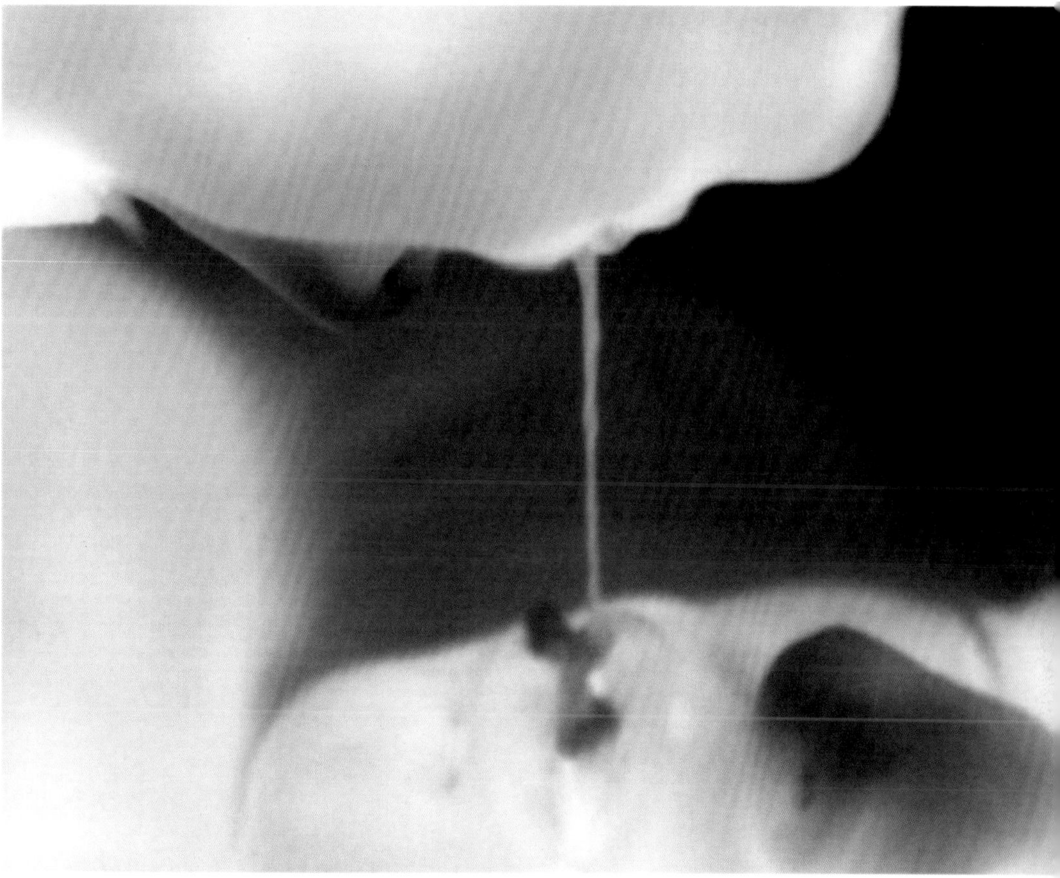

SHAME/HUMILIATION

VIKA KIRCHENBAUER · SINGLE-CHANNEL VIDEO · 2:08 · 2018

CAMERA	RITA MACEDO
MUSIC	COOL FOR YOU

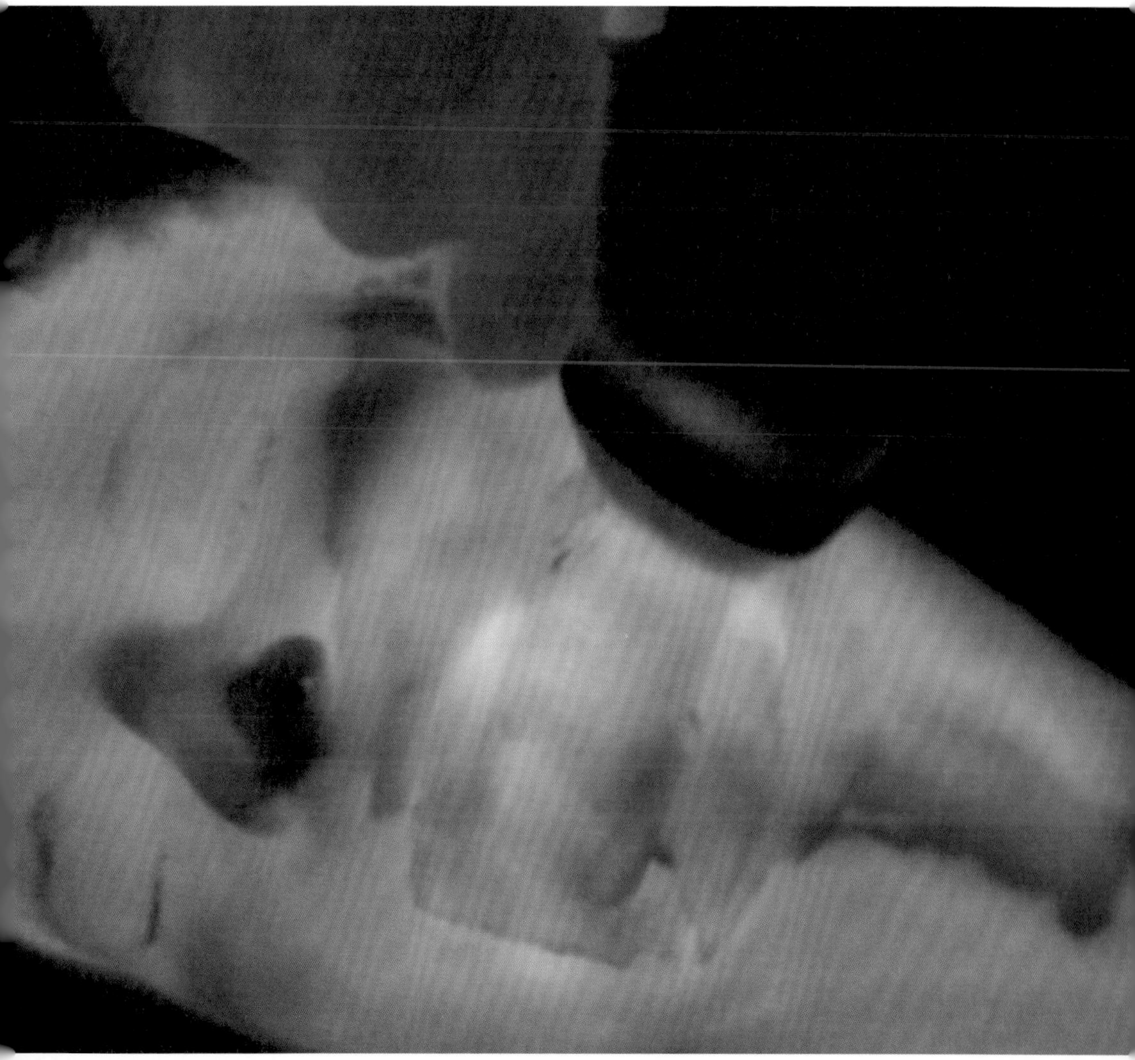

HOW TO MOVE SO CASUALLY?

VIKA KIRCHENBAUER • SINGLE-CHANNEL VIDEO • 2:50 • 2019

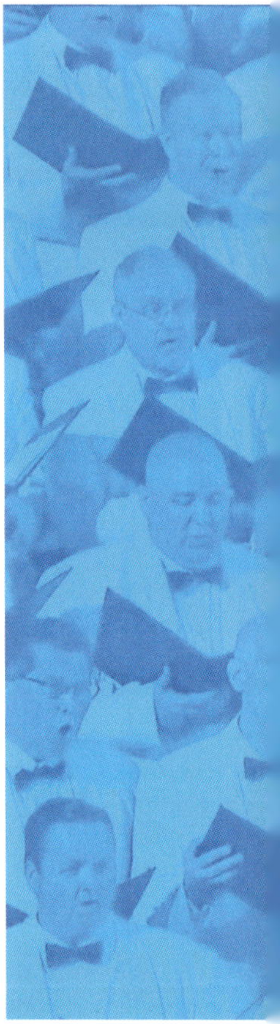

MUSIC

COOL FOR YOU

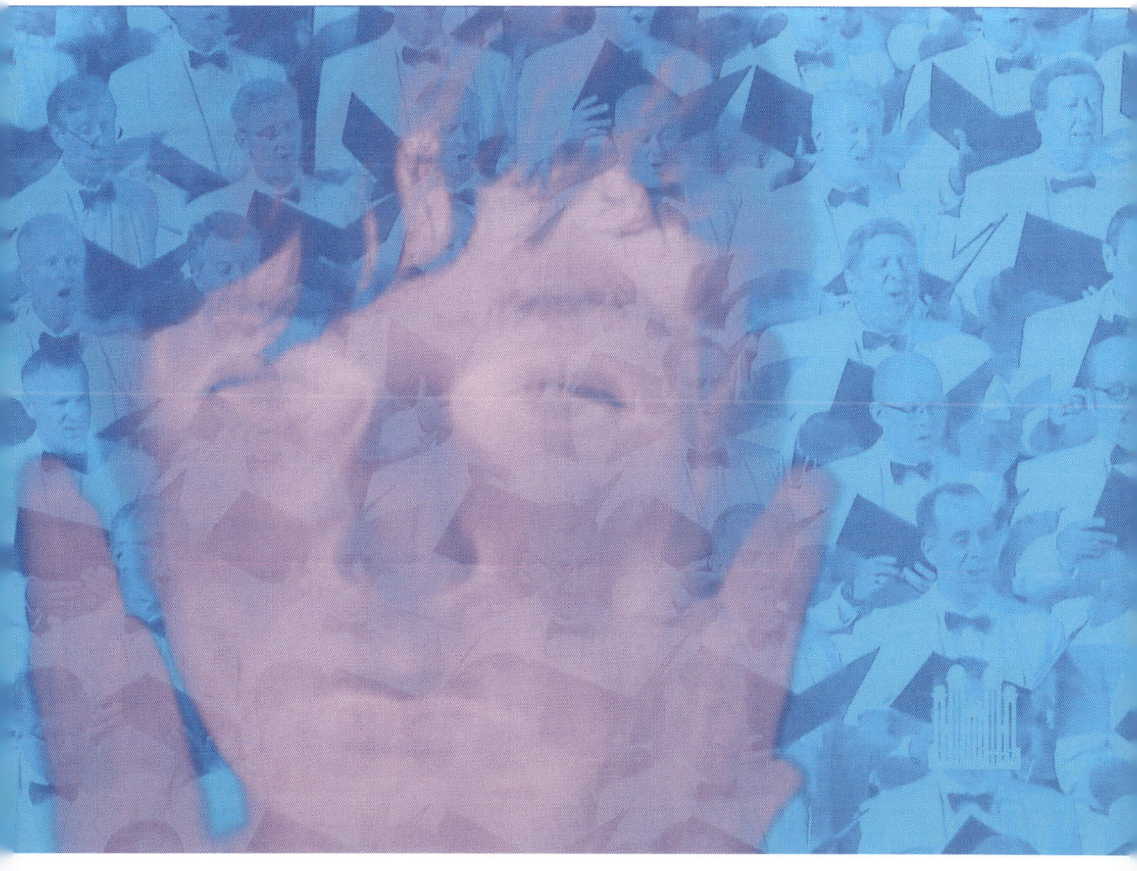

AESTHETICS OF EXPLOITATION: THE ARTIST AS EMPLOYER

VIKA KIRCHENBAUER · 2017

PROJECT ECONOMIES: THE CIRUMSTANCES OF ART'S PRODUCTION

Via social media, an internationally established artist of substantial means advertises a position as a video editor for a piece dealing with social justice issues for an exhibition at a major Berlin art institution. No information is included regarding the window of payment the artist is prepared to offer—common practice with such postings. Interested individuals in possession of a professional skill set for editing artists' moving image are asked to include formal references with letters of recommendation on their behalf as part of the application process. Two days of scheduled interviews with several selected applicants take place during which those invited become provisionally aware of the overall amount the artist is willing to offer for one month of freelance work. For specialised work that requires skills both cognitive and affective—also outside of concrete working hours—the artist offers professionals a total fee of €1,000, a fraction of the established minimum rates for the field. Taking into consideration the time it takes to apply for such positions, the organisational work, the short-term nature of such gigs, as well as the thinking and reading required to help craft complex art works, one would very quickly find oneself working well below minimum wage—which, at the time of writing this essay, is €8.50 per hour in Germany.

/

This case—like all others in this essay not fictitious but anonymised in order to focus on the structural realities—is a particularly ironic instance, since the piece utilises social justice as its central topic. Nonetheless, it points to a larger set of problems connected to a general shift toward art *projects* over the past decades, as well as a misguided understanding of the artist concerning the nature of her labour. / As the scale of art production elevates into increasingly complex and extensive endeavours, specialists, researchers, assistants, editors, etc. need to be employed for the completion of almost any individual art *project*. The expectation from and practice of artists' moving image work, for instance, has developed into pieces that require an independent cinema-like scope of production. Within its relatively short history, video art moved from a person in her studio with a camera to production schemes that make camera and lighting professionals, location scouts and sound technicians essential elements of creation. / The circumstances of art's production are frequently overlooked, probably due to misunderstanding artists as workers. Many artists are not, however, workers, but entrepreneurs who produce upon commission or in hopes of finding a market, be it institutional or commercial. A visual artist desires *to be her own boss*: to hold authority over the conditions of her own work and yet acquiesce in facilitating her own exploitation, while simultaneously overlooking that she takes the role of *being someone else's boss*, mistaking her own exploitative measures over others as gestures of support, shared dedication and sacrifice or *real* political purpose.

HIGHER PURPOSE: THE ARTIST AS AN INSTITUTION

One of several shortcomings of the different waves of institutional critique is the discussion of the artist as, at best, an entangled representative of the institution, while failing to examine the Artist as an institution herself. For successful or even semi-successful artists it is more common to employ than to be employed. Those employed by these artists are frequently creative professionals or less financially successful artists. Overall, it seems fair to estimate that there are more artists working for Artists than there are Artists with direct financial engagements with art institutions. /

Regarding the Artist as an institution helps to better recognise neoliberal restructuring. While there persist highly varying degrees of visibility of different kinds of labour required to complete the Artist's product, the artist-as-institution indeed likens herself to flexible capitalism and frequently obscures power behind oxymoronically flat hierarchies. For those employed, *self-realisation*, personal contact with Artists and intimate identification via one's work all seem at first like desirable attributes, yet these characteristics overburden them with the requisite responsibilities of love and purpose in order to collaborate in their own exploitation. /

Conscious Capitalism, a movement and theory put forward by Whole Foods Market's co-founder John

Mackey, places higher purpose at the core of any ideal corporation. It learns from grassroots organising and volunteer work the ways and reasons for which people tirelessly dedicate themselves to causes they believe in without expecting remuneration.[1] *Conscious Capitalism* deploys the rhetoric of higher purpose[2] as a means to assist the employee in the wilful devaluation of career or money interests, stimulate their passion and understand work as a medium for personal growth and doing good in the world. A similar mechanism might be at work in *political art* and its labour practices, when those supporting Artists with their un(der)paid labour sacrifice their salary for a role within some grand vision for a greater good. / Again via personal platform, a highly successful artist and writer held in major public and private collections offers a studio manager position requiring skills in several fields, each of deep individual specialisation, namely editing and post production software, 3D modelling software, architectural planning software, etc. Simultaneously, the ideal applicant will physically install the exhibitions previously crafted and designed, yet also book flights and execute other, less desirable office tasks. The description mentions merely one guaranteed workday per week while demanding full availability in times of greater workload. Here the Artist provides a characteristic example for a neoliberally designed position: offering no security or stability while demanding everything on call. / Why is it that even artists with a leftist and socially conscious agenda fail so terribly at understanding their roles as *bosses*? A theoretical belief system that positions itself against the hierarchical nature of bosses cannot excuse neglecting the responsibilities of *employing*. If artists identified their (at least partial) role of entrepreneurs —which would mean understanding that they are not part of the union, but often rather its opponent—that would make it harder to mistakenly identify solidarity when in fact there is none, at least not in the invested sense of the word. Critical *practices* are rarely discussed in terms of their own circumstances of production, a flaw in both art criticism and theory. / Within the professional art system, those who publicly denounce their representing gallery's questionable labour practices or directly criticise systematic workings, find themselves at career dead ends, considered untrustworthy traitors too risky to work with. This obscures conversations on labour and exploitation within art systems, as they rarely extend beyond bar talk within smaller circles of friends. How could these shared experiences of exploitation be communicated? How could public platforms be created in which those working for Artists might discuss their working conditions—with the aim of improving them—such as they exist online for, i.e., people working in other fields for

1 John Mackey and Rajendra Sisodia, *Conscious Capitalism: Liberating the Heroic Spirit of Business* (Boston: Harvard Business Review Press, 2013), pp. 54, 87, 156.

2 Mackey and Sisodia, pp. 33-34, 41-43, 46-49.

specific companies and corporations? How could systems of accountability be established that would be constructive and address these problems in structural ways without ending up in bitchy, art world gossip, workplace bullying or scapegoating of individuals? / It is not breaking news to anyone that the entryways to gallery jobs and institutional positions are through un(der)paid internships. Yet most protests on that matter focus almost entirely on art's distribution, sales and presentation system, while ignoring comparable mechanisms also at play within art's production—often much more thickly obscured by the concrete subject matter that a piece or an artistic position might express. / Many people will accept these poorly paid jobs, either for lack of other employment options or because *working for an Artist* is desirable work. *Working for an Artist* is visible and lovable work; it offers higher social recognition than most other jobs within a comparable pay range. Thus many artists, as well as those wanting to work for them, help produce an ideology that rebrands exploitation as self-realisation, presenting work as a pure act of self-love naturally independent from immediate or fair compensation. It is rather ironic that even in Mackey's book *Conscious Capitalism* he and his co-author Rajendra Sisodia at least rhetorically highlight a company's long-term benefits of *happy employees*.[3] In short-term project work such as in art production, in contrast, such long-term benefits do not seem relevant or applicable. / Surely no one is surprised that mostly young professionals from more comfortable backgrounds establish themselves in circles that demand un(der)paid performance in order just to *get in*. These un(der)paid positions also lead art school graduates—those without the convenience of a security net—to abandon their own work, succumbing to exhaustion working for more established Artists under precarious working conditions.

WORKING AESTHETICS: LABOUR PRACTICES FINDING FORM

The question of how an artist structures the circumstances and conditions of her own art production also becomes an aesthetic one. Is it, for instance, worth producing a film about in/visible un(der)paid labour and communist utopias in conditions of production where none of those involved earns a living wage—including the producers? Is that which is being expressed more valuable than the material reality created as part of the endeavour? Will its artistic contribution to political debate naturally outlive and outweigh the pains inflicted for its becoming? / A well-established German director and film professor remarks publicly that if there were unions for film professionals imposing fair

3 Mackey and Sisodia, pp. 72, 75-76, 158-59.

wages and working hours, all European independent cinema production would collapse. His remark makes it clear that he believes the cultural significance to be of higher value than its modes of production. But shouldn't exactly such an insight motivate a person to try harder at finding aesthetics that would not base a whole genre on accepted and "inevitable" exploitation? Wouldn't it be an interesting challenge to not replicate *aesthetics of exploitation*, instead developing alternative aesthetics that don't require as much time, people and expertise?

/ The logistical and financial requirements of project-based work challenge not only the highly established but also those aspiring to become part of the established, in addition to those simply desiring consideration. The ever-greater aesthetic expectations as regards the scale of productions become the gold standard for emerging artists to measure themselves against, not without palpable consequences. For instance, when receiving grants from the Berlin Senate—which are designed as stipends while requiring detailed and competitive *project plans*—one must declare not to pay anyone less than the minimum wage of €8.50. However, there are no checks and balances in place; it is largely understood that within common habits of production artists employing others frequently fail to meet this requirement.

/ In all of this, of course, artists are embedded in larger economic systems of visibility and competition, such as state-of-the-art demands on how art is supposed to look alongside institutional and spectatorial expectations. What kind of scale is considered appropriate for an exhibition to be considered professional, vast and significant? At a Berlin grassroots democratic arts institution with mid-scale funding, where members decide upon the following year's exhibition programme from a number of proposals, it becomes apparent that those who promise the most—those who are most willing and able to exploit themselves and others—will generally find the membership's favour. Rarely does somebody propose a project dedicated to the reasonable allocation of this modest budget for an exhibition's expenses, a handful of artist talks and a catalogue without succumbing to (self-)exploitative strategies since, however, without additional workshop formats, audience-engaging special events, an elevated number of participants, concerts and film screenings, the chances for any proposal to get selected are terribly slim (similar phenomena are observable at biennial or quinquennial expansion projects). All of this is handed down to artists, who are increasingly expected to produce new and site-specific work for each and every exhibition. This leads to an uncomfortable double bind position for the less economically successful artist: to lack the funds to get by herself while having to hand that financial pressure down to co-producers and freelance employees. Even for artists with limited dimensions of support, this creates a split identity of being simultaneously exploiter and exploited. Yet if not only the undeniable precarity of many artists were to remain the sole focus of public debate, but also their simultaneous role as entrepreneurs—modelled in the image of high-profile Artists' practices—wouldn't that create material for interesting works of art negotiating such complexities once they are acknowledged? While not reducing the desired absence of gross exploitation to a *creative obstacle* and whilst not merely considering it a new opportunity to artistically innovate, such an acknowledgement could be the first step towards a conversation in which better conditions could be negotiated and established at large.

CONVENIENT, SACRED, BLESSED

VIKA KIRCHENBAUER • SINGLE-CHANNEL VIDEO • 3:24 • 2015

PERFORMANCE	RITA MACEDO VIKA KIRCHENBAUER
CAMERA	MARTIN SULZER
MUSIC	MAUD

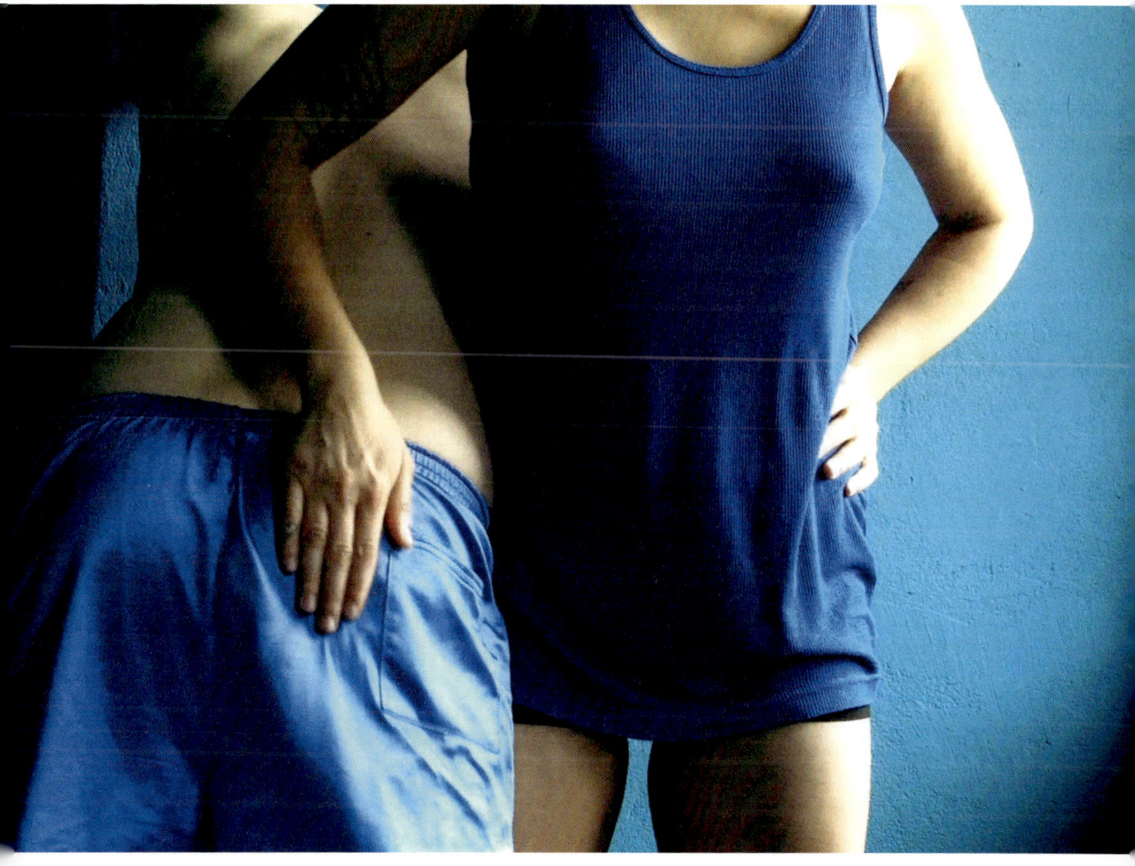

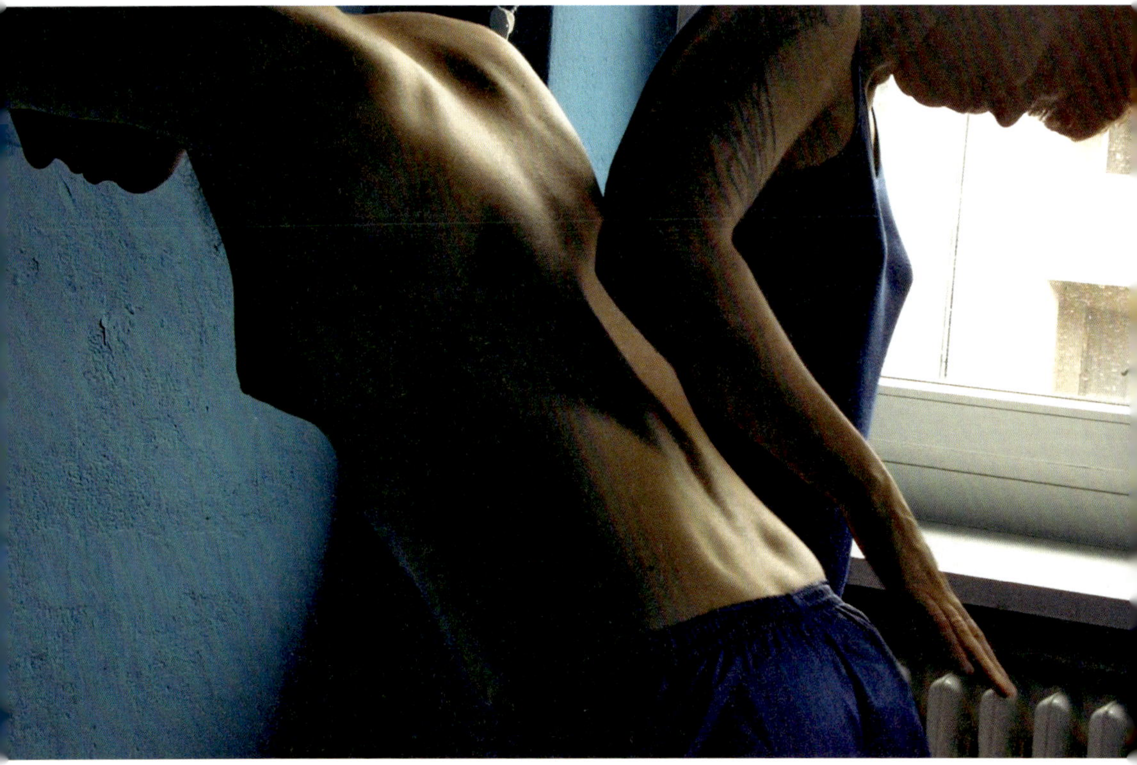

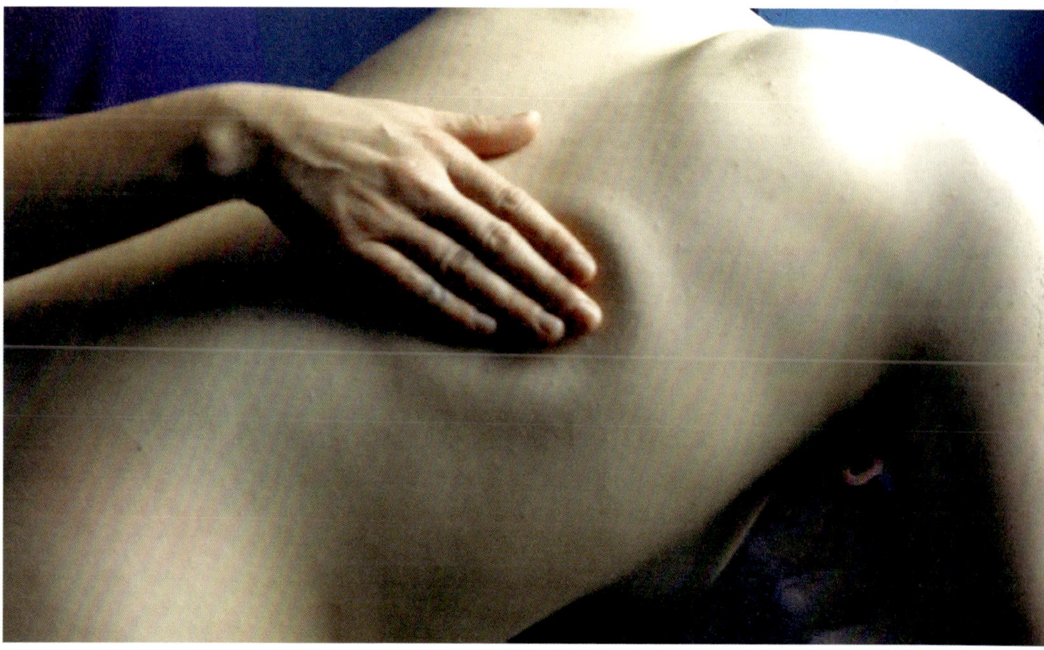

DEATH COACHES LLC

MYSTI & VIKA KIRCHENBAUER · TWO-CHANNEL VIDEO INSTALLATION · 8:39 · 2017

	M	MYSTI
	VK	VIKA KIRCHENBAUER
00:00:07	VO M	What is the outcome of sharing? Sharing hurts? To wound an audience with the revelations of their own oblivion ... What would make the drone of my monologue better memory-making than pyrotechnics? After an identity-forward, full frontal assault of unsolicited disclosures, I shed my victim apron, bend over nude, lighting bottle rockets from my shattered hole ... a final twist in this shit show that need press on only a little longer ... acknowledge my limitation before its mirror of performance ... my volatile content ... pointed at my audience long since drained of their sympathy, exhausted by my use of their evening, now violated ... under fire ... by their own accord ... scrambling for the door ... or maintaining cold dignity knowing that hurts cannot be administered in a theater seat ... ME HOWLING against all sense, aesthetic or justice: Now! Feel my wounds! Feel my wounds! Feel my wounds!
00:01:23	VK	If you could undo either the Holocaust or the AIDS crisis, which one would you choose? Or actually: to which event would you prefer to bear witness? Do you sometimes look to history in yearning for a sense of urgency in your life?[1] Are you bored, so ripe you're rotten?

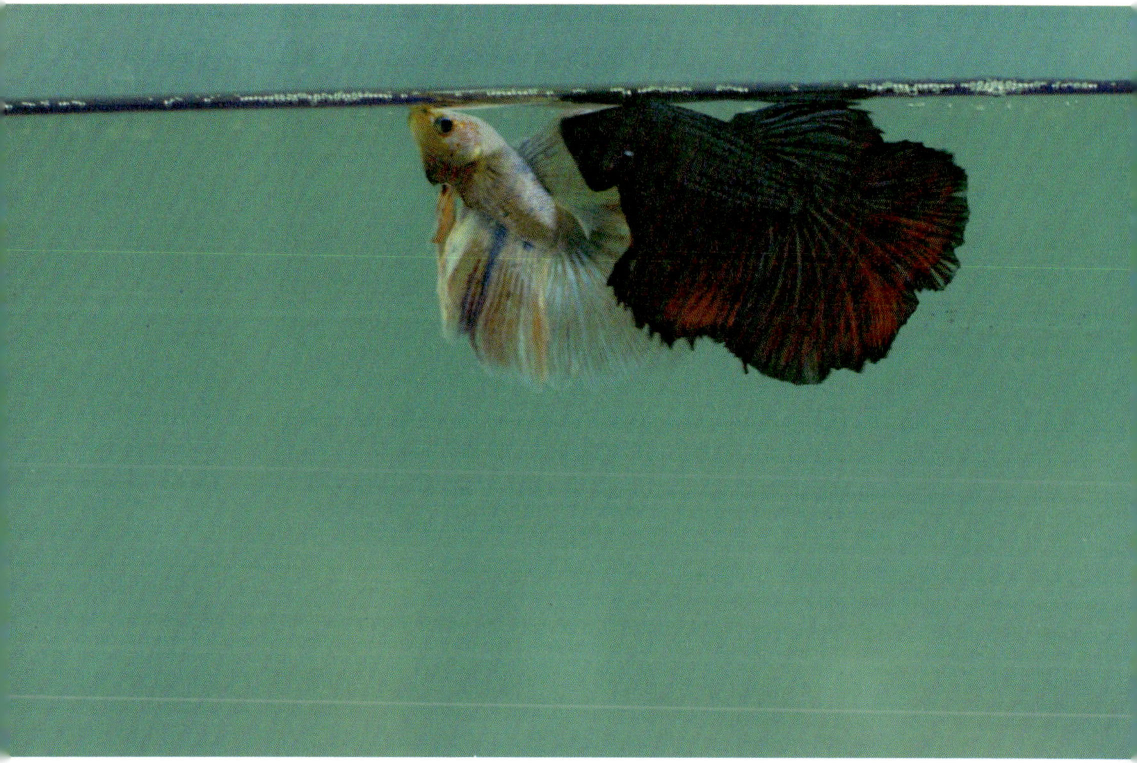

1 Many of Vika's lines are sampled from the websites of life coaches, career coaches, motivational coaches and personality coaches.

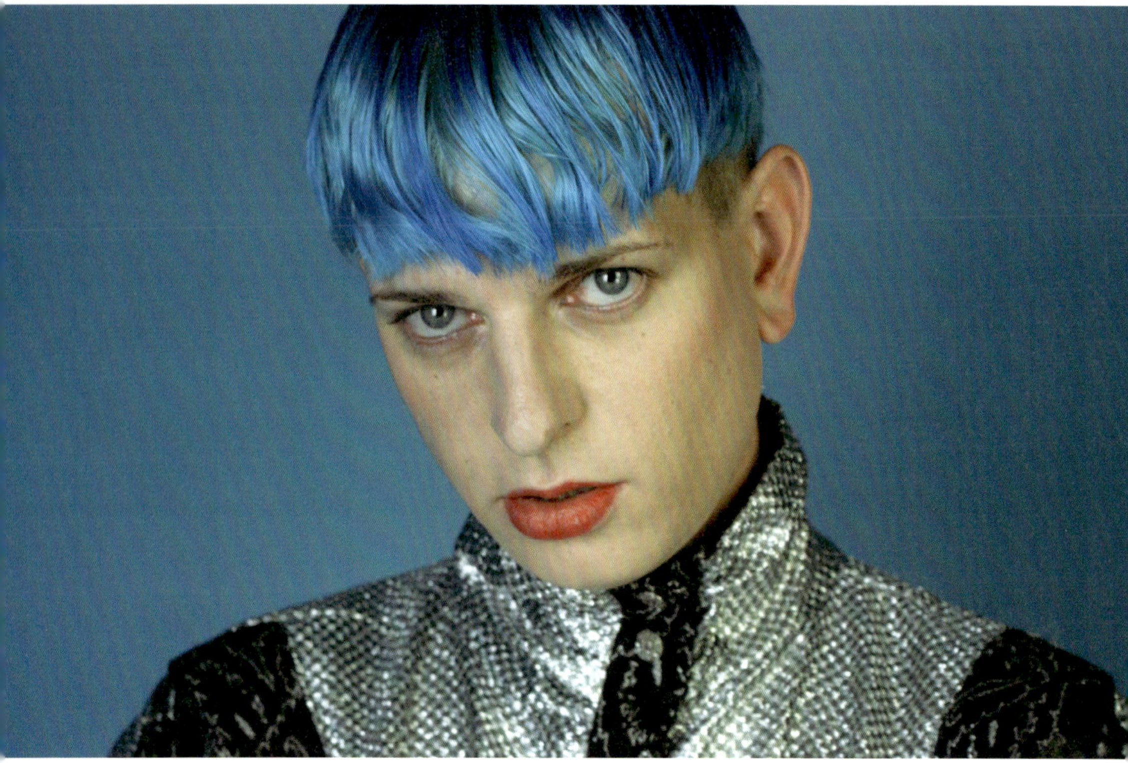

00:01:50	M	... a caustic bottom with a vapid dependence on everyone around you for the completion for even the most inane tasks ... How should I spend my inheritance?
00:02:04	VK	I see you are a person with ideas, a person that sees beyond the mundane of everyday life ... You dream of having a career that inspires, energises, and fulfills you each and every day. And you dream that even in crisis it will feel meaningful and real? You will feel that your work is of social relevance. I for instance love constant human interaction and the fulfillment and satisfaction that comes from helping someone like you solve a problem.
00:02:46	M	My words sound of white noise to you ... only now you find your life cloaked in vanity, oh so devastatingly late in life! Your sense of distance is skewed, making our communication a tiresome struggle to understand together your constant revision of terms.
00:03:12	VK	You shall be looked up to and be adored. Start making the necessary transitions so that you do only what you love to do. Once you discover your true calling, you'll learn how to restructure your life so that you can follow it. You will only work because you want to ... because nothing can stop you. It is hard to be irresistibly attractive if you're worried about paying the bills.
00:03:44	M	History is being recorded like never before. Emails, messages and posts, public and private, will resurface and refuse to explain away the gaps of character ... the balls you dropped ... the relative nature of the resistance you felt. Knowing when to pull out is the best means to secure your investment.
00:04:12	VK	You are suited for success! Why can you only flirt with it?
00:04:23	VO M	Blood art is only interesting if you get the audience to bleed with you. Imagine a single hole in a gallery wall: Put your finger here. Delivering a finger prick to all participants who dare to engage. What do they do with their blood? Dribble it everywhere? Sign their name? Shall I screenprint Band-Aids?
00:04:50	M	You've been bred to sacrifice for work, love and ultimately life. What does that look like to sacrifice for life, a human sacrifice? What wildly ambitious soul has the power to do that and succeed in believing it so? As if there was even opposition to your fantasy ... a fantasy crafted from a soulless child in a padded room ... they covered all the corners ... plugged the sockets ... 'cause they knew you'd hurt yourself.
00:05:43	VK	Are you tired of always ending up with deep contempt for your partner until the only way to tolerate sex with them is to think of somebody else? Nobody sees how truly worthy of love you are, nor do they offer the respect you deserve? None of

the people in your life would sit by your death bed for weeks and say: "Hey handsome ..."? ... And are you somewhat deeply unsatisfied with your sex life? Might it be your fault? Are you a terrible lover? Or simply fucking the wrong people? Or both? There is a way out. Together we can find a plan that you'll be naturally motivated to follow. No need for discipline, willpower or anything other than your inner motivation, because you'll be tapping into your true desires, not versions of someone else's ideal life.

00:07:01 VO M I would probably just install an airbag in a canvas designed to keep you from looking too closely, to save you from searching too long for something that cannot be found in a painting. There is so much wrong with our very tangible present. Are we ready for intricacy? A bloody nose is a better, more meaningful outcome than the study of brushstrokes and shadow. An airbag exploding from a canvas, breaking your neck to save you from the black hole of painting ... Imagine!!!!

00:07:37 VK What's holding you back from being brave? Let me help your ideal self create a solution. Look at the positive sides of this negative situation.

00:07:51 M It's a hard decision for those who lack clarity but you've never gambled in life, you've always known ...

00:07:57 VK Get organised and clear clutter! An elegant and determined end might be the ideal way of getting back at your parents! Learn the importance of being blessedly selfish and conquer your fears by befriending them! With a spectacular death you will no longer be boring but a mythology!

00:08:22 M Walk the plank! You pirated so much of your emotional content.

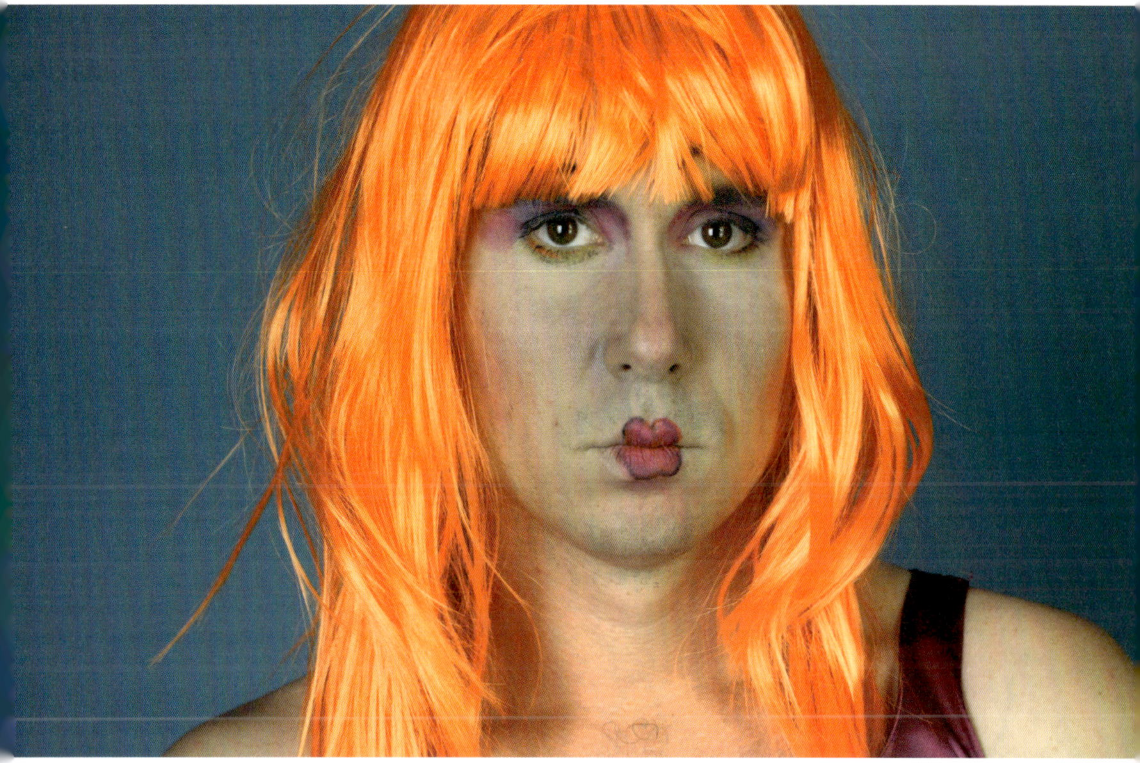

CAMERA, LIGHT	RITA MACEDO
SOUND	MARTIN SULZER
MUSIC	COOL FOR YOU

DEATH COACHES LLC

MYSTI & VIKA KIRCHENBAUER · ACCOMPANYING TEXT · 2017

"Not only could you travel upward toward success but you could travel downward as well; up and down, in retreat as well as in advance, crabways and crossways and around in a circle, meeting your old selves coming and going and perhaps all at the same time."

Ralph Ellison, *Invisible Man* (New York: Vintage Books, 1972), p. 385.

Contrary to rhetoric, being an artist is an outcome-orientated career. Everything done by the artist assumes it will have a future value. Where do artists fit when making work meant to solidify notions of art as higher cultural value worth aspiring to, when conceiving of institutions as generous platforms that exist only to fulfil their exhibitionistic desires?

/ The artist's self-identification with her own work must be produced from a place of authentic attachment and emotion. The mandate to *think outside of the box*, find self-fulfilment in what one does, to share burden and cocktails with one's associates in a way that overcomes the divisions between life and work is found in start-up culture and other forms of the New Economy. These forms draw inspiration from the affective glue with which the art world keeps itself working, and in particular: via the artist's perception of her practice. Love is abuse's most discreet tool, prescribing slow death to the greater workforce. The artist is the deadly cliché that allows for violence to be misinterpreted as passion, or minimally acknowledged as an unpleasant, albeit necessary implement toward an inarticulate, often cagey, vision. /

An intimate connection with the products of one's own labour is now a standard measure of any modern worker's passion, dedication and identification. Uniqueness and independence, always assumed innate within the field of art, now burden contemporary chefs, latte artists, social media managers, receptionists become day-makers, and retail employees as brand representatives. Sharing a belief that unique callings flatten a world of un-equals, everyone is expected to follow their dream or at least perform as if. /

To want to make art is to want to be middle-class. Artists are not workers, but entrepreneurs who produce in hopes of finding a market, be it institutional or commercial. A visual artist possesses relative independence given the autocratic nature of intellectual properties, likening her to those who want to be their own boss: to hold authority over the conditions of her own work and yet acquiesce in facilitating her own exploitation, confusing her own exploitative measures over others as gestures of support, shared dedication or real love. As the status, privilege and drive to do what one loves hold assumed value, there is inevitably a surplus of artist-entrepreneurs offering work that has already been executed (if not finalised, then at least in the form of elaborate project plans forecasting future actualisation upon funding). Thus, artists help produce an ideology that rebrands exploitation as self-realisation, presenting work as a pure act of self-love naturally independent from immediate compensation. /

People choose to enter a winner-take-all market, studying art completely aware of the limited prospects of success, yet must at the same time suspend this knowledge in the name of optimism and self-worth. Those privileged few who manage to make money from their passionate investments are celebrated for bravery and dedication to vision. This heroic understanding of risk reincarnates itself as a daily necessity shouldered by the masses, under the promise of rejuvenating and recharging continually. To not take risks is to accept oneself as a failure—be there a security net or not. /

In the individualistic field of contemporary art, success can only be framed as personal merit, never recognising itself as a form of relative privilege and favourable circumstance because each unique gesture is considered objectively better. Life-coaching is the transformation business, teaching passive people that all they do is wither ... that pathetically failing to act out one's unique calling wilfully cements class distinctions. The role of a life coach is to author a customised transformation of the client, reimagining the client as product whose value is to be determined. So, beyond the experiential value of the service, the customer's aim is their very own commodification, their impulse not dissimilar from the art spectator's impulse in visiting a museum: they are looking for a life-changing event. /

Speed toward deadly dreams, living lies already barely living. Avoiding the upset of yearning for a change that cannot be had without a revision of terms that most certainly reduces one's own value. Will one simply give up on life, life-as-work, which is the only rubric of working in which any value might be ascribed now? Sacrificing the convenient identity of having *made it* for the complexity of not being done just yet ... not quite right ...

INFRARED DREAMS IN TIMES OF TRANSPARENCY: THE LOVE LIFE OF DRONES AND OTHER WESTERN CYBORGS

VIKA KIRCHENBAUER • 2014

DRONE PILOTS AS COMBAT COMMUTERS: WORKERS IN WARFARE

With drones carrying missiles designed to blow up tanks and bunkers, and drone pilots operating them from air-conditioned complexes on a distant side of the globe, it has become difficult to distinguish between civilian and combatant, warzone and workplace. / The drone system is a stealthy achievement of capitalism and the nation state, a schizophrenic, yet efficient and profitable way of organising labour and warfare. It breaks up reality and lets the modern 'combat commuter' experience thrill and spectacle alongside the conveniences of ordinary life. /

With new ways of conceptualising the soldier having been created, the drone technology leads to a de-professionalisation of war. What would be a job first reserved for combat-experienced pilots is now tasked to instructed individuals, usually in their early twenties and often without prior military service experience. Facing a shortage of 'volunteers'—as if any kind of labour was ever 'voluntary' in our economic system—hiring and training of future drone operators is partially outsourced and made attractive through learn-on-the-job or home-training programmes. In times of wars orchestrated between collaborating state military entities and private companies within the federal contracting arena, the war business structurally resembles a branch of the service industry in which life and death, cost and efficiency are manoeuvred as economic values using managerial gestures. /

Enjoying an unobstructed view with total safety and clarity, drone operators carry out missions considered too dull, dirty and dangerous for onboard-piloted aircraft. Between temporary legroom for recreation and off-war normalcy, the 'combat commuters' translate hot and unhot information into clues to obtain 'situational awareness'. /

As opposed to soldiers in field combat where war becomes a shared normal for everyone stationed, drone pilots live in an individualised split reality where contexts perpetually shift. One day they observe a building in Afghanistan, and the next day possibly perform a strike in Pakistan. Between these vastly different workdays they will leave the military base, drive back into the city, have dinner at home and sleep in their own bed, potentially maintain an affair; maybe pick up their children from sports training, or go to a local pub with their pals. / As players in the endless war, the pilot and the sensor operator each observe five screens feeding live footage from the drone's camera, satellite images, data, and additionally infrared vision. Via radio and instant messenger, they are in contact with ground troops and employees of aeronautic companies who launch, land and maintain the drones in regions where they are deployed. / After a strike, drone operators assess the damage, and unlike fighter pilots who fly thousands of feet above their targets, they see in vivid detail what or whom they have destroyed. If their equipment enables them to clearly make out the colour of someone's hair or the brand of shoes that they are wearing, it is indeed not an unusual event for the drone operators to see someone's arm fly off or heads roll around; their gaze and action extend beyond the surface of bodies. While most of their time is spent observing people or buildings, sometimes for weeks on end, and analysing landscape as a container for possible danger and threat, they are used to watching the aftermath, watching someone bleed out, watching their funeral and then possibly launching another 'Hellfire' strike at that funeral. /

In opposition to the common critique of the drone system as a distanced methodology of killing, drone pilots often state that they are not detached but rather often develop close emotional relationships to those whose lives they may eventually take. With their 'targets', the drone operators share a strange cohesion of everyday life and sudden death. When they closely follow the daily routines of their 'targets', watching them eat meals with friends and family, drone pilots are much closer to them than any ground combat soldier could be. / The argument that the drone system dehumanises the 'target' misses the mark. In order to kill, the Other needs to be dehumanised. Therefore, the problem should be framed more precisely as the act of killing itself. In fact, the task of dehumanising those whom the drone operator has observed so closely has emerged as an obstacle to the functionality of the drone system as a new mechanism of death. / Living in a reality marked by excitement and anxiety, intensity and exhaustion, the drone operators are subject to Post Traumatic Stress Disorder, depression or suicidal ideation at a proportion similar to traditional combat aircrews. Consequently, PTSD as a condition is now rephrased as 'moral injury', rather than the formerly prevailing definition of 'fear conditioning'. What is considered trauma in this case nevertheless results from a lapse between active experience and the realisation of the weight of significance of death. / A whole new professional field has since emerged for chaplains and psychologists to convince the 'morally injured' combat commuters that their activity in the killing business ultimately saves lives—and that those in service do a better, more skilled and less damaging job than if replaced by an inexperienced 'newbie'. Informed by motivational language borrowed from the new economy's workshop culture, arguments are formed to elevate the operators' work and fill it with heroic meaning. Ideology ultimately serves as a tool to present killing to the killers in a favourable light. / In a self-congratulatory affirmation, to feel bad about killing is celebrated as a sign of moral intactness, and at its most cynical, the symptoms of PTSD are interpreted as good news and as proof of a remainder of human empathy in the not fully numb and cognitively dissonant killing machine. This feeling of guilt becomes an achievement, while the act of killing is reconciled by the killer's burdened subconscious. / In parallel with the modern worker's reality, overloaded with identification and commitment, the work of the drone operator bleeds into his or her personal life. Their inability to disassociate their so-called 'virtual stress' with the real effects on the lives of people leads a vast number of (former) pilots and sensor operators into alcoholism and drug addiction. Those are respectable and viable choices in life, yet it must be said that countless others manage to pursue such careers successfully without any detours through the killing business.

CYBORGS & HYBRID POSTHUMANS: THE 'VIRTUAL' & THE 'REAL'

In our present moment, to cheerfully announce one's current state of mind, one's inclinations and location has become less a form of expression than a mode of normality. For the human condition to be present everywhere without physical presence marks a society merged with technology. / But why do we awake in shock from this nightmare of drones? Are drones significantly different, more unique or complex compared with other war technologies? Hasn't the cognitive challenge of an image/reality split become our everyday natural task through videoconferences, smartphones and emailing? Do drones perhaps remind us of our own structural attachment to technology? Have we already become hybridised posthumans of technoscience without really noticing? Is our moral shock regarding this new mechanism of killing once again less about those killed than a moment of self-reflection for the West? Is it possible to lead a cyborg existence without physically merging with technological devices? / Technology can be regarded as value-neutral and defined only through human use. Nevertheless, technology defines the possibility of scenarios performed and conceived; we think and act through technology. Drones are tools, instruments, agents or machines, yet at the same time they open up new realms of imagining and executing military actions on a global level. This is not necessarily a shift in terms, but it definitely constitutes a shift in the way we relate to each other and ourselves. / When drone operators report having nightmares in infrared, it should be read as the operators' merging with the drone; it unites the representational experience of reality through images with subjective perception. To dream in infrared is to have taken on the perspective and position of the drone as one's own, to transgress the physical limitations of one's body and to gain the perception of being able to travel through space freely. / If in a sense the drone has emerged as a way of looking over technology's shoulder to see what the future will be, it is important to reflect on how technology works as a means of human enhancement; it increases human capabilities, making life without it inconceivable. Free will and empathy, as characteristics considered to divide humans from machines, are becoming less stable categories. Furthermore, the very idea of a cybernetic organism indeed has been replaced by that of a cybernetic system: one of dispersed brains and components in a wireless era. Implants and a shared organism between technology and human flesh are now outdated tales of the past. Drones are not to be considered a single object but rather hybrid systems distributed across the earth, including aircraft, ground control systems, data distribution terminals, satellite networks, pilots and sensor operators. Thus, the drone system is nothing less than a form of artificial intelligence that functions through the use of human and robotic components, both replaceable. / With screens described as immersive 'drool buckets', drone operators tend to drown in a turbulent stream of raw information. While they are overloaded with live footage, data, instant messages and radio contact it is not unusual to overlook important details, therefore making harmful decisions. The frequent failure to fulfil the simultaneous demands of absolute focus and multi-tasking emphasises the limits of the human component within the drone system. / A 'drone strike' is never a drone striking but a strike conducted by a pilot and a sensor operator in accordance with a ground force commander and in collaboration with the entire drone system. The misunderstanding of the drone as autonomous leads to a hysterical fallacy of understanding the drone as an undead, uncontrollable entity, oblivious to itself, yet driven by an instinct to kill. Whatever alienates us makes easy comparison to the zombie, but while drones are not factually autonomous, it is important not to ignore the human responsibility as the authority of decisions. To present the drone as a new modern monster, mindlessly meandering yet capable of lethal action, is taking fiction as a fact.

/ Not only since the invention of drone technologies have images begun to cover the rupture between the Western media spectators of wars and those physically experiencing armed conflict. The dualistic split between the 'virtual' and the 'real' has become a Western condition. The West experiences only itself as authentic, considering the rest of the world as little more than its virtual body—the provider of resource, labour and image realities imagined to make our lives easier and more entertaining at no cost.

/ No location is actually 'cyber' and nothing is ever 'virtual' but rather deeply real, existing through bodies within concrete political situations and spaces. To imagine a fictional space while remaining oblivious to the notion of real impact of 'virtual action' means dehumanising those not physically present to us. / To argue advocating the 'honourable' way of 'real' combat is misleading and smells of essentialism, bloodthirst and *Abenteuerlust*. To privilege the 'authentic' experience of killing over the 'distanced' experience of killing avoids the understanding of 'virtual actions', romanticises the idea of killing an individual with one's bare hands at risk of one's own life, while forgetting that the act of killing itself is the morally tricky bit, regardless of the means. Even if drones were able to make lethal decisions autonomously in the future, why does the notion of 'human error' make people more comfortable with the deaths of bodies declared 'collateral damage'?

IMAGE CREATORS & SPECTATORS; THE GLOBAL BODY & THE CANCEROUS CELL

Cameras already existed in the cockpits of bomber pilots to evaluate performance; however, the use of images in modern warfare has shifted significantly. Images serve as temporary live-time carriers of truth to mirror the otherwise exported reality TV format in a role reversal play. Still, the bird's eye perspective is present to the spectator as a military perspective, turning life and landscape into abstraction, visual patterns, cues and ornaments. Yet while bomber pilots had little knowledge concerning the extent or details of the damage caused, drone operators see a very clear picture of the effects of their actions. Unless their 'targets' are hidden in architecture, video material exists of everyone killed in a strike performed through a drone. After a strike, operators assess the damage as a means of efficiency control and evaluation. From the point of view of the operators, the strike itself and its analysis unite vita activa and vita contemplativa, protagonism and spectatorship, in a modern manifestation of immaterial labour that materialises through technology. / While the politics of drone warfare have established a 'kill not capture' policy, the execution of 'personality strikes' largely shifted toward 'signature strikes'. The term 'personality strike' is used for strikes where the identity of the target is known and classified as that of a terrorist, whereas 'signature strikes' operate purely on suspicion, based on a behavioural analysis. Driving in a car, meeting with a group of men, carrying a weapon or even a phone with suspicious metadata, or maintaining personal contact with a 'suspected militant' all suffice as justification for a strike. The exact criteria of such categorisations remain murky, and if comparison is drawn to how racial profiling operates, there is little hope that the evaluation processes classifying someone as a terrorist are any more sophisticated than 'male body over 15 who meets with other male bodies over 15 → terrorist'. / The constant and threatening presence of drones ultimately works as a means of disciplining individuals to act for camera, teaching subjects under the lens the potentially deadly consequences of not modifying their behaviour for the camera, compartmentalising life, denying community and mobility altogether. Due to the frequent use of so-called 'double tap strikes', meaning two strikes on the same target within a timespan of only few minutes, people in regions under attack have learned not to approach the scene with humanitarian intent. / The term 'surgical strike', often deployed in official announcements concerning drone warfare, is supposed to suggest medical precision in the elimination of the right individual or cancerous cell from an otherwise intact global organism; a virus that would otherwise corrupt the other cells and justice would not prevail. Remarkably, the notion of a global capitalist organism is now so pervasive in the West that the 'virus' is considered an internal problem, and no longer portrayed as an external threat. / In infrared all people look white, and those who bleed out turn into the same colour as the ground once their heat signature cools down, blending in with the temperature of their environment. After scanning the landscape as a vessel for potentially dangerous bodies, after inserting craters into it, and watching body parts flying around, the infrared view returns the newly unhot bodies to the landscape. Outside this infrared view corpses lay still as a reminder to other subjects marked as 'dangerous bodies or viruses'. / The drone system could be read as the resurrection of god, a new transcendental moment for the West with revival of religion in the public sphere. As god once was, the drone is now a reflection and extreme expression of the sociopolitical state of the earth. In its capacity to see while remaining unseen, and deliver death without warning, legal grounds or judgment, the drone is a morbid reflection of the global inequity of wealth and power in capitalist reality. Installed and brought to power by some in one earthly desert, it is circling overhead others in another earthly desert. At higher altitude, the drone is inaudible and invisible from the ground; however, the drone sound, a monotonous buzz, can serve as a constant reminder of the overhanging threat of sudden death when the drone is descended. Signalling both omnipresence and omnipotence, it strives to discipline into submission the earth-bound creatures who happen to be on the wrong side of the camera. /

Drone technology as a weapon is the installation of an unloving god, one that does not promise immortality of the soul and could hardly be swayed with gifts and sacrifices. He offers only the preservation of one's image as a video document, while holding anally precise views on the proper execution of rituals, fears collective potential and pathologically dislikes men in groups or in cars. Video and the analysis of movement and action are of much higher importance to him than outdated religious media like scripts or books. He rains 'Hellfire' missiles down at supersonic speed on the possibly guilty, and he beams down a ray of laser targeting light to guide the ground troops with what they call 'the Light of God'.

THE NATION & ITS POST-LEGAL 'OUTSIDE'

Through drones, the powerful modern state extends surveillance to the killing of human bodies. Drone conception, fabrication, field deployment, as well as the outsourced pilot training serve as examples of national-corporate fusion. The drone programme marks the perfect marriage between capitalism and formal democracy, constituting the promise of borderless, profitable and permanent war. / Drones in their current state are nearly defenceless when attacked and they are not tailored for air-to-air combat. Their use is exclusively practical for asymmetrical wars in rural areas. This same asymmetry renders obsolete all endgame scenarios that dominated popular culture in the past. While the 'payload' of 'Hellfire' missiles with their ability to blow up tanks and attack bunkers makes them difficult to deploy in urban areas outside an official state of war, 'collateral damage' in rural areas does not exceed a critical point of moral wrong or 'diplomatic embarrassment' in the views of those who oversee their use. Clearly, not only the battles are asymmetrical; they are merely symptoms of a growing global divergence between the rich and the poor. This divergence, a result of global capitalism, is now countered only marginally with alternative imaginations of economic and social organisation. / The modern Western nation state operates with a double standard: internally it performs 'the right to make live and let die', while externally it embodies the more sovereign approach of 'take life or let live'; internally, death is considered private and unavoidable, while externally it is public and potentially desirable. / While the domestic use of drones often constitutes an infringement of privacy, and frequently creates concern about air safety, the state needs an outside-of-the-constitution instance in order to declare others outlaws and kill them without trial or judgment. The drone technology eliminates geography and constitutionality as complicating factors and makes war convenient in a post-legal world. / Over the last decades we have witnessed first the manufacturing industry, and then slowly parts of the service industry relocating the material and immaterial labour to those extra-constitutional terrains beyond the reach of workers' unions and state laws. Similar to the manufacturing or service industry, war is no longer physically located in one space alone. The drone operators as transnational, post-internet workers mirror this flow of labour in the hierarchical (if you will, asymmetrical) setup of capitalist global organisation. / Western democracies prove the ideal breeding ground for capitalism, and those constitutional terrains would be dysfunctional without the outside-of-the-nation-state, where labour and war are executed without legal boundaries. These flows of money, labour and intelligence document forms of neocolonial exchanges, while supra-legal remotely piloted aircraft transgress borders and space to control and kill illegalised bodies.

TOTAL STARING IN TIMES OF UNILATERAL TRANSPARENCY

Drones are masturbatory: they resemble only a self-consuming illusion of total subjectivity, a lonesome wank in the safest place. The drone is the ultimate Peeping Tom of modern warfare. Looking at the world through drones, with no one looking back, the West—former West, Global North or whatever term is considered appropriate—ultimately stares back at itself. The gaze unmet by the observed is lastly directed inwards with self-satisfactory fulfilment. /

This habit of unilateral staring is a form of one-sided transparency motivated by an urge to recognise, and resembles existential crisis. With a total evaluation of the amounts of data, information and images collected being impossible and implausibly beneficial to security, reconnaissance and intelligence are the clearest symptoms of Western neurosis and paranoia, the sheer twitchiness of the manically obsessed. Our reality, not only warfare, is marked by total looking: Market research, online dating, surveillance mechanisms and war strategies have strong similarities in their motives of identifying, understanding and controlling. The idea of transparency subsequently found ways to diffuse into all realms of life. /

With blind trust in the recognisable, in that which is considered understood, the strategies of war have shifted to smaller, more covert bases and operations. The Western nation state reserves for itself the privilege of secrecy while imposing transparency onto the Other as an implementation of hierarchy. Transparency is not a shared condition, but a measure to obtain and consolidate power, to gain and exploit knowledge, to legitimise and delegitimise.

MALE & FEMALE: LOVE AS A COLD WAR SCENARIO

Many criticise the drone system for further contributing to a masculinisation of war, yet their picture of masculinity as an infinite scale remains dubious. While historically war is not a particularly gender-neutral activity, it is complicated to argue against that point without re-enforcing faulty binary gender conceptions of the peaceful female and the aggressive male. / A confused gender perspective stems from the following: Equal to 'Reaper' and 'Predator'—the two most prominent US drones—which are of the MALE category (Medium Altitude, Long Endurance), the European Union is developing a drone of comparable stamina and operational height named FEMALE (Future European MALE). / While the two US MALEs do little to camouflage their use and function, the European idea behind the drone's name remains remarkably opaque. If the FEMALE is the Future European MALE, does this suggest a total feminist takeover in Europe? If the Future European MALE will be FEMALE, is there promise for a total queering of gender on the horizon? And what does this imply for continents as stereotypically gendered entities? Do those European engineers imagine that they are reacting to 'Reaper' and 'Predator'—the standard US American trigger-happy cowboys—with FEMALE, a tough yet caring social-democratic mother drone that kills passive-aggressively? Given the field we are considering, it is safe to assume blatant sexism in an infinite variety of manifestations. /

Against all better judgment, let us agree to anthropomorphise these drones to better imagine a worst-case scenario: FEMALE & MALE dating (assumed heterosexuality seems feasible in this case). Immediately Rae Spoon's pop anthem 'We Can't Be Lovers with These Guns on Each Other' comes to mind. The problem is: we can. What sounds absurd at first reveals itself upon critical observation as the standard situation of romantic relationships between earth-bound, late-capitalist cyborgs. / Love is a power game and the utopia of love overcoming power structures of oppression is at best a naive illusion. What ties romantic lovers together is a pact that while holding guns on each other they refrain from firing them. Each knows they can destroy the other and be destroyed by the other, so they live the classic Cold War scenario of arms race and one touch dial phone calls. At best, this type of relationship describes a more balanced situation than the asymmetrical wars of the present, although it needs to be admitted that, in love as in global politics, a 'Cold War' is never cold but gets very hot in other areas further away from the main focal point. / Just as in war, the knowledge about the other—or 'intelligence' about the other—constructs power; it is the currency that economies of love and war operate on. Nevertheless, the collection of knowledge about the other rarely extends beyond pseudo-factual proof of prior suspicion, most frequently deployed to confirm an identity already inscribed onto the other. The same way the drone pilot translates landscape into targets, potential targets and potentially hidden targets, the jealous boyfriend translates his partner's social media account into betrayal, potential betrayal and potentially hidden betrayal. Change, fluidity, discontinuity and incoherence—if you will, freedom—

in this light become enemies of the dictate of 'understanding'. Love is surely closer to punishment and discipline than it is to liberty. / Like all heterosexual couples of 'Medium Altitude' class background—conscious of the glass ceiling, thus fearful of social and actual descent—MALE and FEMALE would tend to make crisis permanent as a mode of stability. They would pay Ikea an inescapable and compulsive joint visit in an attempt to solidify their mutual commitment against fundamental change, and they could hardly imagine in that moment how deeply they, in a not-so-distant future, will resent each other and their furniture. Would FEMALE and MALE with their weapons drawn be able to overcome narcissism and self-love so as to release each other into freedom? That is doubtful ... /

In the worst case, they would not only further reproduce their wars and conflicts, they would also reproduce themselves; although Reaper, as the offspring of Predator, should be a strong argument against all procreation, and for the end of that precise lineage in particular. Adoption (the freeganism of reproduction, as it is probably euphemised in activist circles) of abandoned drones would probably not suggest itself as a viable practice in this context either. Perhaps the only hope lies in the end of humanity, and consequently the end of its deployment of its sophisticated technological inventions. O apocalypse come forth, o apocalypse arise, o apocalypse ascend, o apocalypse come in.

ENDING ON THE 'OTHER' SIDE

In the West, the emergence of drones is the wet dream of media theorists, the raw material of critical artists and a promising career opportunity for academics, writers and intellectuals of all kinds (this piece of writing is obviously no exception). However, in the regions where those drones are deployed, they signify mostly brutality. They are not a metaphor. / For the spectators, war images of disfigured individuals make us reflect on our own lives, they make us feel physically intact, attractive and blessed. It is even possible to occupy this safe position of cynicism as mere manifestation of helplessness. On the other side of the lens, modern warfare most literally bleeds into the intimacies of people. / While here exists the possibility to poeticise the slowly vanishing heat profiles of bodies declared casualties in a politically correct manner, elsewhere the effects of drone warfare leave individuals unable to distinguish between the corpses of friends and those of livestock. / What in the West can be intellectualised as the interaction of individual and collective experiences on the dramatic level of death elsewhere actually means death.

(Originally published in Married Print #1: Infrared Dream in Times of Transparency, illustrated by Amrei Hofstätter, published by Dicey Studios in 2014.)

KINGDOM COME

VIKA KIRCHENBAUER & MARTIN SULZER · MULTIMEDIA INSTALLATION · DIMENSIONS VARIABLE · 2014

RITUALS, the first of three pieces that make up *KINGDOM* COME, is a large projection of aerial footage that has been shot by pigeons equipped with lightweight digital cameras. With heavy wind and the nervous flapping of wings, the viewer gets only a fractured impression, though immediately identifiable, of a political demonstration. The signature elements of protest are captured only in glimpses: masses of people moving steadily in the same direction, banners, police, police cars, barriers, etc. The political motivations of the demonstration remain ambiguous, as the images primarily highlight the mere shape of political protest. In *RITUALS*, political protest in public space is reduced, presented as a visually uniform and dramaturgically ritualised movement of bodies. /

The video's aesthetics convey a rather painterly or structuralist tone. Between flashes of German flags, the parliament building and the German Chancellery, we can finally make out the protesters carrying white crosses—the hallmark of an annual Christian anti-abortionists' rally. Nevertheless, from the pigeons' perspective the rally looks scarcely different than a reproductive rights demonstration. Some questions arise: can the design and shape of a demonstration show differences in ideology or critical perspective? What might other forms of collective political practice in public space look like? /

While our habits of analysing images lead us to inscribe a *gaze* or *subjectivity* upon their 'creator', the birds compel us to think differently. We neither see what the pigeons see, nor are the pigeons aware that

00:01:49

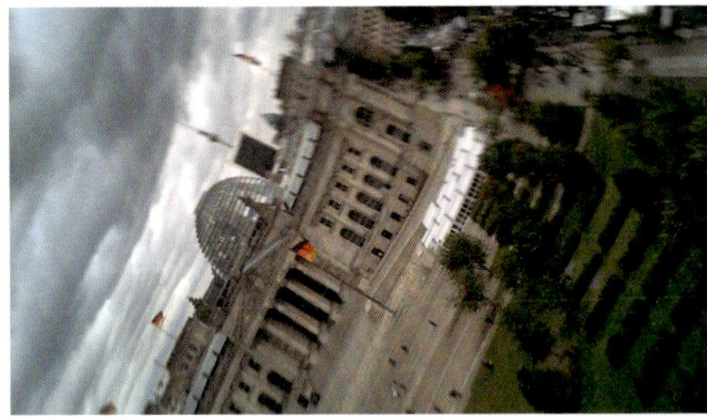

00:01:50

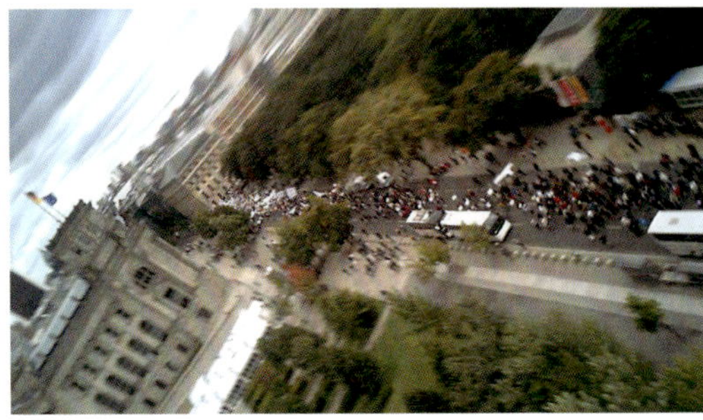

00:02:44

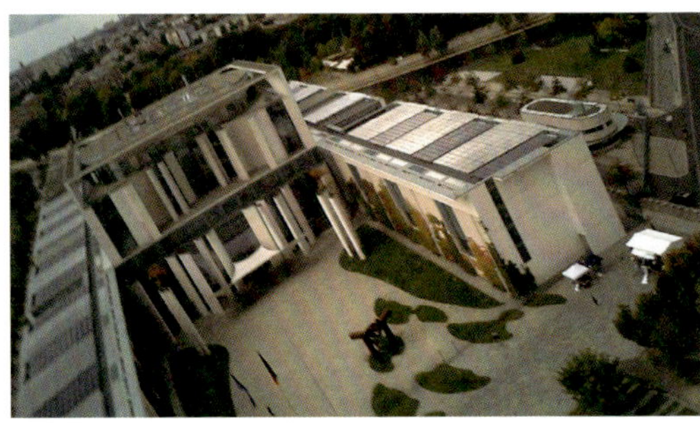

00:03:50

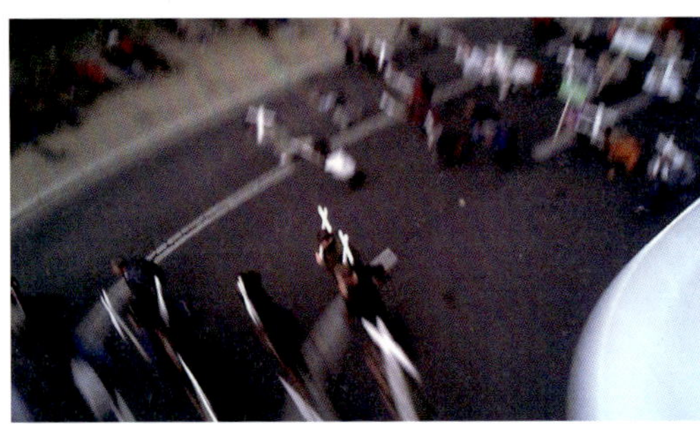

00:04:01

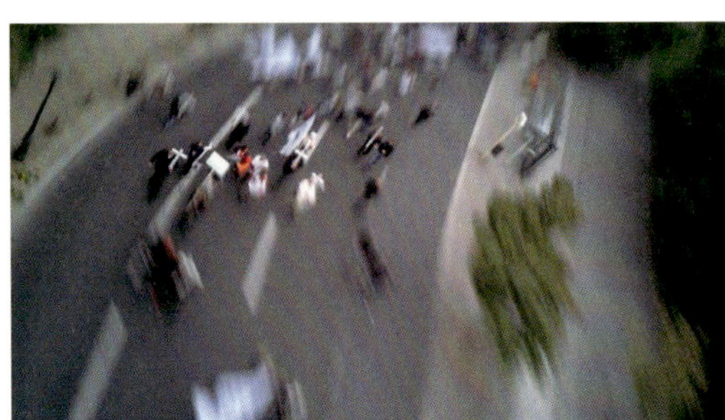

they are filming. Through the pigeons' perspectives of multiplicity, the animal can no longer be seen either as subject or as subject matter, but rather as a medium. The view we get is one of non-participation, an inaccessible anomaly to any form of definition, and following Deleuze and Guattari's concept of *becoming-animal*[1] an achievement of non-identity or post-subjectivity. Here the camera and its perspective no longer occupy a realm of stability and identity, but rather fold into movement and a restless mode of existence. This is the precise perspective *RITUALS* seeks to experiment with when looking at the space and surroundings of what signifies the German political centre, at political geography, participatory democracy and urban landscapes of power. / *KINGDOM COME* was inspired by pigeon photography—a method developed by pharmacist Julius Neubronner nearly a century ago as a way of capturing aerial photographs. This method was used mainly for military purposes during World War I in the field of what would nowadays be called 'unmanned reconnaissance', a precursor of modern drone warfare. This background is reflected in the context of *CENTRE VIEW*—the second element of *KINGDOM COME*. The monitor, placed behind the net of a table tennis training machine, displays images shot by a pigeon perched on top of the German Chancellery for about 20 minutes, near the demonstration. The bird deterrent system on the Chancellery's roof seemingly has no effect, becoming, in fact, one of the main subjects filmed by the pigeon. The method of reconnaissance is ironically folded back against the state and its historical continuities. /

The sovereign power concealed behind the obscure transparency of the democratic order—as displayed in *RITUALS*, with the state as the legitimising entity under which citizens are permitted to protest—finds a twisted *reprise* in *CENTRE VIEW*. Firstly, the state's laws do not affect the movement of the pigeon, nor its reconnaissance activity. Secondly, the installation of the piece actually mirrors the hierarchy of democratic order if we think of an art installation as the artists' definition of a specific space and its modalities—a law, if you will. The meshed net obstructing the view of the monitor keeps the viewer in motion as they continually seek a better perspective. In front of the monitor there is a single hole, making it possible for one person at a time to have an unobstructed view of the video, albeit in an uncomfortable position. This 'sovereign installation' therefore shifts the attention to the exhibition space and initiates reflection on the accidental community that art spectators build. / The third element of the installation, *INTERNAL MARKET*, is an arrangement of one thousand 6cm small plastic foetuses obtained under dubious circumstances from anti-abortionist

1 See Gilles Deleuze and Félix Guattari, '1730: Becoming-Intense, Becoming-Animal, Becoming-Imperceptible...' in *A Thousand Plateaus*, trans. by Brian Massumi (Minneapolis: University of Minnesota Press, 1978), pp. 233–309.

campaigners. The piece thematises the overlap between biopolitical agendas and salvation phantasies, in which national economic interests align with the goals of religious fundamentalists. Continued procreation and unpaid care work are essential to capitalism's need for steady reproduction of both labour force and consumers.[2] The one thousand *white* and identical plastic foetuses bear the marks of Fordist mass production visibly inscribed onto the future post-Fordist subjects, while their inherent reliance on affective and reproductive labour is highlighted through design.

2 See Silvia Federici, *Caliban and the Witch* (New York: Autonomedia, 2004).

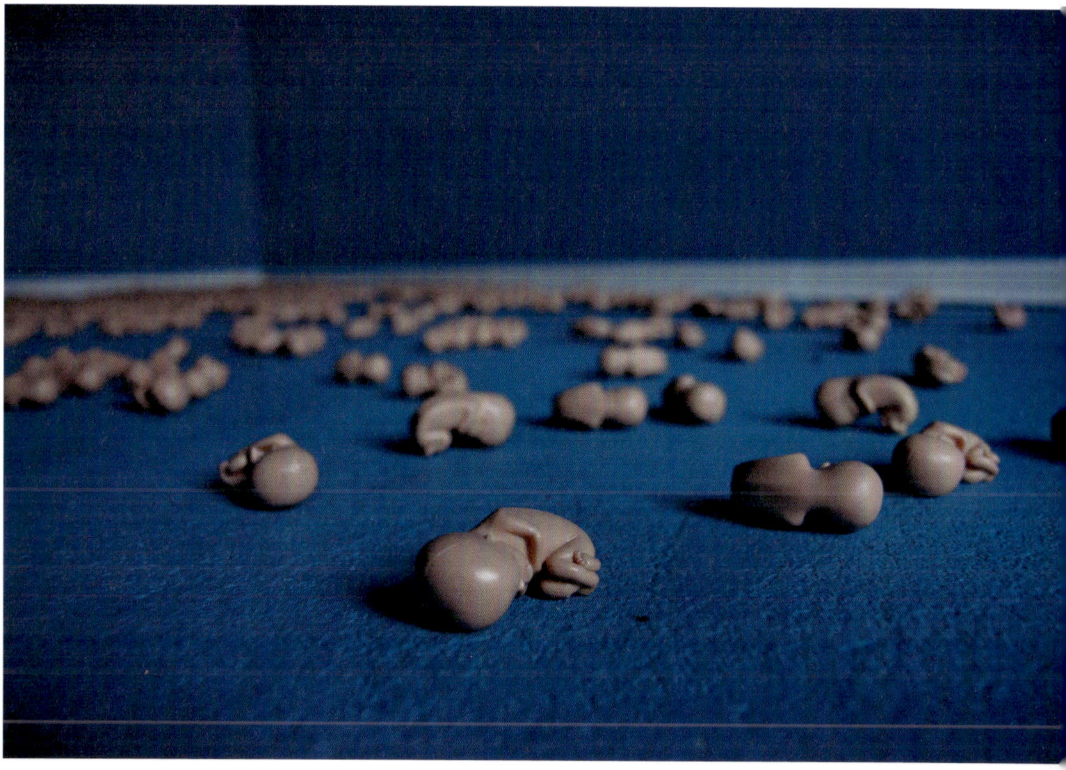

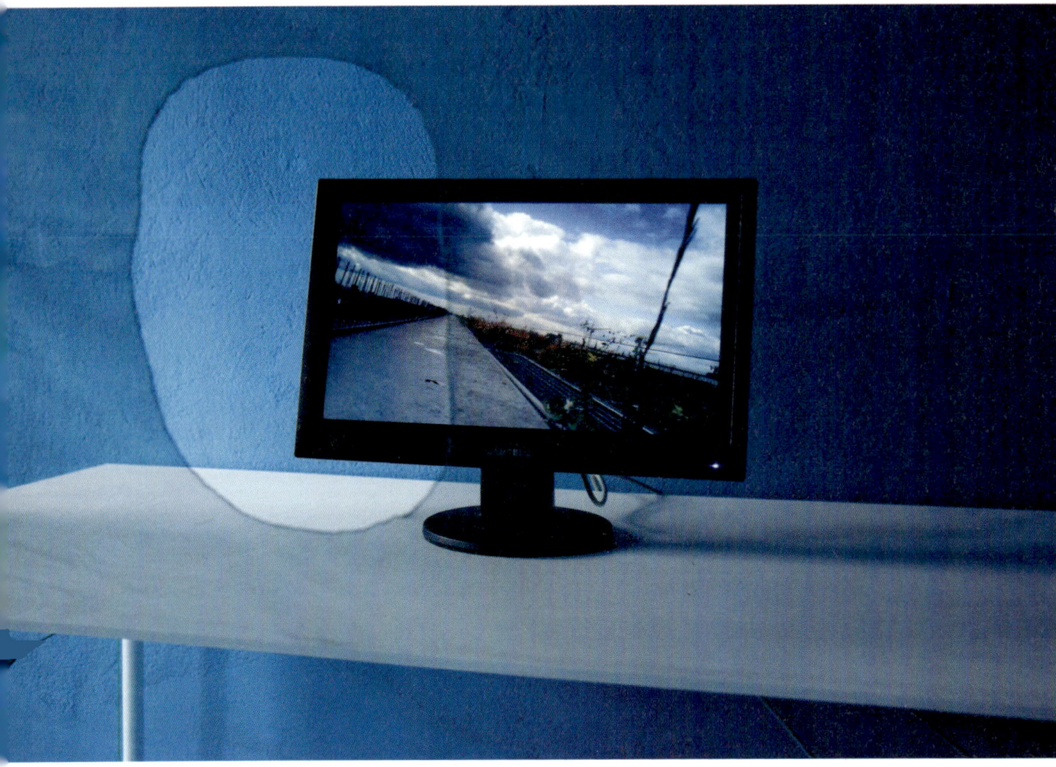

LIST OF ILLUSTRATIONS